Motorcycle Electrical Systems
Troubleshooting and Repair

Motorcycle Electrical Systems
Troubleshooting and Repair

Tracy Martin

MOTORBOOKS

Dedication

To Leslie, whose love and advice is a gift.

Motorbooks titles are also available at discounts in bulk quantity for industrial or sales-promotional use. For details write to Special Sales Manager at MBI Publishing Company, Galtier Plaza, Suite 200, 380 Jackson Street, St. Paul, MN 55101-3885 USA.

To find out more about our books, join us online at www.motorbooks.com.

ISBN-13: 978-0-7603-2716-6
ISBN-10: 0-7603-2716-5

Editor: Jennifer Johnson
Designer: LeAnn Kuhlmann

Printed in China

On the front cover: What may look like a traditional Harley-Davidson V-twin on the outside uses modern electronic fuel injection sharing many of the same types of components used on automobiles. Understanding how EFI works will give owners and technicians alike another tool in the "box" for repairing these systems now and in the future. *Courtesy Harley-Davidson of Frederick*

Inset: Here is the fuse panel installed under the seat of an FJR 1300. The big red wire comes directly from the battery. The big round thing (lower left) is a servo for an aftermarket cruise control. Courtesy Jeff Paries

On the title page: The most difficult part can be getting the bodywork off your bike (in this case a Yamaha FJR) to gain access to the wiring harness. Wiring the BackOFF-Wig Wag module, Signal Dynamics license plate frame, and tailBlazer unit was straightforward. *Courtesy Signal Dynamics*

On the back cover: A relay has been added to this passing lamp circuit. The relay now controls the high amperage load that the passing lamps need to operate.

CONTENTS

PREFACE 6

CHAPTER 1   OHM'S LAW 8

CHAPTER 2   VOLTAGE DROP TESTING 20

CHAPTER 3   ELECTRONIC TESTING TOOLS 28

CHAPTER 4   STORAGE BATTERIES 44

CHAPTER 5   CHARGING AND STARTING SYSTEMS 60

CHAPTER 6   IGNITION SYSTEMS 82

CHAPTER 7   FUEL INJECTION SYSTEMS 99

CHAPTER 8   WIRING DIAGRAMS 118

CHAPTER 9   TROUBLESHOOTING ELECTRICAL SYSTEMS 129

CHAPTER 10   ELECTRICAL ACCESSORIES 139

SOURCES 152

INDEX 158

PREFACE

While the automotive electrical field has always fascinated me, it took me about 25 years to get to the point where I was able to write my first book, *How to Diagnose and Repair Automotive Electrical Systems*, published by Motorbooks, an imprint of MBI Publishing Company. The book covers the same subject matter for motorcycles. I have spent years working in my garage on all manner of cars, trucks, and of course motorcycles, gaining practical knowledge the hard way. In addition to doing all my own maintenance and repairs, I have taught classes for automotive technicians and written about motorcycle-related electrical concepts for power sports magazines for many years. Acquiring this experience has been a long and oftentimes arduous process of trial and error, discovering what works and what doesn't, and how to fashion shortcuts, and how, most importantly, to break it down into simple, easy-to-understand "sound bytes" of information that a reader or beginning technician can quickly understand and digest. Fortunately, to make this process somewhat easier, I have, throughout my career, been taught by some of the best people in the fields of automotive repair and training. Many of the instructional methods used to convey technical information in this book were borrowed from colleagues, friends, and fellow mechanics, and then elaborated upon. However, throughout my experiences I have often been struck by the notion that the related areas of motorcycle and automotive electricity, electronics, and electronic diagnostic testing are needlessly complicated and often confusingly presented. I have endeavored to correct this imbalance in this book.

In the early 1980s, I worked as a lab technician at a large turbocharger manufacturer in Southern California. This company was one of the few pioneering innovators in design and construction of turbochargers for the diesel and automotive markets. It also had the largest engine dynamometer facility on the West Coast. Many automakers introduced the advantages of turbocharging an engine in the early 1980s, and as a technician in the right place at the right time, I was fortunate enough to see new and developing automotive technology years prior to its incorporation into production vehicles. This environment was the setting in which I received an introduction to some of the earliest electronic engine management systems and their modes of operation and inherent "teething" problems.

I, along with fellow technicians, had the opportunity to install test engines into various dyno test cells (soundproof rooms), mounting all the electronics on a plywood board next to the engine. As engine testing progressed, the computer-controlled carburetor or fuel injection system would inevitably "crash and burn" and have to be diagnosed and repaired. Since there were no service manuals available (they aren't written for preproduction engines), automotive engineers were the only source of information about how the systems were supposed to work. And more often than not, the response from engineers to inquiries for more information about why something didn't work out as expected, went something like this: "The system couldn't possibly have malfunctioned—it's made using 'state-of-the-art' electronics, designed by a qualified electrical engineer. *You* must have installed it incorrectly." Although this was not the most ideal environment in which to learn automotive electronics, some technical knowledge rubbed off on me, with the help of fellow technicians.

Some years later, the widespread introduction into the automotive industry of carburetors with wires coming out of them and electronic fuel injection systems gave me the opportunity to teach fellow mechanics (now called "technicians") what I had learned about how to diagnose and repair these systems. I taught classes for many nationwide corporations, including Sun, Allen, Nissan, and Snap-on Tools. Typically, this instruction occurred in the evenings, after everyone had already put in a full day working on cars. Too often, I was faced with a group of tired, hapless students all wishing they were home eating dinner instead of sitting in class listening to me. Keeping these students awake and interested while learning about electricity was a challenge, to say the least. Consequently, over the years I gained invaluable experience and learned—out of necessity—innovative ways of imparting information and keeping things moving during class. As a result, I have been able to incorporate many of these techniques and ideas into this book.

Motorcycles have been behind the "electronic fuel-injected" technological curve and have only in recent years caught up with their automotive counterparts. While electronic ignition systems for the motorcycle have been around for many years, electronic fuel injection (EFI) is a fairly recent development. The widespread use of EFI will quite soon replace carburetors in the power sports industry, and this book hopefully will make the concepts of motorcycle electronics and fuel injection easier to understand.

If these experiences have taught me anything, it's that the more I think I know, the more I know I really don't know much at all. So I'd like to thank some of the people who have helped me in writing this book.

Chief and foremost, I'd like to thank three service managers at three motorcycle dealers who were most generous with their time and advice. Barry Anderson of Twigg Cycles in Hagerstown, Maryland, was most kind in providing me with parts from the big four Japanese manufacturers and access to hundreds of factory service manuals. Josh Neff, service manager at Bob's BMW in Columbia/Jessup, Maryland, provided BMW parts, motorcycles, and advice that was invaluable. Nathan Lewis of Harley-Davidson of Frederick, also in Maryland, let me use the motorcycle featured on the cover and also let photograph hundreds of dollars worth of new parts. Without the help and advice of these three motorcycle experts, my less than perfect of knowledge would have become more apparent in the writing of this book. Fortunately, their generous gifts of time and always-willing-to-help attitude have (hopefully!) saved me from professional embarrassment.

Additional technical information and electrical accessories for the projects in Chapter 10 were provided by many aftermarket companies, and they are listed in the Sources section at the back of this book. Thanks to all—your involvement with this project made this a better book than I could have produced on my own.

And lastly, I'd like to thank my wife of 23 years. I am not only a better writer because of her, I am also a human being.

In closing, I hope you, the reader, are able to gain some practical skills and knowledge, which will help increase your confidence when you're faced with motorcycle electrical challenges.

—Tracy Martin

THEORY

This first section is intended to provide a bare bones explanation of general electrical theory and how basic DC (direct current) electricity operates in a motorcycle. It's not important to understand electricity inside and out—a subject many books cover in excruciating detail—but it *is* important to have a basic understanding of how to apply a practical working knowledge of electricity in order to diagnose and repair electrical malfunctions that may show up on your bike.

An in-depth examination of electrical theory is far more complex and cumbersome than the practical "hands-on" training provided in this book—therefore, apologies must be offered in advance to readers with more than a working knowledge of electricity or electronics, since this book takes certain liberties and shortcuts with electrical science. For all "electronically challenged" mortals, Chapter 1, Ohm's Law, is a "hot rod" version of how 12/6-volt motorcycle electrical systems operate. Chapter 2, Voltage Drop Testing, cuts to the chase by showing you how to apply what you learned in the context of solving real motorcycle problems. In fact, all the subjects covered in each chapter of this book relate in some way to the basic theories discussed in Chapters 1 and 2—thus, if you find brain-fade starting to set in while reading the more detailed sections on wiring diagrams or electronic fuel injection diagnosis, you may want to revisit these early chapters for an electrical theory "tune-up."

CHAPTER 1
OHM'S LAW

Because billions of electrons flowing through a wire at the speed of light are difficult to see, or for most people hard to even imagine, electronics/electrical repair is one area of vehicle maintenance most people shy away from. Unlike disassembling and cleaning a carburetor, changing a flat tire, or bolting accessories onto your bike, repairing electrical systems is a truly cerebral endeavor. However, it is not impossible or even difficult. Electrical systems may seem perplexing when you watch a seasoned technician with electronics savvy diagnose an electrical problem with your motorcycle, especially if you think *you* might have to repeat the process when faced with an electrical nightmare at some later point. However, a little secret will allow you to easily repeat the skills needed to diagnose a starter motor that goes *click*, a dim headlight, or an engine that starts and dies, as well as to find and fix any number of mysterious problems. The secret is practice.

Most people understand the need for practice; playing baseball, riding motorcycles, shooting pool, bowling—anything requiring a specific skill set goes a lot smoother with some experience. If you haven't picked up a baseball bat in a year and it's your turn at bat in the game, there's a good chance you'll strike out. As everyone knows, a little practice before the game goes a long way toward success. Likewise, the day your car or motorcycle fails to start shouldn't be the first time you switch on your new digital voltmeter. Practicing how to apply basic electrical knowledge by using your multimeter on an operating circuit gives you a better-than-average chance of hitting the ball the first time up (electrically speaking) when something goes wrong with your bike. And it's easier than you think.

Applying electrical theory to the real world is simply a matter of knowing what reading to expect from a volt/amp/ohm meter display while it's connected to a working circuit, and *before* connecting it to a problem circuit. Having a picture in your head of what the reading should be, and what the numbers mean, allows you to visualize an otherwise invisible problem. By practicing on operating circuits with known values, you'll gain the necessary confidence to know what to look for in a circuit that isn't doing what it's supposed to. Let's start by dissecting a common 12-volt DC circuit—it doesn't get much simpler.

NOTE: Unless otherwise stated, all of the theories apply to both 12- and 6-volt systems. Where appropriate, differences will be made clear.

A simple 12-volt battery, wires, and light bulb make up a basic DC circuit. This circuit has a power supply, load device (the light bulb), and a ground return. Courtesy Yuasa Battery Inc.

"THREE THINGS" ABOUT 12-VOLT DC CIRCUITS

Everything electrical on your motorcycle is part of a circuit. Circuits are simply layouts or designs of how electrical components are powered and controlled. Electrical components found in motorcycles are usually divided into categories of circuits (though not always). For example, the lighting circuit is composed of headlight(s), taillight(s), and turn signal lights; the charging circuit includes an alternator, generator, or magneto, voltage regulator or rectifier, and storage battery; typical fuel injection circuits have an ECM (electronic control module) and various sensors and actuators.

Within each system are individual circuits that control specific electrical components. Headlights and taillights are part of the lighting system, but each operates via a separate circuit within that system. This system within a system (or subsystem) creates a big stumbling block for many "shade tree mechanics" and power sports technicians facing problems with motorcycle electrical systems. In order to diagnose an electrical problem, the nonoperational circuit must be separated and isolated from the overall larger system of which it is a part, as well as from other operating circuits within that system.

When faced with an electrical repair, most people typically turn to manufacturers' wiring diagrams for help. They wrongly assume, since the diagrams provide a blueprint of the electrical system, that the diagrams will help with the identification of specific inoperable circuits. However, this approach is like looking for a needle in a haystack. Manufacturers' wiring diagrams don't isolate or identify inoperable circuits. In fact, since they could show the entire lighting system with all its circuits, or worse, the complete electrical system for the whole motorcycle, this approach can prove daunting unless you know what to look for.

The ability to simply identify and isolate a circuit allows you to: (1) know where to connect a voltmeter; and (2) know what the respective readings should be. This is not as hard or intimidating as it may sound if you understand the "Three Things" that make up all 12-volt DC circuits. When any one of the "Three Things" goes missing in action, the circuit stops working. While this might seem obvious, it is far less so when you are looking at a complex wiring diagram or the actual wiring harness under a gas tank or behind a headlight. However, once you know what to look for, these "Three Things" are easy to identify as the primary components of every 12-volt DC electrical circuit.

The "Three Things" listed below are necessary, and all must be present in a circuit in order for it to operate.

1. Power Source

Every electrical component must have a *power source* in order to operate. All of the electrical energy needed for the circuit to do its job is provided by the *power source*. For electricity to move along a wire, subatomic particles called electrons (which are invisible to the naked eye) interact so

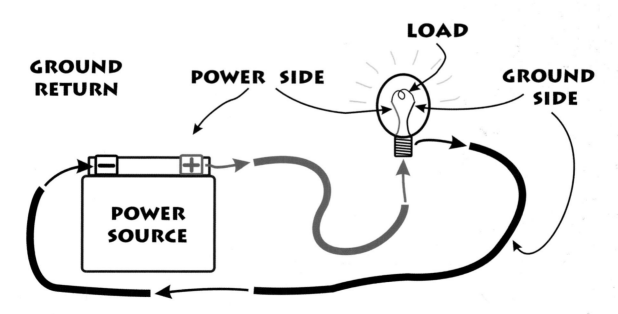

Fig 1-1—"Three Things" that make up a 12-volt DC circuit: (1) the battery's positive terminal and red wire are the power source; (2) the load, or load device, is the filament inside the light bulb; and (3) the black wire is the ground return.

as to transfer energy from one point to another. Electrons provide the power for the circuit. Starting at the battery's positive terminal, electrons are pushed through the circuit. Any problems with connections on the *power* side of a circuit will affect the entire circuit. This seems like a no-brainer, but countless times technicians and home mechanics have spent hours trying to discover why something doesn't work, only to find out later a simple blown fuse was the cause.

The battery and/or alternator/generator are the chief *power sources* for all electrical and electronic circuits in your vehicle. In addition, any wires connected to either the positive terminal of a battery or to an alternator's output terminal should be considered a *power source.* Consequently, relays, fuses, junction blocks, and fuseable links may all provide power to electrical components, because they all connect back to the battery's positive terminal. Other terminology that might be used to refer to a *power source* for a circuit include: plus side, power side, hot or hot side, positive, (+), and battery.

2. Load Device

A *load device* is any component or item that uses up voltage or has resistance to the flow of electrons through a wire. Most *load devices* simply amount to nothing more than electrical conductors of various lengths, sizes, and shapes. For example, starter motors, relays, lights, solenoids, coils, spark plugs, and computers (black boxes) are all *load devices* that have some *resistance* and contain some type of electrical connection. The hundreds of *load devices* appearing in wiring diagrams all perform some type of useful work and are designed into the circuits in which they function.

However, there are types of *load devices* we can all live without. These unwanted *load devices* run the gamut from corroded or loose connections to frayed sections of wire to dirty contacts inside switches or relays. These *load devices* also have resistance to electron flow, use up voltage unnecessarily, and have an undesirable effect on electrical circuits. Worst of all, they don't show up on any wiring diagrams, so you have to find them yourself. Chapter 2 on Voltage Drop Testing will show you how.

3. Ground Return

A *ground return* can be wires, the engine, the transmission, or a motorcycle's frame, all of which provide a route for electrons (electricity) to "return" back to the battery after being used by the load device. Other terminology often used to refer to a *ground return* include: ground, cold, earth, (-), or negative. This sequence of electron flow—*power, load device,* and *ground return* is known as a complete circuit. If any of the "Three Things" gets disconnected, the circuit is broken or interrupted and rendered incomplete.

Because electrons are invisible when flowing through a circuit, it's hard to get an idea of what's going on inside the

Two power sources found in all motorcycles are the storage battery and the charging system. Most motorcycles don't have an alternator like the one pictured, from a Honda Gold Wing, and use a stator, rotor, and rectifier that make up the charging system. Older bikes may use a generator or magneto. Courtesy Twigg Cycles, Yuasa Battery, Inc.

These components may appear different, but they're all really just load devices with resistance to electron flow. Courtesy Twigg Cycles

system. Think of a basic 12-volt circuit consisting of a battery, light bulb, and wires connecting them. The only visual confirmation showing the circuit is operating is that the bulb is on. If everything is connected and the light bulb is off, and one of the "Three Things" is missing, the only confirmation a technician receives that something is wrong is the bulb does not come on.

Let's think of this concept another way. Water flowing through a hose is a "user-friendly" way to conceptualize what's happening inside an operating electrical circuit. Visualize a tank full of water with an internal pump. An inlet and outlet on the tank are connected via hoses to a load device. When water is pumped out of the tank under pressure it's sent to a load device that does some form of work. After the energy from the pressurized water is extracted via the load device, a "return" hose (the ground return in this analogy) sends the water from the load device back to the tank where the sequence starts over again.

However, in order for this process to work continually, water must be returned to the tank at the same rate it's pumped out. The flow of electrons through an electrical circuit works in a similar manner. Starting from the circuit's power side, electrons flow to a load device where they provide energy for some type of work to be accomplished. From the load device they flow through the ground return wire and back to the battery.

"THREE MORE THINGS" ABOUT 12-VOLT DC CIRCUITS

You knew it couldn't be that simple! Only three electrical concepts to keep track of? Don't worry, there's not too much more.

The *power source, load device,* and *ground return* are physical objects that can be seen and touched. In addition to these three physical objects, there are three more elements of a standard 12-volt DC electrical system that are less tangible—they are concepts or principles; however, understanding their significance and interaction is just as important as understanding how the "Three Things" form a circuit. Fortunately, to help you out, so you're not operating totally in the dark, you can observe the net effect of the interaction of these additional "Three More Things."

The "Three More Things" are: (1) *Voltage;* (2) *Amperage;* and (3) *Resistance.* Think of voltage as electrical pressure, amperage as the amount of electricity used in the circuit, and resistance as restriction of the flow of electrons through the circuit. These three principles or concepts represent the electrical values of what's actually occurring inside an operating circuit. Having a clear idea of how these "Three More Things" interrelate allows you to "visualize" what's right or wrong with a DC electrical circuit.

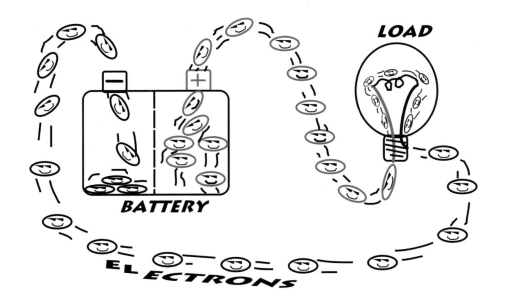

Fig 1-2—*Deliriously happy working electrons are pumped—pushed—out of the battery and travel through a load device back to the battery via a ground return, making a complete circuit.*

VOLTAGE

Voltage can be thought of as the "pressure" needed to push electrons from the battery's positive post through a load device and back to the negative terminal. Voltage, or electrical pressure, is similar to the air produced by an air compressor. The compressor forces air into a tank, where it is stored as an energy source. When you connect an air-powered tool to the tank and squeeze the trigger, the tank's high-pressure air is pushed from the tank through the air hose into the tool so the tool (and you) can do work. The higher the air pressure, the more work the air tool can accomplish (though that is not necessarily true of you!). The same is true of voltage. The more voltage—electrical pressure—present, the harder and more forcefully the electrons are pushed along a wire and through the load device. There are only 12.8 volts worth of "push" in a typical motorcycle battery (6.2 volts on a 6-volt battery). With the engine running, the charging system raises this voltage to around 14.5 volts (around 7 volts for a 6-volt battery). With only these small amounts of "push" present, it's important not to lose any voltage across a connector or along a wire.

However, there is another electrical system in your bike that develops considerably more electrical pressure than the 12.6 or 6.2 volts found at the battery. Ignition systems require high electrical pressure, because the load

device for the ignition system circuit is the spark plug. The spark plug has resistance to the flow of electrons via the small gap of air between two of its parts—the center and ground electrodes. Ignition voltage needs to be high enough to overcome the very high resistance created by the air gap. The high voltage creates a spark as it jumps from the spark plug's center electrode to the ground return electrode. Ignition systems that use points require around 10,000 volts, for the voltage to overcome the air gap's resistance and create a spark.

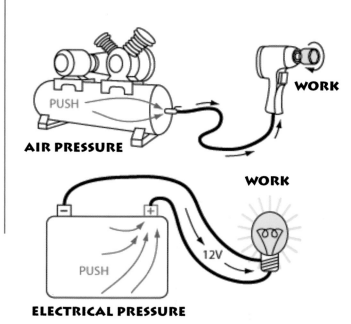

Fig 1-3—*Air pressure and voltage (electrical pressure) are similar in that more push equals more work produced by a load device.* Courtesy Alan Lapp, Level Five Graphics

The voltage output on newer electronic ignition systems is considerably higher, with many producing well over 50,000 volts. If you have ever worked on an ignition system with the engine running and been zapped by a spark plug wire, you know what that push feels like.

AMPERAGE

Amperage, or current, is the amount or volume of electricity (amps) flowing through a circuit. If a starter motor has a high amperage draw, in practical terms it means that lots of electrons must travel from the battery, through the starter, and back to the battery in a complete circuit in order for the starter to get enough energy to turn the engine over. As much as 180 amps are required to crank a large V-twin engine. In a starter circuit, both positive and negative battery cables have to be large enough to not restrict the flow of electrons. In other words, the diameter of a cable in a starter system has to be large enough to offer low resistance to the magnitude of current flow traveling through the circuit.

Conversely, the process of illuminating a taillight requires considerably less energy. Because the bulb used in a taillight circuit is a low-amperage load device, the wires leading from the power source to the bulb and returning back to the negative battery terminal are significantly smaller in diameter than the cables in a starter circuit. The minimal resistance found in the smaller wires will not slow down the electrons substantially enough to prevent the transfer of energy necessary to light up a taillight—only 2 amps. The amount of amperage flow in a circuit is independent of the size of the wires used. Using a wire the size of a battery cable to construct a taillight circuit would have no affect on its operation. However, using a small taillight-sized wire as a battery cable for a starter circuit would not work. The small

wire can't transfer enough electrons (high amperage) into the starter motor—the wire would overheat and melt in half.

RESISTANCE

Resistance is the restriction of electron flow in a circuit. Resistance anywhere in a circuit slows down the flow of electrons. By definition, all load devices have resistance to

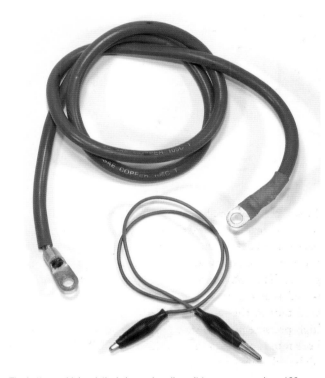

The battery cable's relatively large size allows it to carry as much as 180 amps in a V-twin starter circuit without overheating. The smaller wire will accommodate only up to 20 amps—using it in a starter circuit would melt it in half. Courtesy Twigg Cycles

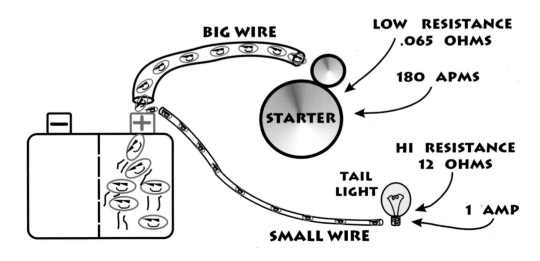

Fig 1-4—A high-amperage, low-resistance starter circuit requires large cables to allow enough energy to reach the starter and return to the battery. However, a taillight's high-resistance, low-amperage design requires only a small wire to carry its electrical load.

BIG WIRE

LOW RESISTANCE .065 OHMS

180 APMS

STARTER

HI RESISTANCE 12 OHMS

TAIL LIGHT

1 AMP

SMALL WIRE

electron flow. The relationship between voltage, amperage, and *resistance* was discovered about 170 years ago by Georg Simon Ohm. The theory explaining the interaction of these principles is known as Ohm's law. The primary measurement of *resistance* is expressed as ohms.

Motorcycles have both high- and low-resistive circuits. For example, a turn signal light bulb may have high *resistance* (12 ohms) to electron flow and therefore use only a small amount of amperage; by contrast, a starter motor has a low *resistance* value (0.06 ohms) and allows a greater number of electrons (high amperage) to flow from the battery to the starter. Because *resistance* restricts the flow of electrons in a circuit, it affects the path (the wire) the electrons travel down. Like most of us, electricity is lazy—it takes the "path of least resistance," going from one point to another in a circuit. For example, if one of the wires going to two light bulbs connected to a battery has high *resistance*, the electrons will flow down the other, lower resistive wire (lighting that bulb only).

RESISTANCE–AMPS RELATIONSHIP

Many electrical gremlins found in motorcycles can be attributed to unwanted, high resistance within a circuit. The presence of too much resistance in a circuit slows down the flow of electrons and causes low performance or nonoperation of load devices.

There is a direct relationship between circuit *amperage* and circuit *resistance*. It's critical you understand this simple cause-and-effect relationship. Knowing how to apply this knowledge is key to helping you solve many electrical problems.

Both a slow-turning starter and a dim headlight are the result of an insufficient number of electrons passing through the circuit back to the battery (creating a complete circuit). Somewhere along the circuit, high resistance has blocked the flow of current (amperage). Thus, an increase in resistance causes a decrease in amperage.

However, the opposite occurs whenever the resistance in a circuit is too low—a decrease in resistance causes an increase in amperage. For example, if a power source wire comes into contact with a ground return (because of a loose connection, frayed wire, etc.), and thereby bypassing the intended load device, the low resistance present in the ground return allows high amperage to flow through the circuit. If the wires are too small to carry the increased amperage, they could overheat and melt, possibly causing a fire. Fuses are used to protect circuits in the event resistance to electron flow becomes too low. The fuse heats up when amperage increases; at some point, amperage gets high enough to melt the fuse in half, causing an incomplete circuit. Fuses provide a margin of safety in circuits, since a burned wire could cause an electrical fire. Also, a blown or melted fuse is easier to replace than burned wires!

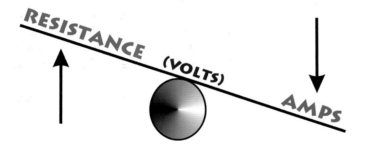

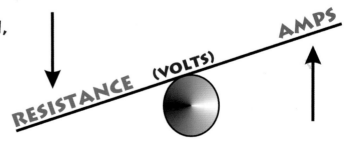

Fig 1-5—If you remember nothing else from this chapter, remembering the relationship between resistance and amps and how they operate within a circuit is worth its weight in gold (or money!) because it will help you diagnose many common electrical problems. If amps are down, the cause has to be unwanted high resistance; if high amperage is present, the circuit resistance is low.

It's important to remember the inverse relationship between *resistance* and *amperage*. When resistance in a circuit is decreased, amperage increases proportionally. Conversely, if a circuit has high resistance, the available amperage is decreased.

DC AND AC CIRCUITS

In a DC (direct current) circuit, the flow of electrical current (amps) is always only in one direction. For ease of explanation (and in conformance with automotive and power sports publications), all diagrams used in this book depict electricity (electrons) flowing through DC circuits in one direction only—from a point of higher (positive) voltage to a lower (negative) voltage. Electron flow, from positive to negative, is called conventional electron theory. (In reality, electron movement at the subatomic level travels only from negative to positive in a DC circuit.) However, since you can't see the electrons while working on a circuit, it doesn't really matter which direction they travel. The important thing to remember for practical purposes (and for the hands-on subject matter of this book), is that the flow of electricity in DC circuits is always only in one direction. For purposes of illustration and ease of explanation, this book uses the conventional view, based on the simple assumption (even if not technically correct) that electrons in a DC circuit always flow from positive to negative.

By contrast, AC (alternate current) circuits (the type typically used in most American homes) reverse the direction of voltage 60 times each second. These alternating cycles of forward and backward electron flow are called Hertz (Hz). This voltage reversal, which also reverses current flow, gives this type of electrical power its name—alternating current. AC circuits operate on higher voltages than DC circuits—120, 240, or 440 volts for an AC circuit versus only 6 or 12 volts for a motorcycle DC circuit.

Once the charging system produces AC voltage, diodes convert it into DC voltage before it reaches the battery because there are no load devices on a motorcycle that operate with AC voltage and current. Furthermore, wiring configurations and components for AC current generally are not compatible with DC circuits.

OH NO, MATH?

Books on electronics are always packed full of mathematical formulas. If you get that glazed, faraway look when faced with cryptic equations like "$E = I/R$," don't worry, this book keeps it simple.

When diagnosing an electrical problem on your motorcycle, understanding the dynamic relationship between *resistance*, *amperage*, and *voltage* is critically more important than any math skills you might have (or not have!). However, some basic calculations come in handy if you intend to add any electrical accessories to your bike. For example, do you have any idea how big the wires need to be to power that 2,000-watt stereo you bought for your Gold Wing? Should you install a larger alternator to accommodate the stereo's power so you get the sound you want? Do you know what size fuse should be used to protect the circuit from meltdown?

The formulas listed in Figure 1-6 will provide you with the basic math necessary to find voltage, resistance, amperage, and watts (power) in any circuit. In general, these should cover most of your average circuitry design needs.

To determine the amount of any unknown voltage, amperage, or resistance present within a particular circuit, you need only know the values of two of the three potentials—the third unknown value can be determined based upon the values of the other two. Performing these simple mathematical computations allows you to calculate electrical loads.

Fig 1-6—These are the basic math formulas needed to figure out the numbers in any 12- or 6-volt DC circuit. To solve for any one unknown value, you only need to know two of the three values—volts, amps, or ohms; the unknown variable can be determined by the simple mathematical equations at right.

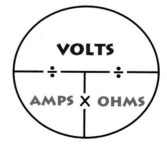

VOLTS = AMPS TIMES OHMS

OHMS = VOLTS DIVIDED BY AMPS

AMPS = VOLTS DIVIDED BY OHMS

WATTS = AMPS TIMES VOLTS

AMPS = WATTS DIVIDED BY VOLTS

To find the voltage used in a circuit, just multiply existing amps by ohms. Similarly, ohms can be calculated by dividing amps into voltage. Likewise, amps can be determined by dividing ohms into voltage. If that electric vest you intend to use is rated in watts and you want to find out how many amps will be used in the circuit, just divide watts by volts. Conversely, if you want to find watts, it's amps multiplied by volts.

RULES OF OPERATION FOR THREE TYPES OF CIRCUITS

Three types of electrical circuits are used in motorcycles: series, parallel, and series/parallel. Series and parallel circuits are by far the most common and can be found on both new and older bikes. Each type of circuit follows a set of operational rules that govern how the circuit works. Some rules apply to more than one type of circuit; others apply to only one type. Knowing these rules and understanding how each circuit operates gives the added advantage needed to diagnose most electrical problems.

SERIES CIRCUITS

Naturally, there are "Three Rules" regarding how a series circuit operates.

The First Rule of Series Circuits is: All available voltage in a series circuit will be used up by the load device.

It's important to remember this rule. By keeping it in mind, you'll be able to determine what the voltage should be at any point in a series circuit; then, if your voltmeter gives you an unexpected result, you'll know where to look for the problem. Here's why:

Figure 1-7 shows a positive battery terminal and the wire connecting it to the light bulb as the circuit's power source. The light bulb is the load device. All 12 volts from the power source are present at every point along the wire between the battery and load device (and can be measured by a voltmeter). When 12 volts reach the light bulb (the load device), the light bulb uses up all the voltage in the circuit. Since the greedy light bulb uses up all the

available voltage by turning 0n, no voltage is present on the ground return wire all the way back to the battery. (Caveat: Not quite true! The ground return wire also has an inherently small amount of resistance to current flow, which causes a small amount of voltage to be present.) Consequently, the ground wire will measure close to 0 volts. Chapter 2 on Voltage Drop Testing provides more in-depth explanations of what to expect from voltage readings on ground return wires. For now, consider the ground wire to be essentially 0 volts.

The Second Rule of Series Circuits is: When more than one load device is present in a series circuit, the individual resistance of each load device divides the available voltage and adds to the total resistance of the entire circuit.

Think of load devices in a series circuit like a strand of Christmas tree lights along a wire—they are connected in a series. Because each bulb has resistance to current flow, each adds to the total resistance of the entire circuit. This cumulative increase in overall circuit resistance correspondingly decreases the amperage available for all the bulbs, thus keeping the strand of Christmas tree lights at a nice, fire-safe, low-level amperage. In addition, each of the bulbs must share or divide the available voltage because all need some voltage to light up.

Voltage in a series circuit is not a constant. It is shared or divided between all the load devices in the circuit. Voltage is divided based on the individual resistance of each specific load device. It's important to remember that each load device(s) in a series circuit requires both a power source and ground return in order to operate. Because the load devices are linked together, the power source for one load device simultaneously acts as the ground return for another.

For example, consider three light bulbs connected in a series circuit (see Figure 1-8). The first bulb (Bulb No. 1) is powered by the originating power source—a 12-volt battery. The ground return for Bulb No. 1 becomes the power source for the second bulb (Bulb No. 2). Bulb No. 1 uses 4 volts of power from the 12-volt power source (to light up)

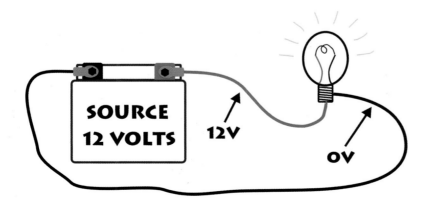

Fig 1-7—Twelve volts are present on the red wire between the battery and light bulb (load device). The light bulb uses up all available voltage. Thus, the ground return wire reads 0 volt all the way back to the negative battery terminal.

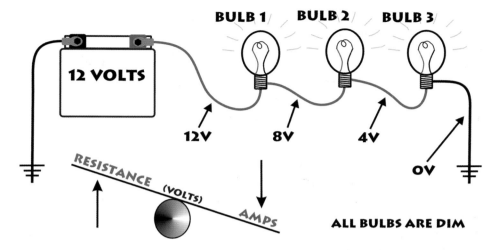

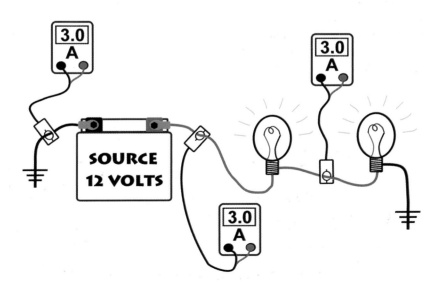

Fig 1-8—Each 12-volt bulb (load device) has a given identical individual resistance, resulting in equal sharing of the overall available voltage. The difference in voltage between the power source and ground return for each bulb is 4 volts. Consequently, each bulb has only 4 volts of electrical pressure with which to operate. Since all the bulbs are designed to operate on 12 volts and not 4 volts, this shortfall in voltage for each bulb causes all of them to be dim.

and then passes the "leftover" 8 volts into its ground return. Similarly, Bulb No. 2 takes (and uses up) 4 volts of the available voltage from the ground return of Bulb No. 1 (Bulb No. 2 uses the same voltage as Bulb No. 1 to operate). The remaining 4 volts of power pass into Bulb No. 2's ground return (Bulb No. 3's power source). Bulb No. 3 takes the last 4 volts and uses up all the voltage left in the entire circuit; consequently, its ground return has 0 volt.

Figure 1-8 illustrates the application of this division of voltage along a series circuit. It also proves the First Rule of Series Circuits still holds true—the load device uses up all the available voltage since all the individual light bulbs combined cumulatively use up all the available voltage in the circuit (equivalent to a single combined load device). Thus, the ground return wire at the *last* load device will measure close to 0 volts. Figure 1-8 also introduces the ground symbol—three horizontal lines at the end of the ground return wire. The placement of this symbol indicates

a particular wire is returning back to the negative battery terminal. The ground return symbol might also be used when a ground strap, engine, or motorcycle frame is used as a ground.

The Third Rule of Series Circuits is: Amperage is the same at all points throughout a series circuit.

This rule is true on both negative and positive sides of a circuit. Figure 1-9 shows three amp meters measuring current in a series circuit. As you can see, the amperage remains constant on both the power and ground return sides of the circuit. Rule Three illustrates the simple concept (but unwanted result!) that a bad wire or poor connection (unwanted resistance) will affect circuit amperage no matter which side of the circuit it's located on.

PARALLEL CIRCUITS

Nearly all of the electrical circuits designed for motorcycles are parallel circuits. Fortunately, the rules for parallel circuits

Fig 1-9—Amperage will be the same on both the power and ground sides of a circuit. All three amp meters indicate the same amount of amperage (current) is flowing throughout the circuit.

are basically the same as for series circuits, but with a couple of notable exceptions.

The first exception is: Voltage will be equal (the same) everywhere on the positive side of the circuit and will not be divided between load devices as in a series circuit. This is because each load device has its own wire (conductor) connecting it to the power source. The same is also true on the ground return side—each load device has its own ground return. As a result, the ground return side of each load device registers 0 volts because each individual load device uses up all the original source voltage.

Figure 1-10 displays how 0 volts are present on the ground return side of each individual bulb (load device) because all of the original power source voltage is used up by each bulb. The ground return side of each bulb operates just like the ground return side at the end of a series circuit. However, in a parallel circuit, it is helpful to think of each bulb as a simple series circuit itself—it has a separate power source (the 12-volt battery), a load device (the bulb), and a ground return (the wire). Consequently, as more load devices are added to a parallel circuit, the greater the amperage from the power source to the load devices needs to be—because total resistance of the entire circuit decreases as overall amperage increases. Remember? (See Figure 1-5 on page 14.)

The second exception is: Each additional load device in a parallel circuit lowers the total overall resistance of the circuit and increases amperage. The second exception requires *ALL* the power for the entire circuit to come from the same power source (the battery). Referring to the diagram in Figure 1-11, the total amperage used by all the load devices must pass through the 20-amp fuse. Since

each of the 12-volt bulbs in the individual circuits uses 6 amps, the total combined amperage for all the bulbs (3 bulbs x 6 amps = 18 amps) must pass through the 20-amp fuse. This isn't a problem, because the fuse won't melt until amperage exceeds 20 amps.

Figure 1-11 illustrates how the addition of more load devices to a *parallel* circuit causes the resistance of the entire circuit to decrease and a corresponding increase in amperage—the teeter-totter effect (unlike what occurs in a *series* circuit, where the resistance of each load device adds to the total resistance of the circuit). It shows how each "leg" or individual circuit within a parallel circuit operates like a series circuit. Each has a power source, load device, and ground return.

To understand this concept better, consider the following analogy: Imagine there are 20 people in a room with only one exit door. Someone yells "fire" and everyone tries to exit through the only door, creating lots of "resistance." The people represent amperage, the room is the circuit, and their effort to get out is the resistance. Because there is only one door to use to escape, very few people actually get out because of the net effect of their combined resistance. Now assume the same 20 people are in a room with 20 doors. The same fire occurs. Everyone is able to exit the room easily because each leaves through a separate door. Because there are more doors, there is less resistance in the flow of people. The extra doors in the room represent additional load devices in a parallel circuit. Resistance to electron flow is reduced because a parallel circuit has more "doors" for the electrons to exit (more load devices). As stated before, when resistance decreases in a parallel circuit,

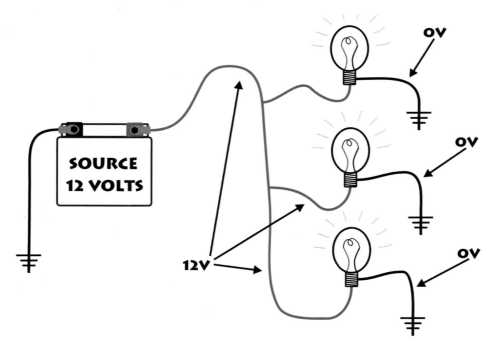

Fig 1-10—Parallel circuits do not share or divide voltage between load devices, as in a series circuit. Unlike series circuits, where the light bulbs (load devices) divide the total voltage between them, the bulbs in a parallel circuit are each individually brighter because each bulb operates on 12 volts and uses all of the power source voltage.

amperage increases (and more people get out); so, adding more load devices (doors) lowers total resistance and increases circuit amperage.

Referring to Figure 1-11 again, the end of the circuit is an electric radiator fan motor (another load device), requiring 12 amps to operate. As long as the motor switch is open, the circuit uses only 18 amps to light the bulbs and the fuse is adequate for this application. However, if the motor switch is closed the motor connects to the parallel circuit and the amperage requirement for the entire circuit increases to 30 amps (18 amps from the bulbs + 12 amps from the motor = 30 amps). This amount exceeds the rating of the 20-amp fuse, so the fuse overheats and melts in order to protect the circuit by cutting off power to the entire circuit. Thus, in order for this circuit to work, the 20-amp fuse has to be replaced with a fuse with a rating of more than 30 amps.

SERIES/PARALLEL CIRCUITS

Series/parallel circuits are rarely designed for motorcycles. However, they can be created whenever a poor connection is present in a parallel circuit. Remember, any form of resistance is considered a load device. Loose or corroded connections have resistance; therefore, whenever they are present, a series or series/parallel circuit is formed. The load devices in circuits with unwanted high resistance operate with less voltage and amperage than intended. Consequently, *all* load devices connected to the circuit could be affected by the resulting reduced voltage and amperage.

Figure 1-12 illustrates a series/parallel circuit designed to operate a headlight and taillight. The addition of a light bulb between the battery and other load devices represents a bad connection, which is in series with other load devices. The presence of the bad connection (bulb) adds resistance, lowering the available voltage and amperage necessary for the intended load devices (headlight and taillight) to operate. Because the bulb uses some voltage from the power source, less than 12 volts are present on the wires going to the two lights (their power source). Since the headlights and taillights are designed to operate on 12 volts, and not less, they won't work as intended, and are consequently dim.

Replacing a headlight, taillight, or battery won't solve this problem either—but you'd be surprised how often this is the attempted "fix." The only way to fix what's really wrong is to find the bad connection; in this example, simply replacing the small bulb with a section of wire will eliminate the unwanted high resistance so both headlights and taillights will shine brightly again. The trick is to find the bad connections without unraveling wiring harnesses or removing parts, and that is what Chapter 2, Voltage Drop Testing, is all about.

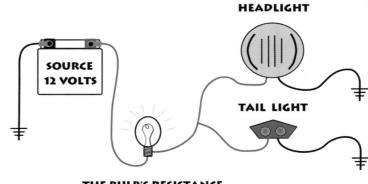

HEADLIGHT

TAIL LIGHT

SOURCE 12 VOLTS

THE BULB'S RESISTANCE REPRESENTS A POOR CONNECTION

Above: *Fig 1-12—The presence of loose or corroded connectors (represented by the small light bulb) have turned this parallel circuit into a series/parallel circuit. The bad connection/bulb is in series with the headlight and taillight and divides the voltage between them. Thus, the originally intended load devices won't have enough voltage or amperage to operate properly.*

Left: *Fig 1-11—In a parallel circuit, each additional load device lowers the circuit's total number of ohms (resistance), inversely raising the overall amperage flowing through the circuit. A higher-rated fuse and larger wires are required so this circuit can operate without melting wires or blowing the 20-amp fuse.*

RESISTANCE (VOLTS)   AMPS

20 AMP FUSE

BULB 1 (6 AMPS)

BULB 2 (6 AMPS)

BULB 3 (6 AMPS)

SOURCE 12 VOLTS

MOTOR SWITCH

MOTOR (12 AMPS)

CHAPTER 2
VOLTAGE DROP TESTING

WHAT VOLTAGE DROP TESTING DOES

Consider the following scenario: The owner—let's call him Bob—of a six-year-old Gold Wing tries to start the engine on a cold morning. The starter cranks slowly then makes a clicking sound. Bob finds his jumper cables and using his truck, jump-starts the Wing. Bob takes the bike to a local dealer who claims he can fix the problem by replacing the battery. He does so, and the engine starts right up. Problem fixed? Maybe. Lucky for Bob, his motorcycle starts and runs okay every morning for a few weeks. Bob is happy the problem has been fixed. However, several weeks later, the same thing happens again—the engine cranks too slowly and won't start. Bob, now angry, takes the bike back to the dealer and demands an explanation. He gets one. This time the mechanic says it has to be a faulty starter. Bob reluctantly replaces the starter, having lost confidence in the mechanic. The Gold Wing works fine again for a few more weeks. However, several weeks later, Bob gets the same result. Sound all-too-familiar? After spending $100 on a new battery, $538 for a new starter motor and $150 for labor, not to mention all his wasted time and aggravation, the original problem is still there.

As it turns out, the cause of the slow-turning starter was a loose bolt that attaches the battery ground cable to the engine block. Poor electrical connections are the most common cause of many electrical problems. While this statement might seem obvious, in reality, very few mechanics think to look to electrical connections first for the source of an electrical-related problem. In fact, this scenario can happen with just about any electrical component—alternators, generators, radiator cooling fans, headlights, brake lights, etc. Home mechanics and many professional technicians have the same difficulty diagnosing this type of problem.

Above right: *Voltage drop testing this starter solenoid is the only reliable way to determine if the high-voltage contacts inside are good. Voltage drop testing determines if a circuit's connections and wires can pass enough amperage to operate correctly.* Courtesy Fluke Corporation and Twigg Cycles

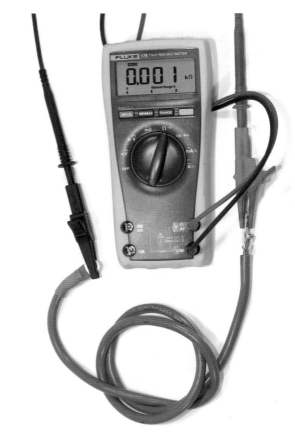

Right: *Even a good ohmmeter, like this Fluke 175, is only able to indicate that a battery cable is essentially not cut in half. While continuity can be shown on an ohmmeter, the battery cable could still have unwanted high resistance, which can only be measured via a voltage drop test.* Courtesy Fluke Corporation and Twigg Cycles

Fortunately, there is a simple and easy way to test for bad connections, switches, or wires as the likely cause of a problem with an electrical circuit. The method is called voltage drop testing. A voltage drop test measures resistance within a circuit using a voltmeter (not an ohmmeter). Voltage drop testing is the easiest method to confirm that wires, connections, battery cables and terminals, relays, and switches are not the cause of an operating problem with an electrical circuit. The major advantage of performing a voltage drop test is that nothing needs to be disconnected to perform the test—no unraveling of the wiring harness and no removing starters, alternators, or any other components.

Simply because a wire or electrical connection "looks good" doesn't mean it is good. The only way to determine if unwanted resistance is slowing down the flow of electrons passing through a connection, or along a wire, is to measure the drop in voltage within the circuit as it operates.

DON'T USE AN OHMMETER

Many shade-tree mechanics and even some professional technicians insist that finding a bad wire, switch, or connection can be accomplished using an ohmmeter. While this is partly true, it is certainly not the best method (or even a good one!) for diagnosing loose connections and other similar electrical resistance problems. Attempting to test a wire using an ohmmeter can reveal only one limited fact—whether the wire has continuity (a connection exists) between the two points being measured. However, it's the *quality* of the connection that will determine if the circuit can carry enough amperage to operate.

When checking continuity using an ohmmeter, the meter's internal battery sends only a few milliamps (thousandths of an amp) of current through the wire or connection, thereby enabling the meter to read in ohms. Battery and charging system cables and wires are capable of carrying hundreds of amps. Even a radiator cooling fan motor may require 15 or more amps to operate. The few milliamps from an ohmmeter do not simulate the operating condition that the wire being tested is subjected to by high-amperage load devices.

Figure 2-1 illustrates the problem of using an ohmmeter to check a bad battery cable. While the ohmmeter registers continuity, obviously this cable still does not have enough capacity to carry the current required to start an engine. Unwanted high resistance in the battery cable will not show up using an ohmmeter for testing.

Another problem with attempting to use an ohmmeter to measure a wire's resistance is its inherent inability to measure *low* resistance. Attempting to check the resistance of any wire or load device, such as a starter motor, using an automotive ohmmeter will not work, because the starter motor's resistance could be as low as 0.05 ohms. To accurately measure resistance of less than one-tenth of an ohm requires a laboratory grade ohmmeter, which costs thousands of dollars. Since resistance measurements in this low range are affected by temperature and humidity, an automotive ohmmeter simply does not have the required sensitivity.

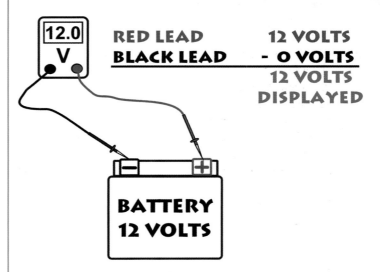

Above: *Fig 2-2—A voltmeter measures the difference in electrical pressure between its two leads. The value of the negative meter lead (0 volts) is subtracted from the positive lead (12 volts) to display the battery's total voltage—12 volts.*

Left: *Fig 2-1—High resistance equals low amperage flow in this battery cable. The ohmmeter registers continuity between the ends of the cable, but obviously the cable won't start a motorcycle engine because of its high resistance to current flow.*

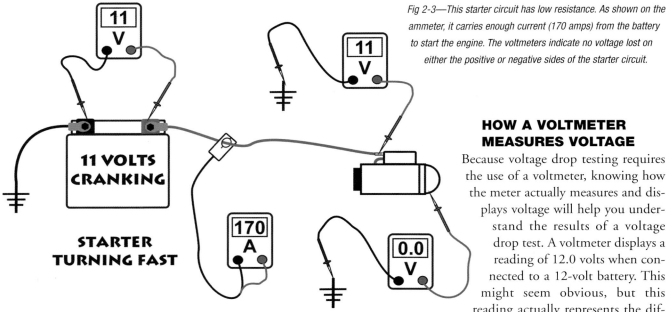

Fig 2-3—This starter circuit has low resistance. As shown on the ammeter, it carries enough current (170 amps) from the battery to start the engine. The voltmeters indicate no voltage lost on either the positive or negative sides of the starter circuit.

HOW A VOLTMETER MEASURES VOLTAGE

Because voltage drop testing requires the use of a voltmeter, knowing how the meter actually measures and displays voltage will help you understand the results of a voltage drop test. A voltmeter displays a reading of 12.0 volts when connected to a 12-volt battery. This might seem obvious, but this reading actually represents the difference in electrical pressure between the positive and negative battery terminals. The red meter lead senses 12.0 volts; the black meter lead senses zero volts. The computer chip inside the voltmeter simply subtracts the value of the black lead from the voltage level present on the red lead and displays the difference. Figure 2-2 (on page 21) illustrates the math taking place inside the voltmeter. An analog voltmeter (one with a needle) uses the voltage difference between the red and black leads to power a small internal motor that swings the needle across a numerical scale.

The only reliable method to locate a poorly conducting wire or connector is to use a voltmeter to measure the voltage drop across the section of the circuit being tested. Voltage drop testing works because even an inexpensive digital voltmeter can accurately measure small amounts of voltage—as low as 1/1,000th of a volt, (1 millivolt). Voltage drop testing provides a comparison of the voltage between two points in an operating circuit by displaying the difference or loss in voltage between them. The greater the unwanted high resistance, the greater the voltage drop.

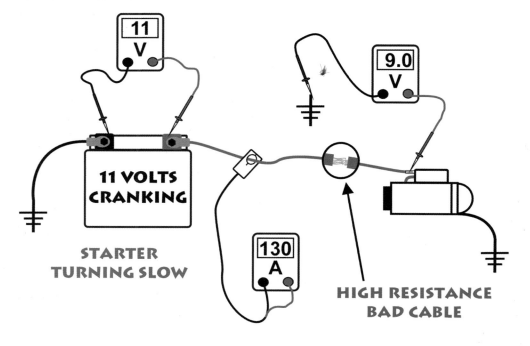

Fig 2-4—A bad battery cable can prevent sufficient amperage from reaching the starter. As a result, the engine turns too slowly to start, because the positive cable looses 2 volts between the connection at the battery and the starter motor. The voltage loss causes only 130 amps to flow through the starter circuit instead of the 170 amps needed to crank the engine fast enough to start.

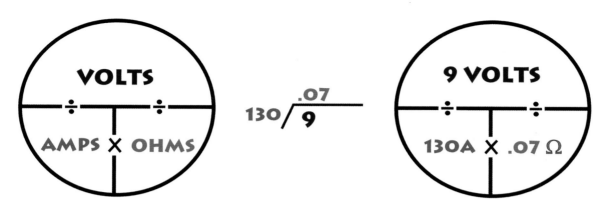

Fig 2-5—With only 9 volts and 130 amps measured in this starter circuit, resistance is calculated at 0.07 (7/100th) ohms, far too low for an automotive type of ohmmeter (even an expensive one) to measure or record accurately.

TESTING CIRCUITS DYNAMICALLY

Dynamic testing occurs when the circuit being tested is actually operating. This type of testing stresses all the components within a circuit and is more indicative of real-world operating conditions than other forms of testing. Current must be flowing through the circuit in order to measure voltage drop. Figure 2-3 illustrates the voltage present at various points in an operating starter circuit. With the starter cranking the engine, an amp meter reads 170 amps flowing throughout the starter circuit. Battery voltage normally drops to around 11 volts because of the amperage load from the starter. Voltage measured at the starter is also 11 volts. This demonstrates that the positive battery cable has low resistance and no voltage is lost between the positive battery terminal and the starter. The voltmeter reading for voltage drop on the ground return side of the starter circuit is 0 volt—this also indicates the ground cable and all the connections back to the battery have low resistance and no voltage is lost. The reason the ground side of the circuit reads 0 is that the load device (the starter) uses up all available voltage.

Figure 2-4 shows what happens when high resistance (in this case, a bad battery cable) is present in a starter circuit: The starter cranks the engine too slowly for it to start up. The positive

battery terminal has 11 volts, but only 9 volts reach the starter motor—not enough electrical pressure to crank it fast enough to start the engine. The starter motor is designed to operate on a minimum of 11 volts, not 9. High resistance in the positive battery cable causes a loss of 2 volts between the battery and starter. Because resistance is high in the circuit, amperage decreases, and only 130 amps flow through the circuit (indicated by the amp meter) instead of the 170 amps the starter requires.

As mentioned before, an ohmmeter simply cannot accurately measure the high resistance present in the battery cable shown in Figure 2-4. Figure 2-5 illustrates why: To find the actual resistance present in the battery cable, both voltage and amperage must be measured. The math is simple: 130 amps divided into 9 volts equals a resistance of 0.07 ohms, or 7/100th of an ohm—far too low a value for an automotive ohmmeter to measure.

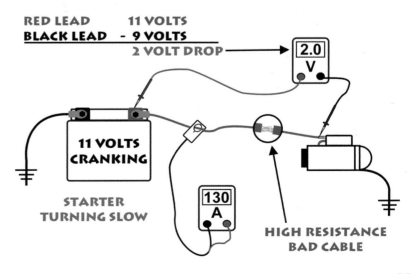

Fig 2-6—When performing a voltage drop test on the positive side of a circuit, connect the positive meter lead to the source of highest voltage, in this case, the battery's positive terminal. The negative meter lead is connected to the point where the voltage is trying to get to, in this case, the battery terminal on the starter. The meter displays the difference—2 volts.

23

VOLTAGE DROP, POSITIVE SIDE

In the examples of voltage drop testing presented so far, it would be necessary to use several voltmeters to determine voltage drop in a starter circuit. However, only one voltmeter is needed to perform a voltage drop test. Figure 2-6 (on page 23) shows how the test is accomplished using only one voltmeter to measure the voltage drop on the positive side of the starter circuit. The red meter lead is connected to the voltage source or highest point of potential voltage (in this case, the positive battery post), and the black meter lead is connected to the point the voltage is trying to reach—the starter's positive terminal.

The potential difference in voltage between the battery's positive terminal and the cable's connection at the starter is 2 volts, which is displayed on the meter. Remember, the voltmeter reads the value on the red lead, then subtracts it from the value of the black lead and displays the difference. If, by mistake, you connect the meter leads backward (red to the load device and black to the positive battery post), a digital voltmeter will display a negative number—this isn't a problem if you simply ignore the minus symbol when you read the display. However, if an analog meter is connected backward, the needle will go to the far left, past zero, and no reading is possible. A simple rule to remember to connect voltmeter leads properly when performing a voltage drop test is that the red lead gets connected to the point where voltage is highest. This will always be the source of voltage for the load device—usually the battery's positive terminal. The black meter lead gets connected to the lowest point of voltage or where the source voltage is going to—the load device.

VOLTAGE DROP, GROUND SIDE

It is important to understand that when you have performed a voltage drop on the positive side of a circuit, you are only half finished with the test. Don't forget to voltage drop test the ground return side of a circuit! Checking for resistance on the ground return is equally important to testing for it on the positive side. Remember the Three Rules of DC circuits? One of them states: "All available voltage in a circuit is used up by the load device." While we are using an example of testing a starter circuit, this rule is true for voltage drop testing any circuit. If the ground return side of the starter circuit has low resistance, there should be no voltage lost on its ground return path. This path consists of the starter's metal case, negative battery cable, and the negative battery terminal. There should be a 0-volt difference between the starter's metal case and the negative battery terminal, indicating low resistance to current flow. The bad positive battery cable in Figure 2-7 will have no effect on the ground side voltage drop test.

To measure voltage drop on the ground side of the starter circuit, connect the red meter lead to the point with the highest potential source of voltage—in this case, the metal housing of the starter motor (see Figure 2-7). When voltage drop testing another type of load device, the red meter lead would be connected to the ground return wire. The black meter lead is connected to the negative battery post—the lowest point of voltage. Once the starter is cranked, the voltmeter will display the difference

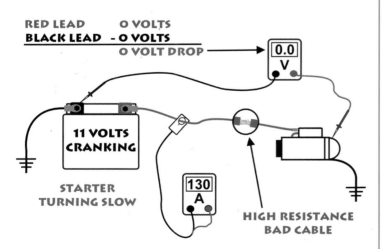

Fig 2-7—The starter should use all the available voltage when it's operating. The starter's metal case is part of its ground path back to the battery's negative terminal. The voltage drop between the starter case and negative battery terminal should be 0 volts, indicating no voltage loss.

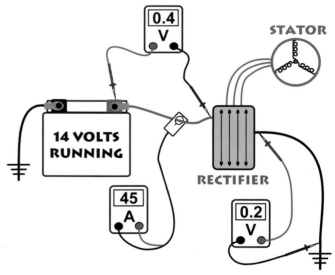

Fig 2-8—With the charging system operating, the wire between the rectifier/regulator and positive battery terminal shows a voltage drop of 0.4 volts, indicating that the connectors and wire are good. Ground side voltage drop is 0.2 volts—a low-resistance ground.

between the voltage potential on the red and black meter leads. In this example, the voltage drop on the ground side of the starter circuit is 0 volt. In other words, the ground side of this circuit has low resistance, because no voltage is lost. In the "real world," some loss of voltage will always occur between connectors and along wires or cables within a circuit. This is because there is always some resistance to current flow, even in circuits that are operating properly. How much voltage drop is too much is always a matter of opinion and interpretation.

HOW MUCH, IS "TOO MUCH"?

There are two reasons voltage drop numbers vary. The first is that the greater the amperage present in a circuit, the greater the acceptable voltage drop. For example, an alternator producing 45 amps will only have a maximum voltage drop of 0.4 volts. Some motorcycles' charging systems produce only 25 to 35 amps and will have voltage drop numbers around 0.2 volts or less. The other factor affecting circuit voltage drop is wire length and/or size. The longer the length of wire, the more its resistance increases thereby lowering the voltage present at the end of the wire. This is not much of a problem on motorcycles, because wire lengths aren't that long. However, if you tow your motorcycle with a trailer, the wires from the tow-vehicle's battery to the trailer's lights are quite long and could cause a voltage drop great enough to cause the trailer brake lights to be dim. Using a heavy gauge wire will solve this problem, because of the wire's low resistance to current flow.

In general, voltage loss on the ground side of a circuit is almost always less than on the positive side of the same circuit. Ground return circuits are often composed of the motorcycle's frame or engine/transmission. These large metal components of a bike can be more simply thought of as really BIG wires, and as such, they will have low *resistance* to current flow causing a smaller voltage drop. A circuit's positive (power) side will always be a wire or cable of some length and size, and therefore, will have greater resistance to current flow than the ground side of the same circuit, thus creating a greater voltage drop.

The following is a ballpark guide to use when performing voltage drop tests on various electrical circuitstypes of motorcycle electrical circuits.

Starter Circuit, Maximum Voltage Drop
Positive side, small starter/800-cc engine size or less,
    0.4 volts
Positive side, large starter/1,000-cc engine size or more,
    0.8 volts
Negative side, 0.4 volts
Starter solenoids, 0.2 volts
Battery terminals, 0.2 volts

Charging Circuits, Maximum Voltage Drop
Positive side, 0.2 volts (system charging at 25 amps)
Positive side, 0.4 volts (system charging at 45 amps)
Negative side, 0.2 volts

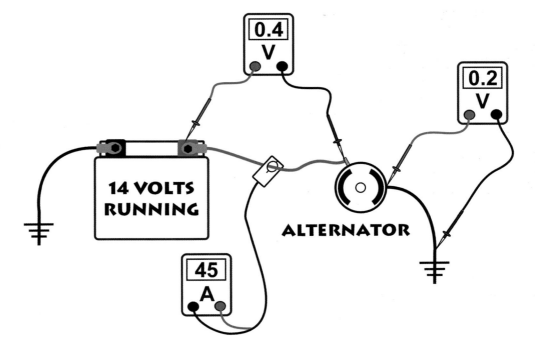

Fig 2-9—The red voltmeter lead is connected to the power wire on the back of the alternator. The black voltmeter lead is connected to the positive battery post. A second voltmeter is used to measure voltage drop on the starter's negative side. With all electrical accessories on and the engine at 4,000 rpm, the voltage drop on both the positive and negative sides of the alternator circuit are shown.

This 2006 Yamaha Star's rectifier/regulator is located just behind the front fender so it can be cooled off during operation. This makes getting to the wires relatively easy for voltage drop testing. Courtesy Twigg Cycles

Accessory Circuits (headlights, brake lights), Maximum Voltage Drop

Positive side, 0.2 volts

Negative side, 0.2 volts

Computer Circuits (ignition modules and fuel-injection sensors), Maximum Voltage Drop

Positive side, 0.1 volts (computer circuits operate at low amperage)

Negative side, 0.06 volts (computer grounds are very sensitive to loss of voltage)

LOCATING THE BAD SPOT

Figure 2-10 provides an example of how a voltage drop test can be used to locate a bad switch in a circuit. To isolate a point of high resistance in this light circuit, a voltmeter is connected to the positive battery post and the light bulb. The voltage drop is 0.5 volts. This drop (resistance) is too high and it causes the light to be dim. To determine if the switch or connector is at fault, a voltage drop test is performed across the switch and connector. A minimal drop in voltage of 0.1 volts at the connector indicates there is no excessive resistance to current flow—thus, the connector is good. However, the voltage measured across the switch is 0.4 volts—way too high. The switch is causing the light bulb to be dim. Simply cleaning the switch would lower its resist-

ance and increase the voltage going into the bulb, thereby making it shine brightly. This method of moving the voltmeter test leads along the circuit to locate the point of high resistance will work on any circuit.

Voltage drop testing is a good way to save a great deal of time and money in the quest to solve many electrical problems. The entire length of both positive and negative sides of a circuit can be checked without disconnecting any wires or connectors. For example, if the headlight on a motorcycle was dim, it may only take two or three measurements to find the point of high resistance. By connecting a voltmeter's red lead to the ground wire for the headlight and the red meter lead to the negative battery post, the drop in voltage for the entire ground side of the circuit can be determined (don't forget to have the headlight on—the circuit must be on and operating for a voltage drop test!). If the voltage drop on the ground side is acceptable, high resistance will most likely be found on the positive side of the circuit. Since headlights on many motorcycles use a relay to control power to the light, performing a voltage drop test across the relay is the most likely place to find high resistance. After connecting the red voltmeter lead to the power source for the relay, and the black lead to the relay's output side, the resulting voltage drop will reveal if the relay high-amperage contacts have high resistance.

TEST, DON'T GUESS

There are a few simple things to keep in mind when performing voltage drop tests: (1) Make sure the circuit you are testing is operating, or on. If no current is flowing in the circuit, there is no voltage drop to measure. (2) Test both the positive and negative sides of the circuit. If you find a voltage drop that is too high on one side of the circuit, start isolating where the point of high resistance is located by moving your test points along the circuit. (3) Most importantly, practice voltage drop tests on circuits that are working properly. When you have to actually do the test on a problem circuit, you'll know what's normal and what's not. (4) Finally, voltage drop testing is far easier than removing a starter or alternator, or replacing a battery. Test, don't guess, before you waste your time or money.

This negative cable connection to the battery looks okay, but it still might have high resistance. Performing a voltage drop test while the starter motor is cranking the engine can expose a poor connection without the need for removing the battery cable from the terminal. The positive side is tested in the same manner.
Courtesy Twigg Cycles

Fig 2-10—By moving the voltmeter along the circuit, the point of high resistance can be located. The switch in this circuit has an unacceptable voltage drop of 0.4 volts—time for a new switch!

CHAPTER 3
ELECTRONIC TESTING TOOLS

Using your car's factory jack and lug wrench is okay for changing a flat tire, but the job would be a lot easier using a hydraulic floor jack and 1/2-inch impact gun connected to an air compressor. Both sets of tools will get the job done, but the latter is less work, and who likes to work? Working with motorcycle electricity is no different. Using only a test light will get you only limited results when trying to solve an electrical problem. Add in a $10 voltmeter and your diagnostic potential dramatically increases. Your friends or loved ones might complain that you own every tool known to mankind (or wish you did!), but you can tell them that you have only scratched the surface—you have only enough tools needed exactly for the job at hand. When the next job comes along, you just might have to buy more. Just like wrenches, sockets, and screwdrivers, you may never finish purchasing electronic test tools.

You might wonder if a $500 digital multimeter is really required to work on motorcycle electrical systems. The answer depends upon your diagnostic goals. If you're working toward becoming a professional technician, or already are, time is money. So an expensive DVOM (digital volt ohmmeter) with all the bells and whistles can, and will, save you hours diagnosing a problem. Home technicians usually don't have the time constraints professionals do and can make do with less elaborate test equipment, so the cost for an expensive multimeter might not be warranted. However, you should always buy quality tools. If you've worked around motorcycles for any length of time, you know that the inexpensive socket set you bought at your local mass retailer is good enough for the toolbox in the trunk of your car or under the seat of your pickup, but using it for anything other than emergency repairs is problematic. Well, then, what tools should you buy? Buying a

An analog meter (right) uses a needle to display readings. The meter's dial must be set to the right scale to read correctly. Modern digital meters (left) provide readings with electronically displayed numbers. Some, like this Fluke 175, have an analog bar graph that acts like an electronic needle— the best of both old and new.
Courtesy Fluke Corporation

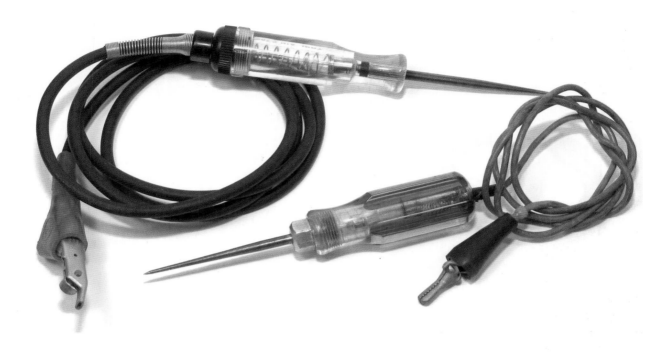

In addition to using heavier gauge wire, a quality test light (upper left) has a strain relief (metal spring or rubber) guard located where the wire exits the test light's body. This guard prevents the wire from breaking, even after years of use.

quality digital multimeter and test light is a good starting point. Adding a logic probe to your electronic toolbox will also increase your ability to solve electronic ignition and on-board computer dilemmas. Let's start with the most basic tool—a 12-volt test light.

TEST LIGHTS

An automotive test light is a bulb mounted inside a plastic housing (it looks kind of like a screwdriver) with a pointed probe at one end; a length of wire exits the other end and has an alligator clip attached to it. With the alligator clip attached to ground, the pointy end of the test light can be used to probe wires or fuses to find the presence of voltage. As soon as the probe of a grounded test light (alligator clip attached to *ground return*) touches a wire with 12 volts, the internal bulb lights up.

Automotive test lights have been around a long time and are great tools for testing for the presence of voltage. However, a test light will not indicate levels of voltage, and anything below 8 volts may not even make one light up. Test lights are also useful for activating relays and solenoids. The probe of a grounded test light can be touched to the "trigger" terminal/wire of a relay to energize it. A grounded jumper wire will do the same thing—however, a test light is safer because if you touch the probe to the

wrong wire/terminal at the relay, the test light will just light up instead of causing a spark which could possibly damage the circuit.

Test lights can also be used instead of an AC pickup coil, Hall-effect switch, or optical trigger to send a signal to an ignition module. When used in place of one of these components, the test light fools the ignition module into reacting as if the engine is turning. If the module is working, it will produce a spark from the coil—this is known as a tap test, and it is covered in more depth in Chapter 6, Ignition Systems. Additionally, test lights can be used on an ignition coil to check whether an ignition system's primary circuit is switching on and off, as well as for a fuel injector pulse from a motorcycle's on-board computer. (All of these tests are covered in later chapters.)

Not all test lights will work for all of these tests, because some have bulbs with too much resistance and can't pass enough current to provide a trigger for ignition modules or relays. Test light bulbs should have less than 10 ohms of resistance in order to trigger relays and perform ignition tap tests. If the test light you're using has more resistance, replace the bulb with one of higher wattage (lower resistance). Many of the more expensive test lights by Snap-on, Mac, and Matco use high-resistance bulbs.

Test lights range in price from as little as $5 to more than $25. So, what's the real difference between them? The more expensive ones use quality wire for the lead and a better alligator clip. In addition, a metal spring or rubber strain relief guard protects the wire where it exits the plastic body of the test light, preventing wire breakage—even after hard use. Most importantly, quality test lights use steel probes that have been hardened and don't require frequent sharpening, and the plastic housings are strong and durable. Cheap test lights may break if dropped or banged about and by the time you've bought several replacements the cost of a good one will have been far exceeded. While both inexpensive and quality test lights do the same job with the same degree of accuracy, you'll get more life out of a quality tester; so, save up and spring for the better quality—it's worth it in the long run (or handle your cheaper test lights carefully!).

Always test your test light before using it to check a circuit. Ground the lead and touch the pointy end to something you know is "hot"—such as a positive battery terminal or fuse. Remember, the bulb will eventually burn out. If you don't check your test light once in a while, you'll go crazy wondering why everything you test doesn't seem to have power.

MULTIMETERS

The term "voltmeter" is practically a misnomer today since it's almost impossible to find a meter that reads only voltage, unless you're in an antique shop. The new terms for voltmeter include digital multimeter, digital voltmeter, or DVOM. If you're serious about diagnosing and/or repairing electrical problems on your motorcycle, a good digital voltmeter is as basic and necessary a tool as a 3/8-inch-drive ratchet or socket set. Many amateurs and even some professional technicians try to find their way around a problem circuit using only a test light. Depending on the type of information sought, this method can have its place—but more often than not, knowing only that voltage is present, but not how much, is simply not enough information to figure out what's wrong with a problem circuit. A good multimeter is essential if you don't want to waste a lot of time.

Over the last 20 years, voltmeters have followed the pocket calculator (and most electronic technology) by continually dropping in price and increasing the number of extra features available. Multimeters used to come in two basic flavors—analog and digital, but today, most multimeters are only digital.

Analog meters use a needle and a fixed numbered scale to display readings. Analog meters are difficult to read

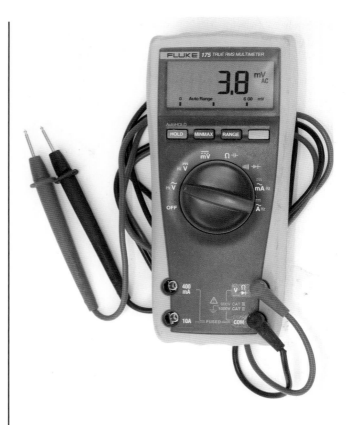

In addition to reading voltage and ohms, the Fluke 175 is a true RMS type multimeter that can accurately read frequency produced by motorcycle AC pickup coils. Courtesy Fluke Corporation

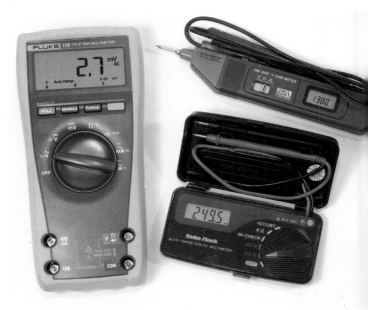

The Fluke 175 Digital Multimeter (left) has a bar graph feature not found on less expensive digital meters. Radio Shack's Pocket Digital Multimeter (lower right) does more and gives more bang for its buck than other meters costing several hundred dollars a few years ago. Courtesy Fluke Corporation

accurately because it's hard to line up the needle with the numbers on the meter's face. In addition, if the meter gets dropped, the mechanical movement of the needle can be damaged, producing inaccurate readings without the user being aware of the problem. Nowadays, you have to look hard to find a new analog multimeter (try the antique shop again), since most have been replaced by digital electronics.

A DVOM offers several advantages over old analog meters. DVOMs display electronic numbers via a liquid crystal display (LCD). Even if the meter gets banged about a bit, as long as the display is working, the meter's probably still okay. Another major difference between the two types of meters is their internal resistance. Analog meters have low internal resistance (usually only around 100,000 ohms) while digital meters typically have 10 meg ohms (10,000,000 ohms). Consequently, an analog meter will give false readings if used to measure high resistance computer circuits and could even cause damage to certain electronic fuel injection components.

Voltmeters, multimeters, and DVOMs are all capable of measuring a variety of electrical inputs. All read volts (both AC and DC) and ohms. Other test functions they perform include amperage, frequency, continuity, capacitance, and temperature. Additional features include auto shutoff, digital smoothing, internal fuse protection, display backlighting, and analog bar graph display.

You can spend as little as $10 or as much as $500 for an automotive-type DVOM, and just as a $50 car stereo plays the same music as a $2,000 stereo, all digital voltmeters will read electrical values, but all are not created equal. The one that works for you will depend on the level of automotive diagnostics you want to pursue. Spending more money on a quality DVOM will buy durability, ease-of-use, extra features (oftentimes the only way to figure out a problem), quality meter leads, availability of accessories, and product support.

AUTO-RANGING FEATURE

The majority of DVOMs sold today have an auto-ranging feature that senses volt or ohm input levels and automatically displays correct readings, including rounding off numbers and correct placement of a decimal point. Using a meter without this feature requires the user to choose the correct scale before a meter reading can be interpreted. For example, to read voltage from a 12-volt battery on a DVOM without auto-range, the 0–20-volt scale must be selected, thus allowing the meter to read between 0 and 20 volts.

Measuring resistance can be more difficult when using either an auto or nonauto ranging meter, since resistance values can cover a wide range, from 1 to more

Before reading voltage or resistance, this Yuasa Digital Meter without an auto-ranging feature must be set to the correct scale. The meter is set to read between 0 and 20,000 ohms—the 20k scale. Courtesy Yuasa Battery, Inc.

than 1 million ohms. There are a few simple rules to help you interpret ohm readings on both types of meters. We'll use an ignition coil to show an example of how to do this.

In this example, an ignition coil's secondary windings have a resistance of 11,800 ohms. Using a DVOM with auto-ranging feature, the meter leads are connected to the coil's secondary terminals and the function switch set to ohms. A reading should be displayed. The meter's auto-ranging feature senses the coil's resistance and displays the correct reading—11.80k ohms. The "k" (thousands) symbol means you should move the decimal point three places to the right (there are three zeros in the number 1,000), making the reading 11,800 ohms—not 1,180 ohms; if the k symbol is not displayed, the reading would be complete—1,180 ohms. If the coil's secondary windings were open, the reading would be 11.80m ohms. An "m" (millions) symbol has replaced the k symbol and you know to move the decimal point six places to the right (there are six zeros in a million and the display does not have enough room to show this, so you must visualize the number in your head). The reading is now 11,800,000 ohms. These same rules apply to meters that are not auto-ranging. If you use the 2k scale when measuring ohms, you can read between 0 and 2,000 ohms. If you select the 20k scale, the meter will read between 0 and 20,000 ohms; similarly, the 200k scale reads from 0 and 200,000 ohms.

The Fluke Corporation has been manufacturing digital meters for the automotive and power sports market for years. Their Series 170 is a good example of the type of automotive digital multimeter available in the midprice range (around $190).

There are two basic designs of voltmeters: averaging and true RMS (root mean square). Both meters measure voltage and ohms, but the RMS model measures distorted sine waves more accurately. AC pickup coils and other AC voltage-producing speed sensors have lopsided waveforms (sine waves). An averaging meter may not be able to read the output from a distorted sine wave. The Fluke 175 is a true RMS meter and can accurately read frequency produced by automotive-type AC pickup coils used on many motorcycles.

Another feature that makes a difference between the two types of meters is an analog bar graph. Meters with this feature provide both digital and analog displays. The bar graph acts exactly the same as an electronic needle, only much faster. The bar graph on a Fluke 175 updates about 40 times per second—10 times faster than the digital

display. This allows the user to detect changes in readings that occur too fast for a meter not equipped with a bar graph feature to display. This feature is useful when checking for a bad throttle position sensor (TPS) signal or for watching the performance of a speed sensor with an intermittent problem—both tests are only possible using a meter with an analog bar graph display.

A Fluke Model 175 Digital Multimeter is a good example of a meter loaded with features. The various features and functions can be accessed via a rotary switch and buttons found on the face of the meter. Other manufacturers offer similar bells and whistles. By way of example, to show the range of functions a modern digital multimeter is capable of performing, the following is a description of the various features found on a Fluke 175 Digital Multimeter.

ROTARY SWITCH POSITIONS

The rotary switch is the dial on the face of the meter, which the user rotates to select various meter tests and functions. Rotary switch selections are identified by yellow and white letters or symbols. Functions indicated in yellow are accessed by pressing the yellow function button located at the top-right of the meter face just under the display. Pressing the function button a second time returns the meter back to the tests and functions indicated by white symbols or letters, which are accessed by simply turning the rotary switch. Here are the common rotary switch positions and their corresponding functions:

1. **Off:** Switches the meter off. If no input readings change for 20 minutes, the meter automatically enters into sleep mode, thereby saving its battery. This feature can be enabled, or disabled for recording voltage over time.

2. **AC Volts/Hertz:** Measures AC voltage between 0.1 mV (millivolt) and 1,000 v. Pressing the yellow button (see No. 12) switches the meter to AC capabilities, enabling it to read AC voltage frequency or hertz. AC voltage frequency testing is useful when checking AC pickup coil sensors.

3. **DC Volts/Hertz:** Measures DC voltage between 1mV and 1,000v. Pressing the yellow button (see No. 12) switches the meter to DC mode, enabling it to read DC voltage frequency or hertz. DC voltage readings

In addition to reading volts, amps, ohms, and frequency, this Fluke Series 170 multimeter has Hold and MinMax features. The yellow button switches the meter's reading modes between white- and yellow-lettered dial functions.
Courtesy Fluke Corporation

are the most commonly used function on any meter. DC voltage frequency testing is useful when checking sensors with digital (on/off) outputs.

4. **DC Millivolts:** Measures DC voltage between 0.1mV and 600 mV. This setting performs essentially all of the same functions as No. 3 (DC Volts/Hertz), except this function is useful for measuring voltages on a smaller scale, usually measurements less than 0.6 volt.

5. **Ohms/Farads:** Measures resistance in ohms between 0.1 and 50 million. Pressing the yellow button (see No. 12) switches the meter to Farad mode, enabling it to read in Farads. This function is used to measure capacitance in Farads or capacitors; however, the capacitance function is seldom used in power sports applications. The ohms function is useful for measuring resistance of sensors, relays, switches, plug wires, and other components.

6. **Beeper/Diode:** The meter beeps whenever the meter leads touch each other—the test for continuity. Continuity testing is useful for determining if a wire is broken. Pressing the yellow button (see No. 12) switches the meter to test diodes such as those used in alternators or spike diodes used in other types of circuits.

7. **AC/DC Milliamps:** Measures AC/DC milliamps from 0.01 to 600 milliamps. It's used to measure small current draw, and is useful for checking parasitic amperage draw from on-board computers, radios, clocks, etc. Pressing the yellow button (see No. 12) switches the meter to read AC frequency from 2 hertz to 99k hertz.

8. **AC/DC Amps/Hertz:** Measures AC/DC amps from 0.01 to 10 amps. The amp function is protected by an internal fuse and is useful for checking circuits up to 10 amps. Pressing the yellow button (see No. 12) switches the meter to read AC frequency up to 99k hertz.

BUTTONS

The following are the common buttons and their typical functions:

9. **HOLD:** This button holds or freezes the display when pressed. Pressing the hold button twice switches the display to Auto Hold. In this mode, the meter holds the reading until it detects a new stable reading; then the meter beeps and displays the new reading. This feature is useful when you can't see the meter but want to know if you've probed a wire with power or other signal on it.

10. **MINMAX:** Pressing the MinMax button lets the meter record minimum, maximum, and average values over time. By pressing the button once, the meter takes three stepped readings over time. Holding the button for one second ends the min/max/avg recording. The meter's sleep mode is disabled when in min/max/avg record mode. This function is useful for reading changes over time when you can't keep an eye on the display—works really well when trying to figure out intermittent electrical problems.

11. **RANGE:** The meter powers up in auto-range mode. Pressing the range button changes the meter to manual range. This feature allows you to change where the decimal is located. Pressing the button moves the decimal point one place in the display. This feature is useful when you only need to know large changes in voltage or resistance.

12. **Yellow Button:** The yellow function button simply switches the meter between different modes on the rotary dial. This button also disables sleep mode if pressed when the meter first powers up.

TERMINAL JACKS

The Fluke 175 meter has four terminal jacks. The COM jack serves as the ground return for all measurements. The volt/ohm/diode jack (on page 28) is for testing voltage, continuity, resistance, diodes, capacitance, and frequency measurements. Both jacks on the left are for measuring amps; each is protected by an internal fuse that can be tested just by using the meter leads. By touching the leads

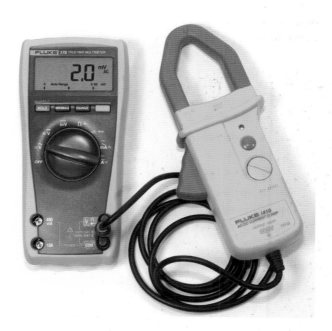

The Fluke i410 AC/DC Current Clamp can be used with any digital multimeter capable of reading in millivolts. This current clamp will measure up to 400 DC amps and is useful for checking starting and charging systems. Courtesy Fluke Corporation

together, the fuses can be checked without taking off the meter cover. Also, the meter has a built-in safety mechanism, which warns the user against inadvertently connecting the leads incorrectly. For example, if the leads are plugged into the jack for voltage testing but the meter is accidentally switched to read in amps (or vice versa), the word "lead" is displayed to warn the user the meter leads need to be moved in order to prevent internal damage to the meter.

MEASURING AMPERAGE

There are two types of ammeters used to measure current—series and inductive. Some digital voltmeters are designed with built-in series ammeters that can measure as much as 20 amps (10-amp capacity is more common). A series ammeter is helpful to use when trying to find a parasitic amp draw (battery drain). They can be connected in series with a circuit that is causing a drain on the battery. The Fluke 175 has two ranges for its series ammeter: 400-milliamp (mA) and 10-amp. The 400-mA range can be used to monitor current used by on-board computers, clocks, and radio memory; the 10-amp range can help locate a stuck relay or other components. Both amp ranges are protected by internal fuses.

If you ever need to measure starter motor or alternator output amperage, an inductive current probe should be used. Current probes are self-powered (usually by a 9-volt battery) and produce output in millivolts. As current flows through the starter cable or alternator output wire, a magnetic field forms around the wire. The inductive amp probe measures this field and converts it to a millivolt signal, which can be read directly on a voltmeter (one mV equals one amp). The Fluke i410 AC/DC

Current clamp (on page 33) can measure AC or DC amps from 1 to 400 amps. The clamp plugs into any voltmeter that accepts a banana-plug style jack. Be careful when considering a purchase of an inductive amp clamp, as most will only measure AC amperage, which is not useful for power sports equipment. The Fluke i410 costs about $155 and is well worth the money if you anticipate diagnosing starter or charging system problems.

LOGIC PROBE

One of the most useful and inexpensive electronic test tools for digital signals on motorcycles is a logic probe. Previously exclusively used for electronic board testing, the logic probe has finally made its way into automotive/power sports use. These handy little tools are sometimes referred to as "red and green" test lights. A logic probe can only sense two things—high and low voltage. However, its real value is its ability to detect either digital or analog electronic pulses. The outputs from the following components can all be detected (though not measured) using a logic probe: AC pickup coils and digital square wave crankshaft speed sensors, optical speed or ignition sensor outputs, and fuel injector pulses from a motorcycle's on-board computer. Because of its high internal resistance, a logic probe is a safe tool to use on any sensor or computer-generated output.

A logic probe is powered by connecting the probe's red lead to any 12-volt power source on the motorcycle being tested, and the black lead to any ground return. The pointy end of the probe is used for detecting pulse outputs from various sensors. A green LED (light emitting diode) display indicates the input voltage level is below the threshold level of 0.8 volts—a red LED lights up if voltage

This Radio Shack Logic Probe can detect signals from AC pickup coils and Hall-effect switches. It can also sense a fuel injector pulse from the electronic control module (ECM) to the fuel injector.

Snap-on and other manufacturers market red and green test lights. This tester is simply a heavy-duty version of a logic probe.

is above the high threshold of 2.2 volts. If a pulse is present at the probe tip, the LED will flash or flicker.

Radio Shack's Logic Probe (Part Number 22-303) costs about $20 and has an orange LED that flashes if a pulse is detected. In addition, it has a beeper that changes tone depending on voltage level. If you search the Internet under "logic probe" or "red and green test light" you can find others that may suit your needs as well. They all do about the same thing and all are invaluable tools for working on electronic ignition and fuel injection systems.

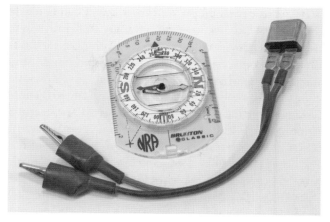

This homemade short finder consists of a 5-amp resetting circuit breaker, wire leads with alligator clips, and a compass.

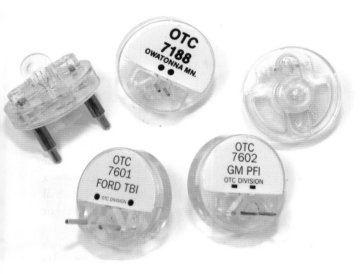

Each of these noid lights fit different fuel-injection wiring harnesses. When connected, they flash when an injector pulse is present. While this set from SPX/OTC is used for automotive applications, it will work on many motorcycle EFI systems as well. Courtesy SPX/OTC Service Solutions

NOID LIGHTS

A noid light is a specialty tool, specifically used for checking for the presence of a fuel injector pulse at the injector wiring harness. A noid light plugs into the wiring harness in place of the fuel injector. When the engine is cranked over, the light flashes or flickers if a pulse is received. You can purchase a set of noid lights on the Internet or at most auto parts stores for about $20. Most sets typically have a number of different lights with different connectors to accommodate the varying sizes of fuel injector connectors. However, as mentioned earlier, a test light can also perform this same function and is equally safe to use on all electronic EFI systems. However, some EFI systems use a series resistor with the injectors; these systems may not pass enough current to make the test light light up. Noid lights usually require less voltage/current to light them up and may work better in that respect.

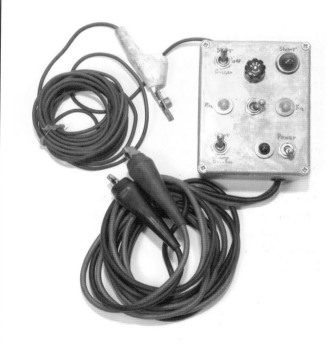

Another homemade short finder uses a switchable 5- or 10-amp resetting circuit breaker. In addition, it flashes a light and beeps. Other functions include a 20-amp breaker for testing wiring harnesses or powering up a fuel pump.

SHORT FINDER

If the same fuse keeps blowing, it's easy enough to look at a wiring diagram to determine the accessories powered by that circuit. However, it's another matter altogether to actually find the section of wire or connector that has shorted to the ground. Sometimes service manuals provide wiring harness routing locations, but one still has to locate the shorted wire. To do so, it's often necessary to remove fairing panels, gas tanks, or fenders.

The task of finding a short in a circuit can be made much easier by making a simple short finder at home, using a resettable circuit breaker and compass. (Self-setting circuit breakers can be purchased at most auto parts stores, and sporting goods' dealers can supply you with a compass.) The circuit breaker connects directly to the fuse box and takes the place of the blown fuse. The bimetallic strip inside the circuit breaker heats and cools as current passes through it, causing the circuit to turn on and off. Each time the circuit receives and loses power, a magnetic pulse is generated in the wire. Placing the compass near the wire will cause it to deflect each time the breaker resets. By moving the compass along a wiring harness, the location of the short can be determined, because the needle movement in the compass is always about the same strength until it is placed just beyond the shorted wire. The less the compass needle moves, the farther away it is from the shorted wire. With a little practice, and a little more practice, you should be able to narrow down to within 6 inches the location of the shorted wire. Also, it helps that the compass can sense the magnetic pulse through sheet metal, plastic, and just about everything else. You can make your own short finder (as described above) or you can purchase one online by searching the Internet under "automotive short finder" to locate this tool—the cost should be around $20.

JUMPER WIRES AND ACCESSORIES

Various lengths of wire with alligator clips connected to the ends are commonly called jumper wires. Jumper wires have numerous uses and a serious technician always has at least two (red and black) clipped to the outside of a toolbox. The best jumper wires can be easily made from silicone wire and good quality alligator clips. Also, heavy lamp cord (14 gauge) with larger clips works well when you want the convenience of having both power and ground sources at the rear or front of a motorcycle. If you don't want to make your own, packages of jumper wires in most sizes can easily be purchased at Radio Shack or through the Internet.

Measuring voltage or other outputs on wires that disappear into a connector or sensor can prove problematic. Picking up a knife or wire stripper to scrape off wire insulation is not a good idea—it's not a good way to tap into a wire, since it could cause damage to the wire. A better method for testing connector or sensor wires is to use a seamstress dress pin, available at most fabric stores. These dress pins have a T-shaped end that can be inserted between a wire and a connector until contact with the terminal inside the connector is made. The T-shaped end also provides a place where meter leads can be attached. Furthermore, when the pin is removed, there's no damage to the wire or connector.

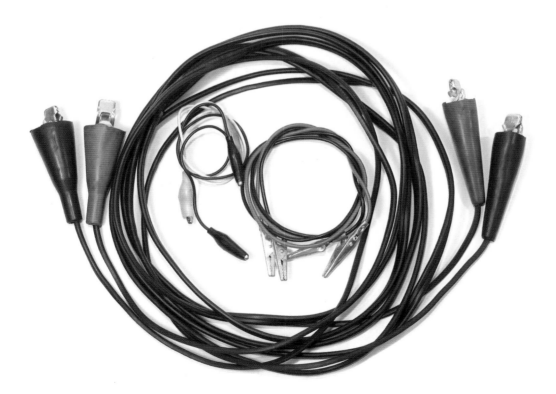

A guy or gal can never have too many jumper wires. They come in all different sizes, as shown here. The large set of jumpers was homemade using 14-gauge lamp cord; it comes in mighty handy for getting power from one motorcycle to another.

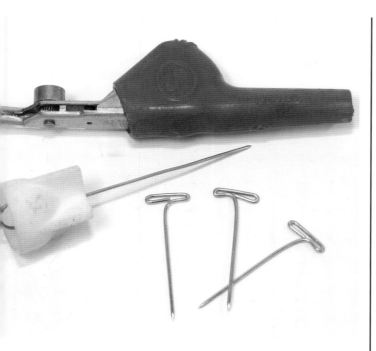

The best tool around for tapping into a wire with no connector is a JS Popper Alligator Clip made by the Mueller Electric Company. The JP-8783 Alligator Clip is equipped with a "Bed-of-Nails" (sharp spikes clustered close together). These clips are designed to reach the conductor inside a wire by piercing the insulation without causing damage to the wire. They can attach directly to meter leads or jumper wires. Search for this specialty tool on the Internet under "JS Popper" or "Mueller Electric."

COIL TESTER

Testing an ignition coil can be problematic. If you use an ohmmeter to measure the coil's primary and secondary winding resistance and they check out okay, does it mean the coil will work? Not necessarily. Sometimes an ignition coil with internal resistance that meets specifications won't produce a spark when connected to the motorcycle's ignition system. A better way to test a coil to determine if it can produce a spark is by using a universal coil tester. A universal ignition coil tester can be simply made using an automotive points-type condenser and some jumper wires. A coil tester basically functions like a set of ignition points and can be used to fire any type of ignition coil. When connected to an ignition coil that has battery power, the

A JS Popper Alligator Clip (top) equipped with a "Bed-of-Nails." This tool can pierce wire insulation and provide a place to connect a voltmeter. The T-shaped pins (bottom) are available from any fabric store and work well to backprobe connectors.

An old test light body, condenser, wire, and some alligator clips can be combined to create a homemade coil tester. If a coil is good, this tool will make it produce a spark.

Left: *By observing the distance a spark jumps on the spark tester on the left, you can get some approximation of spark plug firing voltage. The air gap's width can be set by the user to increase or decrease the firing voltage required to jump the air gap. The HEI Spark Tester on the right has a fixed air gap that requires about 25,000 volts from the ignition coil to jump. This is a good indication of coil strength on most electronic ignition systems.*

Below: *The IgnitionMate is a unique tool that can diagnose ignition problems, including primary voltage output up to 400 volts. This will test 12-volt systems as well as off-road motorcycles with CDI ignitions. In addition, secondary spark voltage can be measured up to 40,000 volts. The tool can detect ignition misfires as well as spark strength. Ignition triggers including AC pickup coils and Hall-effect sensors can be diagnosed as well. The unit is compact enough to be mounted on a motorcycle's fuel tank for test rides to detect misfires.* Courtesy TecMate

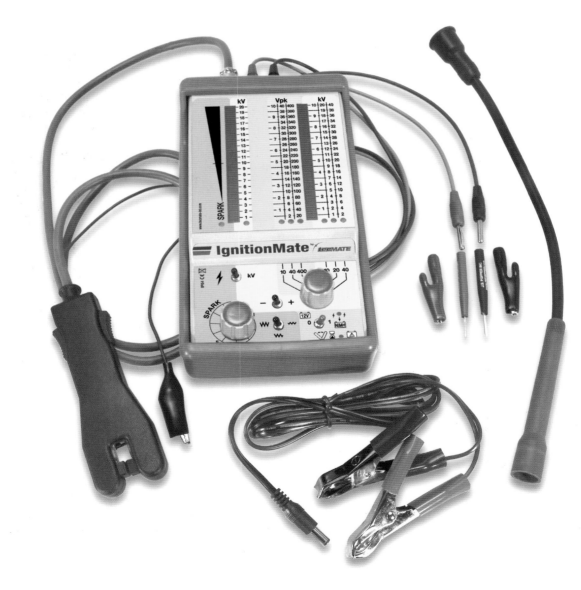

coil tester can cause the coil to produce a spark. This dynamic test is a much more effective tool for discovering a bad coil winding that may break down when under an electrical load. A more complete description of how a coil tester works can be found in Chapter 6, Ignition Systems, under "Generic Coil Testing."

IGNITION SPARK TESTER, HEI AND OTHERS

Using a jumper wire held close to a ground as a method of testing for ignition coil output will work, but it can zap you if you're not careful. A high energy ignition (HEI) tester is a safer device to use. It is basically a spark plug with no ground electrode and an alligator clip welded onto it. About 25,000 volts are needed from the ignition coil in order to produce a spark at the tester. This indicates a good coil that should be capable of producing enough energy for the ignition system. Consequently, this tester may not work on some points-type ignition systems because their secondary voltage output is too low.

An adjustable spark tester will work also, but it will only provide you with an approximation of spark output in thousands of volts. This tester has an electrode that can be adjusted to increase the air gap the spark has to jump. A printed scale on the tester indicates how much voltage is required to jump the resulting air gap. The two testers work equally well, and both sell for less than $8 and can be found at most auto parts stores.

IGNITION TIMING LIGHT

In addition to checking ignition timing, an inductive timing light can also be useful for detecting ignition misfires. By installing the inductive clamp on the coil wire and then pointing it at your face you can actually "see" misfires because the light skips a flash whenever a misfire is detected. Thus, the human eye and the timing light serve to create a poor-man's ignition scope. A timing light can also be used to detect an ECM that is not firing a fuel injector. By clamping the inductive probe around one of the wires going to a fuel injector, injector misfires can be observed in a similar manner to ignition misfires. Any inductive type timing light will work for these tests. Timing lights are available at most auto parts stores and online.

Any inductive timing light can also function as a poor man's scope. When connected to an ignition wire, the flashing light will skip a flash whenever a misfire is detected. Timing lights can also be used to detect injector pulse.

An OTC 3180 Stinger Battery Tester pulls a 100-amp load during battery testing. Hand-held battery testers are more convenient than using the engine's starter motor. Both 6-volt and 12-volt batteries can be tested. Courtesy SPX/OTC Service Solutions

BATTERY TESTERS

Using only a voltmeter and starter motor to test a battery is a very time-consuming task. There are a number of hand-held automotive battery testers on the market that make this job a whole lot easier. The Owatonna Tool Company (OTC) makes several types of battery testers. Its Model 3180 Battery Tester can load a battery to 100 amps. The tester consists of a voltmeter, relay, and heavy-duty resistor. After connecting the tester's cables to a battery, the load switch is turned on for 3 to 5 seconds. Before releasing the switch, read the voltage display to determine if the battery is good or bad. The battery has to be at least 75 percent charged in order for all load-type testing to produce reliable results. Hand-held battery load testers can be found at most auto parts stores and online.

If you want something a little more high-tech, there are several solid state electronic "conductance" battery testers on the market. These testers indirectly measure the available plate surface area of a battery needed to produce the chemical reaction that creates current. Thus, conductance testing provides a reliable indication of the overall battery "state-of-health" (how much life is left) and has a direct correlation to a battery's capacity to start an engine. Conductance testing can also be used to detect bad cells, shorted plates, and open circuits within a battery. Furthermore, unlike a load-type battery tester, digital testers can also test a discharged battery. Testing takes only

a few seconds, and the digital display includes cold cranking amps (CCA), open circuit voltage, and battery health. Unfortunately, conductance type testers don't come cheap! Priced at $300 and up, conductance testers are mostly used at dealers by professional technicians.

LAB SCOPES

Analog oscilloscopes are mostly used in laboratory settings, but have also been widely used in the automotive industry since the 1950s to diagnose ignition system problems. In the late 1980s, the digital lab scope was introduced as a tool that could "see" various inputs and outputs from electronic fuel-injection systems. These tools could not only view electronic signals but also could record and store them for later review. With the proliferation of electronic fuel injection used in motorcycles and

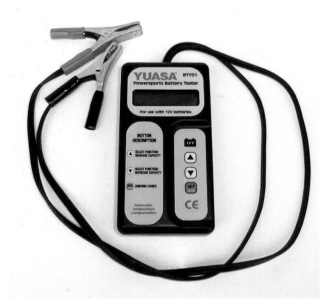

Yuasa's BTY01 Powersports Battery Tester eliminates the problem of charging a battery before testing. The tester will test powersports batteries of both maintenance-free and conventional designs, with amp hour ratings from 2 to 35. Courtesy Yuasa Battery, Inc.

A Fluke 98 ScopeMeter can record and play back both analog and digital electronic fuel-injection signals. It can also measure secondary ignition voltage and display spark plug firing patterns. Courtesy Fluke Corporation

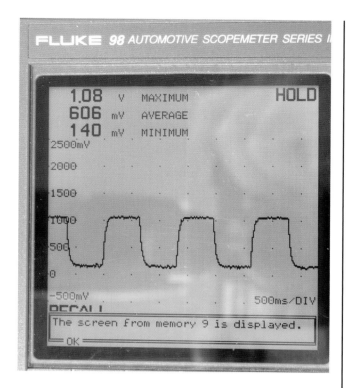

other power sports vehicles, lab scopes are showing up more and more in power sports dealerships.

The advantage of using a lab scope over more conventional electronic testing tools is its ability to view intermittent electronic faults and evaluate the quality of an electrical components output. Computer sensors, including MAP, BARO, AC pickup coils, hall-effect switches, and optical sensors, all produce waveforms, which are shapes derived from displays of voltage-over-time for a signal output. A lab scope can view and display computer sensor waveforms. Take, for example, a crankshaft position sensor, used on many EFI motorcycles to input engine rpm to the fuel-injection computer. Some of these sensors produce a square wave that a multimeter displays as frequency or hertz. As engine speed increases, the crankshaft sensor's signal changes as the number of hertz increases. However, if the sensor has an intermittent problem the multimeter will not be able to detect it—but the lab scope can record and display the intermittent fault. In some instances, use of a lab scope is the only way to actually

Above: *The ability to play back this recording of a crankshaft position sensor is sometimes the only way to see an electrical glitch that could cause an ignition misfire.* Courtesy Fluke Corporation

Below: *Analog scopes are not designed for use on motorcycles and they have limitations. They can only operate in real time and can't record waveforms. They can be purchased new for as little as $350.*

ELECTRONIC TESTING TOOLS

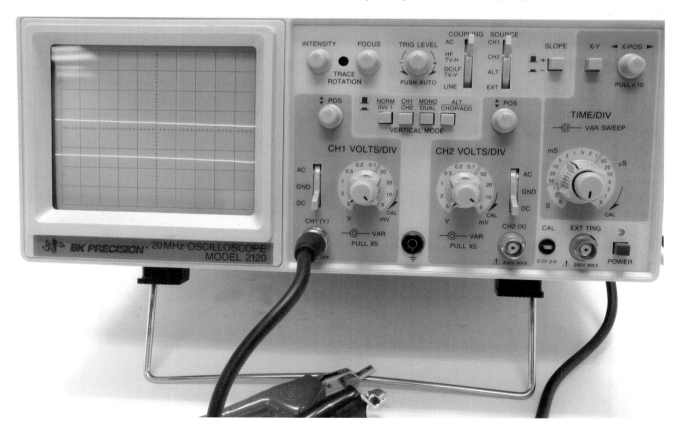

This Weller Dual Heat Range Soldering Gun Kit (Model 8200PK) is standard issue for doing electrical work on motorcycles. Soldering guns heat up quickly, are easy to work with, and some even have a work light to illuminate what you're soldering. Courtesy Weller

"see" the square wave break down. This is particularly useful when the quality of the signal is of greater importance than the fact that the signal is present. Another good example of when a lab scope is a preferred tool is when measuring fuel injector pulses from the ECM. A flashing noid light, test light, or logic probe connected to the injector harness will only tell you a signal is being sent. Again, the quality of the signal cannot be determined by these test methods. However, a lab scope will not only verify an injector signal is present but how long the injector on time is. By analyzing the scope's digital display, you can determine if there is a problem with the fuel injection computer's injector circuit. In addition to viewing sensor waveforms, a lab scope can also measure and record waveforms from actuators, including those from fuel injectors, idle controllers, solenoids, and relays.

About 70 percent of the time, the use of a logic probe or multimeter is sufficient to determine if a computer sensor or other electronic component is working. However, it's the exceptions that really cause diagnostic headaches. Most home mechanics won't have the need—or can justify the expense—of owning a lab scope. By contrast, professional technicians work on a wider variety of motorcycles with more computer-related issues, and a lab scope can save hours of time when trying to solve stubborn electrical problems. The price of digital lab scopes has come down in recent years, but they are still expensive—ranging from $800 to well over $3,000. If you search the Internet under "automotive lab scope" you'll get an idea of what's available.

There is, however, a new interesting alternative to a digital lab scope if you already own a PC, laptop, or PDA. There are scope interfaces (a box with leads coming out of it and a USB port) that plug into a PC or PDA. With the included software installed, you can view, record, and store waveforms on your personal computer or PDA. The software and interface are about $300 and can be found on the Internet. Another alternative is to use an analog lab scope. However, these tools are not designed for automotive use

Weller's Heavy-Duty Soldering Iron Kit (part number SPG80L) produces 80 watts of power and comes with two tips. A safety indicator light lets you know the iron is on. Courtesy Weller

and do have limitations. Analog scopes operate in "real time," so they cannot record waveforms. Consequently, finding intermittent electrical glitches is difficult. Analog scopes can be purchased new for as little as $350, and even less if used.

SOLDERING TOOLS

Having the right tools to repair electrical problems is as important as having the right electronic testing tools to find the problem in the first place. Soldering tools are basic and essential for repairing and splicing wiring, adding connectors, and general electrical repair. The electric soldering gun has been around for years; having a quality one will make your electrical work go smoothly. Weller, a division of Cooper Tools, has manufactured a variety of soldering tools for many years and is considered the standard in automotive and electronics industries.

The Weller Model 8200PK Multi-Purpose Soldering Gun Kit features a dual heat range (100/140 watts) element. By pulling the trigger to the first position, 100 watts of power and heat are produced at the gun tip. This setting works well for smaller wires (up to 14 gauge). When working with larger wires (12 and 10 gauge), the second trigger position is capable of producing 140 watts. This range works best for most motorcycle electrical work. If you need to work with heavier wire or terminals,

the Weller Model D550PK develops 200/260 watts of power. Both models have built-in lights—great when working in a dark garage. Pencil type soldering irons are also available; they get into those tight spaces (under your bike's seat) and make soldering much easier. Weller makes electric—and for the ultimate in portability—butane-powered soldering irons.

Weller's Portasol is a completely portable, butane-powered soldering iron. This tool is convenient and invaluable when working on trailer wiring, under the dash, at the racetrack, or for those dreaded roadside repairs. Heat is adjustable and ignition is via a piezoelectric system—just flick the ON switch. The tool can be charged with butane using the same canisters that fill cigarette lighters. One fill lasts several hours—more than enough time to solder entire wiring harnesses. Courtesy Weller

CHAPTER 4
STORAGE BATTERIES

Typically, most people don't spend a lot of time worrying about the battery in their motorcycle until the engine won't start—then it gets 100 percent of the attention. Fortunately, you can usually jump-start the engine using another vehicle, but the bigger problem is whether it will start again once you get where you were going. Charging the battery may only be a temporary fix. In addition to not starting the engine, a weak or old battery can also lead to drivability issues with EFI bikes, and can cause problems with the charging system. In fact, as stated in Chapter 5, Charging and Starting Systems, the battery should be charged before diagnosing potential charging-related problems. An understanding of how a battery works, and how to test one, will help solve other electrical-related issues on a motorcycle.

Batteries have three jobs: (1) to provide electrical power to start the engine; (2) to supply additional current when the charging system can't keep up with electrical demand; and (3) to act as a voltage stabilizer for the motorcycle's charging system.

A battery's primary job is engine starting, and in this case, size does matter. Engine displacement is the determining factor of amperage requirements for engine starting and related battery capacity. The amperage required for starting an engine varies, depending upon the type and size of motorcycle engine. Battery size is rated in two ways: amp hour (AH) and cold cranking amps (CCA). Amp-hour rating is the battery's ability to deliver current for an extended period of time, while cold cranking amps is the battery's ability to produce current in low ambient temperatures.

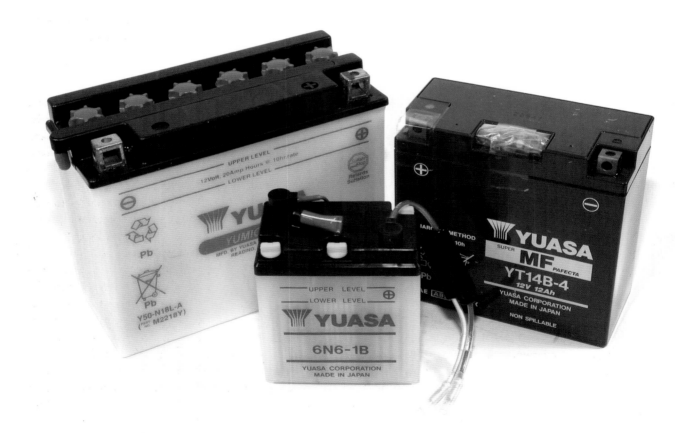

Three common types of batteries: 12-volt conventional (top left), 12-volt maintenance-free (top right), and 6-volt (bottom). There are several advantages to the maintenance-free battery—no fill caps, water doesn't have to be added, and it can be mounted on its side. Courtesy Yuasa Battery, Inc.

Here are the parts that make up a Yuasa maintenance-free battery. The polypropylene plastic case, cover, and filler caps form the container for the battery. The cell group (lower left) consists of positive and negatives plates with glass mat separators in between each plate. The three odd-shaped lead lugs are intercell connectors that attach the cell groups to the two battery terminals. Courtesy Yuasa Battery, Inc.

How batteries are rated is covered later in this chapter. In general, the larger the surface area of the plates inside the battery, the greater the AH and CCA ratings.

A battery's cold cranking amperage rating is directly proportional to engine size, as each engine requires a minimum level of amperage for starting which must be met or exceeded by the battery's capacity. Batteries with less capacity are capable of starting a large displacement engine, but they may not do so reliably, especially in colder climates. Other factors contributing to starter current demand (and related battery size) include: engine/starter cranking ratio, internal starter gear reduction, oil viscosity, ambient temperature, and overall starter circuit resistance.

A battery's second job is to supply current when the charging system is overworked. This usually occurs (though not always) when the engine is being operated at speeds of less than 3,500 rpm (below 1,500 rpm on a Harley-Davidson). If the motorcycle's electrical system is creating a high demand—headlight(s) on, heated vest, gloves, etc.—and the engine's speed is too low for the alternator/generator to supply enough current, the battery makes up the difference. This can also occur once after-market electrical accessories have been installed, since high-wattage sound systems, driving lights, and excessive Christmas lights on a Gold Wing can all exceed the charging system's current-producing capacity. When the charging system is at maximum capacity, the battery supplies any additional current required, but only for a short time. The overworked charging system is already unable to keep up with the bike's electrical loads, and therefore, it can't also supply current for battery charging for long.

The last function of a battery is to act as a voltage stabilizer for the charging system. Alternators need something to *push* against to keep from producing excessive voltage. As a result, a battery should never be disconnected on a bike equipped with an alternator, since the charging output voltage can increase to over 20 volts—enough electrical pressure to take out many (if not all) solid state components such as ignition modules, computers, stereos, etc. In addition to acting as a voltage stabilizer, a battery provides other electrical system protections. High-voltage spikes may be produced when turning on or off certain electrical circuits; these fluctuations in voltage are partially absorbed by the battery, which further protects solid state components from damage.

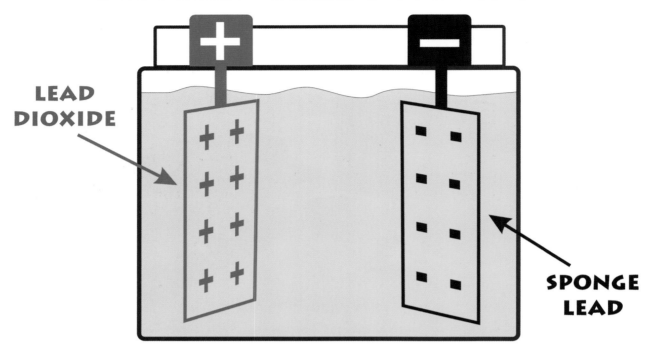

SINGLE CELL BATTERY

LEAD DIOXIDE

SPONGE LEAD

SULFURIC ACID + WATER = ELECTROLYTE

Above: *Fig 4-1—This single cell battery has one positive and one negative plate. The plates swim in an electrolyte solution of sulfuric acid and distilled water. Each cell in a motorcycle battery has multiple plates and produces about 2.12 to 2.2 volts.*

Right: *Pictured is a one of six cell groups that go into a battery case to form a working battery. Intercell connectors are used to connect the cell groups together between positive and negative battery terminals.* Courtesy Yuasa Battery, Inc.

CHEMICAL REACTIONS

A battery is basically nothing more than a simple chemistry set that stores electrical energy. It's important to understand that a battery does not store electricity; rather, it only stores the chemical energy necessary to produce electricity. When a battery is required to produce current (to start an engine, for instance) it converts its chemical energy into electricity. This is simply accomplished by a change in the form of energy that a battery stores, and while the process might seem mysterious (since it's occurring inside the battery), the following explanation should take the mystery out of it.

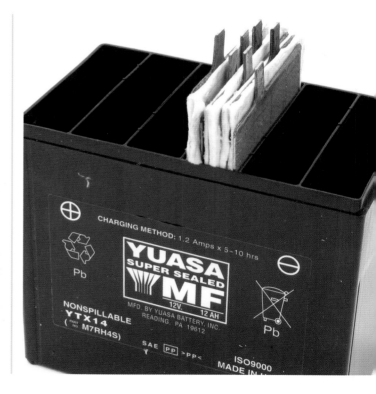

12 VOLT BATTERY (SIX CELLS)

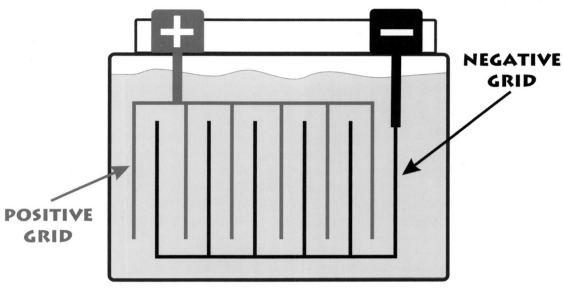

NEGATIVE GRID

POSITIVE GRID

EACH CELL IS 2.1 VOLTS

Above: *Fig 4-2—Six cells, producing approximately 2.2 volts each, are connected in series to create a 12-volt battery. Depending on battery type, the total open circuit voltage of all the cells is between 12.8 and 13.0 volts.*

6 VOLT BATTERY (THREE CELLS)

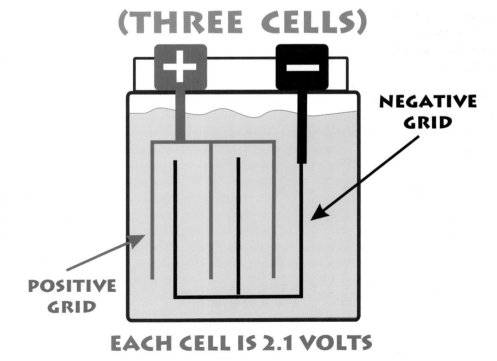

NEGATIVE GRID

POSITIVE GRID

EACH CELL IS 2.1 VOLTS

Right: *Fig 4-3—Each of the three cells in a 6-volt battery produces 2.1 to 2.2 volts—total voltage is around 6.3 volts.*

Just like holding a hand of cards. One negative plate, a glass mat separator, and one positive plate make up the cells inside a maintenance-free battery. The glass mat absorbs the electrolytic solution of sulfuric acid and distilled water. Courtesy Yuasa Battery, Inc.

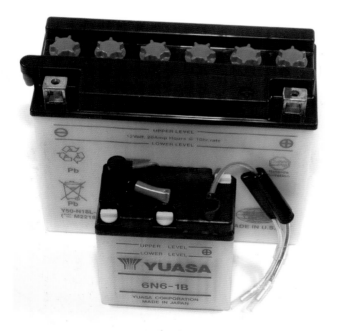

The 12-volt battery (top) has six fill caps, one for each cell. The six-volt version only has three fill caps (yellow caps). Both of these batteries are conventional design and require periodic topping-off with distilled water. Both must be externally vented so harmful out-gassing does not corrode any metal parts near the battery. Courtesy Yuasa Battery Inc.

Batteries are made of separate compartments called cells, each containing a pair of negative and positive lead plates. In each set, one plate is made from lead dioxide that has a positive charge, and the other is made from sponge lead that has a negative charge. The plates are stacked alternately (negative, positive, negative, positive, etc.) and immersed in an electrolytic solution of sulfuric acid and distilled water. The active material in these positively and negatively charged plates (lead dioxide in the positive plate and metallic sponge lead in the negative plate) produces electricity when immersed in the electrolytic solution.

Each of the six cells in a 12-volt battery produces 2.12 to 2.2 volts for a total of 12.8 to 13.0 volts (see page 47, figure 4-2). The variance in voltage is because of different battery designs. A 6-volt battery has three cells and a total voltage of around 6.3. The amount of electrical energy a battery is capable of producing is dependent upon the surface area of the plates contained in the cells. The lead plates in the cells are supported by a cast lead framework called a grid. The grid not only holds the plates together, but also facilitates the flow of electrons between negative and positive plates during charging and discharging.

DISCHARGING

One of two chemical processes is always occurring inside a battery at any given time—either discharging or charging. The electrolyte solution contains charged atomic particles called ions, made up of sulfate and hydrogen. The sulfate ions are negatively charged, while the hydrogen ions have a positive charge. When you place a load (starter motor, headlight, horn, etc.) across a battery, the sulfate ions travel to the negative plates and give up their negative charge, causing the battery to discharge. This excess electron flow out of the negative side of the battery, through the load device, and back to the positive side of the battery is what creates DC current. Once the electrons arrive back at the positive battery terminal, they travel back into the cells and reattach themselves to the positive plates. This process of continuous discharge occurs until the battery is dead, and there is no chemical energy left. The actual flow of electrons from negative to positive battery posts is contradictory to the popular notion that electricity moves from the positive post of a battery through an electrical device and back to the negative post (general electrical theory—see Chapter 1).

When a battery discharges, the ratio of sulfuric acid to water in the electrolytic solution changes to mostly water. At the same time, battery acid produces a chemical byproduct called lead sulfate, which coats the plates,

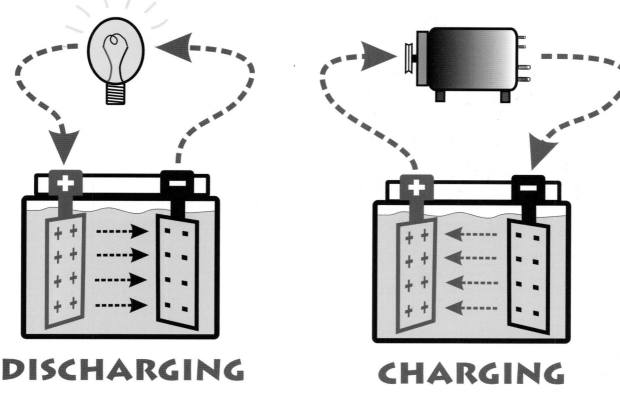

DISCHARGING   CHARGING

Fig 4-4—The battery on the left is discharging as its positive ions travel from the positive to the negative plate. The process is reversed (right) when the battery is being charged. In order for charging to take place, charging voltage must always be higher than open circuit battery voltage.

thereby reducing the surface area over which chemical reactions can occur. As the surface area of the battery plate shrinks, current-producing capacity lessens as well. For this reason, an engine's starter motor can't be cranked for long periods of time, nor can other electrical loads be left on indefinitely.

It's a fact that a battery will weaken from just sitting around. Self-discharge is always taking place, even if the battery is not connected to anything. A modern lead-calcium battery will self-discharge at a rate of 1/300 volts per day, depending on temperature. This means that at 77 degrees Fahrenheit a fully charged battery will be dead in 600 days. As ambient temperature increases, the self-discharge rate increases. At 104 degrees F, it takes 300 days for the battery to reach 100 percent discharge, and at 32 degrees F, a battery will take as long as 950 days to die. The bad news takes place at temperatures of 130 degrees F

This maintenance-free battery uses an AGM (absorbent glass mat) design. Because it's leak-proof, it can be mounted in almost any position on a motorcycle and does not require filling with water. Courtesy Yuasa Battery, Inc.

and higher. These temperatures can be reached if the battery is stored in a garage or shed, and they will "kill" the battery in short order.

A common misconception about battery storage is that if one is left on a concrete floor, it will eventually discharge rapidly. This was true about 35 years ago or more, when battery cases were made of hard rubber—the moisture from concrete caused this type of battery to discharge more quickly. However, modern battery cases are made of polypropylene plastic and can be stored on concrete surfaces without concern for excessive discharge.

ELECTROLYTE SOLUTION

As previously mentioned, a battery's negative and positive plates "swim" in an electrolyte solution of sulfuric acid and water—one of the ingredients necessary for electrochemical processes to occur inside a battery. Whenever the ratio of sulfuric acid to water is measured, the resulting value is expressed as specific gravity, or SG. The specific gravity for pure water is 1.000. Sulfuric acid has a specific gravity of 1.835. Combined, their SG is about 1.265 to 1.280 (indicating a fully charged battery at 77 degrees F). However, as the battery discharges, the ratio of acid to water changes so there is less sulfuric acid and more water; thus, the specific gravity of the electrolyte solution is lowered. The process is reversed when the battery is charged. The SG becomes higher as the ratio of acid to water changes back to mostly acid. Specific gravity also can be used to determine the state of charge of a battery (see "Battery Testing" in this chapter).

Temperature also has an affect on a battery's ability to produce current—the lower the temperature, the lower the specific gravity and the lower the current-producing potential. In addition to producing less current, a lower SG allows the electrolyte to freeze at higher temperatures. A battery with an SG of 1.265 typically will not freeze within the continental United States, because the electrolyte solution can be subjected to minus 75 degrees F before it turns into a solid chunk of frozen acid. However, batteries should always be kept charged in cold climates to prevent damage. As a battery becomes discharged, its SG is lowered, and so is the freezing point of its electrolytic solution. A dead battery with an SG of 1.155 has a freezing point of about 5 degrees F—at which point it could freeze solid and damage the battery beyond recovery.

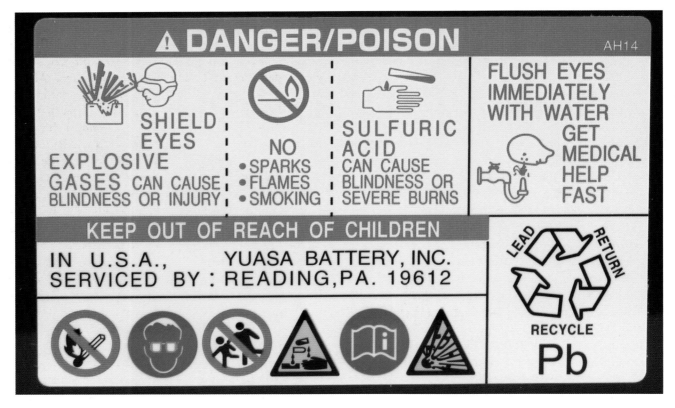

Because all batteries contain sulfuric acid and lead, they are required to have a warning label similar to the one here. Not only will battery acid burn your skin and eyes, it's explosive when being charged or discharged. Lead is a no-no for the environment. Dead batteries should be recycled and not thrown into the trash. Courtesy Yuasa Battery, Inc.

CHARGING

Charging a battery reverses the chemical reactions that occur during discharge. The sulfate and hydrogen ions basically switch places. The electrical energy used to charge a battery is converted back to chemical energy and stored inside the battery. Battery chargers, including alternators and generators, produce a higher voltage (higher electrical pressure) than the open circuit voltage of the battery they are charging. This electrical pressure pushes the current back into the battery (overcoming its open circuit voltage) in order to charge it. The charging device (alternator, generator, or battery charger) produces excess electrons at the negative battery plates where positive hydrogen ions are then attracted to them. The hydrogen ions combine to form sulfuric acid and lead, which ultimately reduces the amount of water in the electrolytic solution and increases the battery's specific gravity.

Applying a charging current to a battery—without overheating it—is called the natural absorption rate. Because of their smaller size when compared to automotive types of batteries, motorcycle battery are more sensitive to how much current they can safely absorb. When charging a motorcycle battery, don't exceed 2.5 amps. Most automotive battery chargers are not suitable for charging a motorcycle battery. A rule of thumb is to divide the battery's amp hour rating by 10. For example a 14 AH battery should be charged at 1.4 amps (14AH/10=1.4 amps). See "Battery Chargers" later in this chapter for more details.

When charging amperage exceeds the level of the natural absorption rate, the battery may overheat, causing the electrolyte solution to bubble and create flammable hydrogen gas—hydrogen gas, when combined with oxygen (from the air), is very explosive and can easily be ignited by a spark. Consequently, always remember to turn the power off before connecting or disconnecting a battery charger to prevent a spark at the battery terminals! Many solid state "smart" battery chargers designed for use with motorcycle batteries have a "no spark" feature, even when being connected or disconnected, when plugged into AC power outlet. In addition to excessive "outgassing" during charging, a battery that has been rapidly discharging (cranking an engine over until it's dead for instance) may also produce excessive hydrogen gas.

A spark can also be created when connecting jumper cables to a dead battery; though rare, this can also cause an explosion. Figure 4-5 (on page 52) illustrates the correct method for connecting jumper cables from a motorcycle with a dead battery to one with a good battery. Always follow these four steps when jump-starting a motorcycle: (1) Connect the red jumper cable to the dead battery's positive terminal; (2) attach the other end of this same cable to the charged battery's positive terminal; (3) connect the black jumper cable to the good battery's negative terminal; and (4) connect the other end of the negative black jumper cable to the dead motorcycle engine, transmission or a frame/engine mounting bolt. The last connection is the one that has the potential to spark. This method will keep all sparks away from both batteries. Because motorcycle frames are painted, or powder coated, don't connect any cables to the frame, or the paint or frame could be damaged. Start the bike that you're jump-starting from and run the engine at 3,000 to 4,000 rpm. Now start the dead bike and let the engine run for a few minutes before disconnecting the two motorcycles. Remove the jumper cable connected to the frame of the dead bike first. The steps for connecting a dead motorcycle battery to a car or truck are the same, but *DO NOT* start the car's engine. The charging system in an automobile can overwhelm your motorcycle's dead battery and may cause damage.

Designed for jump-starting motorcycles, these eight-foot jumper cables are easy to take along when you ride. The 8-gauge diameter cable has enough capacity to jump-start even the largest motorcycle. A nylon storage bag is included. Courtesy Yuasa Battery, Inc.

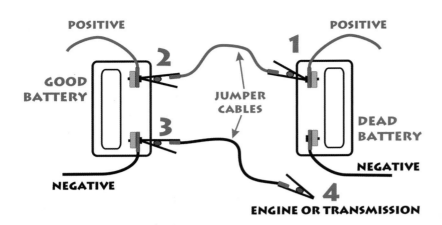

Left: *Fig 4-5—For safety when attempting to jump-start your motorcycle, always make the last jumper cable connection (step 4) to the engine or transmission of the bike with the dead battery. This will prevent a spark from occurring at the negative terminal of the battery, possibly causing an explosion.*

Below: *Fig 4-6—Yuasa's YuMicron battery features a unique cover design that minimizes electrolyte spillage. They also have two extra plates per cell that provide extra cranking power for large displacement motorcycle engines.* Courtesy Yuasa Battery, Inc.

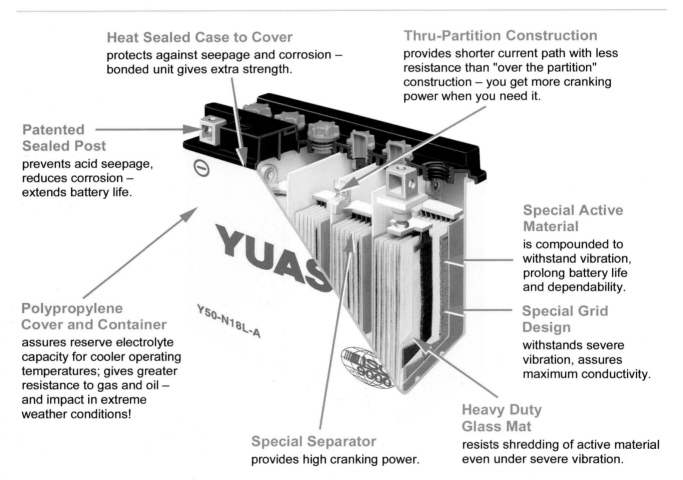

Heat Sealed Case to Cover
protects against seepage and corrosion – bonded unit gives extra strength.

Thru-Partition Construction
provides shorter current path with less resistance than "over the partition" construction – you get more cranking power when you need it.

Patented Sealed Post
prevents acid seepage, reduces corrosion – extends battery life.

Special Active Material
is compounded to withstand vibration, prolong battery life and dependability.

Polypropylene Cover and Container
assures reserve electrolyte capacity for cooler operating temperatures; gives greater resistance to gas and oil – and impact in extreme weather conditions!

Special Grid Design
withstands severe vibration, assures maximum conductivity.

Special Separator
provides high cranking power.

Heavy Duty Glass Mat
resists shredding of active material even under severe vibration.

TYPES OF BATTERIES

There are two basic battery designs available for motorcycles and power sports equipment—conventional and absorbent glass mat (AGM). Because a battery can potentially leave you stranded, you should always only buy high-quality brands. Rebuilt or "bargain basement" batteries may start your bike for a while, but are sure to leave you stranded sooner rather than later.

CONVENTIONAL BATTERIES

Sometimes referred to as "flooded" batteries, these are the most basic design. Many batteries use lead-antimony as a material for the plates, while others use lead-calcium, adding much improved self-discharge properties. When these types of batteries charge and discharge, some of the water in the electrolyte solution evaporates, causing the acid level of cells to become low. Conventional batteries have filler caps on top of the cover allowing each cell's electrolyte level to be checked. The individual cells need to be topped off with distilled water periodically due to inevitable water loss as a result of the charging/discharging process. When charging a conventional battery, always remove the caps to let the hydrogen gas produced escape.

ABSORBENT GLASS MAT (AGM) BATTERIES

Unlike conventional batteries, AGM batteries are designed so no free unabsorbed electrolyte solution can spill or evaporate. Also, they never need water added to them. Hence, these batteries are commonly referred to as "maintenance-free." The electrolyte "soup" is fully absorbed and permanently held in capillary attraction by glass-fiber mat separators between the lead plates or grids. This design gives antivibrational support to the battery plates, keeping them from short-circuiting between negative and positive grids. AGM batteries will hold a charge longer when not in use—winter storage for instance. In addition, AGM batteries can be physically smaller—yet provide the same or more cranking power—than conventional designs. AGM batteries require charging systems that produce a regulated output of 14.0 to 14.8 volts to fully charge. Older motorcycle charging systems produce slightly less

voltage (around 13.5) and are not suited for use with AGM designs. In addition, some motorcycle battery chargers are not able to produce sufficient charging voltages to work with an AGM battery. The AGM design can be somewhat confusing, as battery manufacturers come up with all sorts of marketing names for their batteries. These include: gel cell, gel, sealed, dry charged, maintenance free, dry cell, and others. Whatever they are called, all of these batteries are an AGM design. This is similar to blowing your nose with a Kleenex, handkerchief, tissue, hanky, Scottie, or nose rag—they all refer to the same thing.

GEL BATTERIES

The term "gel" battery is often confused with an AGM battery design. True gel batteries contain electrolyte solution in a gel form but have conventional style construction with paper or polyethylene insulators separating the plates. The electrolytic solution is a mixture of sulfuric acid, water, and silica, which has a toothpaste-like consistency. Until recently, gel-electrolyte construction was limited to what is known as deep-cycle batteries. Deep-cycle batteries can be used until dead and recharged with little loss in overall capacity. Conventional and AGM batteries have shorter life spans if allowed to completely discharge. Gel batteries are primarily used in mobility equipment (wheelchairs),

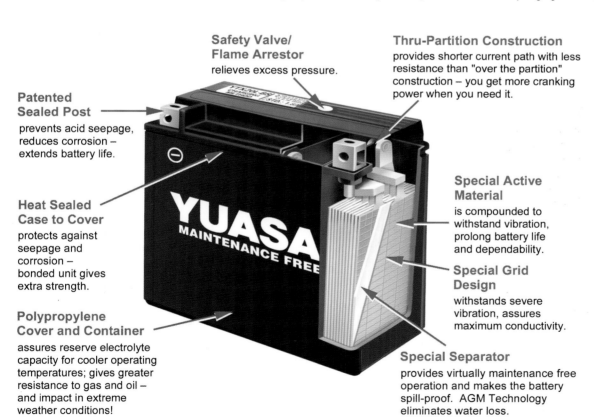

Safety Valve/ Flame Arrestor relieves excess pressure.

Thru-Partition Construction provides shorter current path with less resistance than "over the partition" construction – you get more cranking power when you need it.

Patented Sealed Post prevents acid seepage, reduces corrosion – extends battery life.

Heat Sealed Case to Cover protects against seepage and corrosion – bonded unit gives extra strength.

Polypropylene Cover and Container assures reserve electrolyte capacity for cooler operating temperatures; gives greater resistance to gas and oil – and impact in extreme weather conditions!

Special Active Material is compounded to withstand vibration, prolong battery life and dependability.

Special Grid Design withstands severe vibration, assures maximum conductivity.

Special Separator provides virtually maintenance free operation and makes the battery spill-proof. AGM Technology eliminates water loss.

Fig 4-7—Yuasa's VRLA (valve regulated lead acid) AGM batteries are maintenance free and do not require the addition of water. This type of battery is ideal for occasional use or storage because they hold a charge longer than conventional batteries. In addition they can be mounted on their side, saving space under a motorcycle's seat. Courtesy Yuasa Battery, Inc.

53

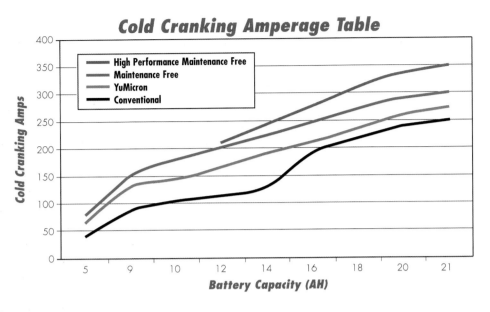

Cold Cranking Amperage Table

Cold Cranking Amps (y-axis: 0, 50, 100, 150, 200, 250, 300, 350, 400)

Battery Capacity (AH) (x-axis: 5, 9, 10, 12, 14, 16, 18, 20, 21)

Legend:
- High Performance Maintenance Free
- Maintenance Free
- YuMicron
- Conventional

Fig 4-8—This chart illustrates a comparison between amp hours (AH) and cold cranking amps (CCA). To ensure consistent engine starting performance, always consult a battery application chart before you replace the battery in your motorcycle. Courtesy Yuasa Battery, Inc.

golf carts, RVs, marine applications, and automotive racing. I have yet to find a true gel battery specifically designed for use in a motorcycle with the exception of some late-model BMWs. The on-board computer used on BMW bikes places additional loads on the battery when the bike is not running, and the gel battery provides a longer storage period without going dead. The bottom line on gel batteries is that they have higher internal electrical resistance than AGM batteries and don't offer as high a rate of performance. In other words, what works well on your golf cart, won't necessarily start a medium- to large-displacement motorcycle engine, especially in cold weather.

BATTERY RATINGS

Since a battery's basic job is to power the starter motor while maintaining sufficient voltage to also run the ignition and fuel systems, there has to be some way to rate their ability to perform this job. Motorcycle batteries are rated in amp hours (AH) or cold cranking amps (CCA). Amp hour ratings are the most common and are usually found on the battery case. A battery's ability to discharge a given amount of current over a specific length of time is its AH rating. For example, a 14 AH battery discharges at a rate of 1.4 AH for 10 hours. At this point, the overall open circuit battery voltage drops from 12.6 (fully charged) to 10.5 volts or 1.75 volts per cell. A 6-volt battery with the same AH rating drops from 6.3 volts to 5.25 volts.

The other method to rate a battery is cold cranking amps, although this rating method is mostly used for automotive batteries. CCA represents the discharge load in amps that a new, fully charged battery at 0 degrees F can continuously deliver for 30 seconds while maintaining 7.2

volts. CCA battery ratings for cars and light trucks are generally in the range of 300 to 1,000 CCA. The largest motorcycle batteries have CCA ratings of around 385. Generally, as displacement per cylinder increases, so does the CCA or AH rating. The following are AH and CCA recommendations for motorcycle applications: engine sizes over 1,500-cc—19 to 30 AH (250 to 300 CCA); large engines, 1,000- to 1,500-cc—11 to 18 AH (180 to

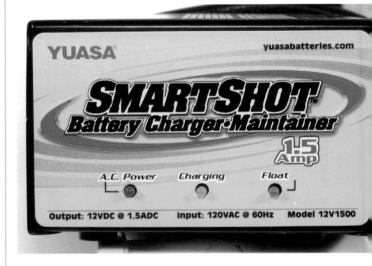

Yuasa's Automatic, 1.5-amp SmartShot charger can maintain your battery for long periods of time. In addition, it can diagnose multiple shorted cells and high sulfation conditions. It will charge all types of batteries including absorbent glass mat (AGM) designs, because the charging voltage cycle will reach 14.4 volts before tapering off. For winter storage the charger reevaluates the battery's condition every 28 days. Reverse polarity protection and spark-free operation make it safe to use while the battery is on or off your motorcycle. Courtesy Yuasa Battery, Inc.

250 CCA); medium size engines, 500- to 1,000-cc—10 to 17 AH (160 to 180 CCA); and small engines, 200- to 500-cc—6 to 16 (85 to 150 CCA). Because starter design varies widely between manufacturers, always check a service manual or with the battery manufacturer for the correct size battery for your motorcycle.

BATTERY CHARGERS

Quality battery chargers available today for motorcycles are sometimes known as "smart chargers," because they use a microprocessor to control multiple charging functions. Smart chargers monitor the battery's state of charge and will automatically start charging when the battery falls below a specific voltage. This "smart" technology also is used to prevent batteries from being overcharged, causing water loss in conventional batteries. Some chargers have diagnostic features and indicate if a battery is worn out and needs replacing. In addition to these features, many smart chargers will not spark when connected to a battery and will tell you if they are connected backward—something you *never* want to do with an older charger or when jump-starting a battery. Battery chargers used to provide a maintenance charge for motorcycle-sized batteries should not exceed 2.5 amps. Many of these chargers won't even charge a battery if the open circuit voltage is less than 6 volts. The charger's internal electronics won't allow the charger to switch on. A conventional battery charger would have to be used to initially charge the battery past 6 volts before connecting the smart charger. Be careful using automotive chargers, as they can overcharge and damage motorcycle batteries.

Least effective for charging a motorcycle battery are the "trickle" and automatic taper battery chargers. Both are similar in that their voltage is fixed. The taper charger reduces charging current while the trickle charger keeps both voltage and current constant. These chargers are slow in charging even moderately discharged batteries. Another problem is that they are not safe to leave connected to a battery for long periods of time—they can overcharge or undercharge a battery.

Constant current battery chargers are a better choice for battery charging. Constant current chargers continuously increase voltage during battery charging and can charge twice as fast as the constant-voltages or taper types of chargers. The best chargers combine both these designs. The strong charging characteristics of a constant current charger are used to initially charge the battery; then the charger automatically switches to a constant voltage mode to float-charge or maintain the battery. This type of charger is also know as a "smart" battery charger because it uses a microchip (computer) in its circuits to determine when to switch from charging mode to maintenance, or float, modes of charging.

Most motorcycle battery chargers come with clips to connect the charger leads to the battery and some have an additional SAE quick-disconnect plug that allows permanent connection to your bike's battery. To charge the battery, just plug the lead in. This is especially helpful if your battery is hard to get to. Others are available with BMW type sockets that can plug into BMWs, Triumphs, and some Ducatis.

Kisan Technologies chargeX solid state smart charger is small enough to be mounted on-board your motorcycle. All you need to charge your bike is a 120v extension cord. The charger can detect what type of battery (conventional or AGM) it's connected to and adjust its charging program accordingly. Not much larger than a pack of gum, the charger puts out 2.2 amps. Courtesy Kisan Technologies

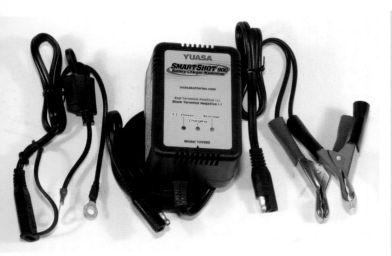

Left unattended, batteries lose up to 1 percent of their charge each day at 70 degrees and more if the ambient temperature drops. Electronic fuel injection, computers, clocks, and radios also drain batteries, even when the ignition is off. Even if a motorcycle is ridden often, charging the battery between rides will keep the number of discharge cycles to a minimum. In addition to keeping a bike ready to start, using a battery charger has an additional benefit—prolonged useful battery life. While there does not appear to be any "scientific" evidence available to support it, and this theory may be at odds with some battery manufacturers' supplied technical information but, it does seem to be true (or a hard fact) that connecting a "smart" battery charger to the battery every time you park your motorcycle causes the battery to last longer. For example, the Yuasa battery that was factory-installed in my 1997 Harley-Davidson Road King was still going strong after four years of constant use. Many owners of large displacement bikes only get one or two years before they have to replace their batteries. I have found this to be true of other motorcycles I've owed as well.

BATTERY ACTIVATION

New batteries require an initial charge before they are put into use. When a motorcycle dealer fills a conventional battery with acid, it's only about 80 percent charged. This is also true for AGM (sealed) batteries that you can purchase via the Internet or through the mail. Both types of batteries when new must be charged to reach their full life expectancy, as well as a 100 percent charge. Failure to charge a new battery can prevent it from ever becoming more than

Fig 4-11—Designed for long-term use, Yuasa's SmartShot 900 Automatic smart battery charger will not overcharge motorcycle batteries. The charging cycle reaches 14.4 volts then switches to "float" mode (indicated by a green LED). If a load is applied to the battery (turning on the key, etc.) while charging, the charger automatically switches back to charge mode, then to a maintenance float charge. The charger plugs directly into a wall outlet and comes with a 12-foot output cord. Courtesy Yuasa Battery, Inc.

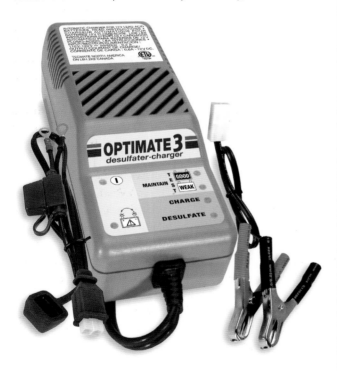

The OptiMate III smart battery charger has a unique algorithm specifically designed for power sport starter batteries. A combination of both voltage and current sensing technology double-checks to ensure that the battery is fully charged during constant-current stage of charging. If the battery is OK, the charger goes into the float mode charging and can maintain a battery for many months. Courtesy TechMate

The case on this AGM, maintenance-free battery states the charging method as "1.2AX5~10h." That means 1.2 amps for 5 to 10 hours of charging time. The capacity of the battery is 12 AH. "NON SPILLABLE" is also printed on the case as this AGM type of battery can be mounted on its side. Courtesy Yuasa Battery, Inc.

STORAGE BATTERIES

80 percent charged. Many motorcyclists prefer to fill (with acid) and install their own batteries to make sure they are charged before being put into service. If you don't do this yourself, ask your dealer to make sure the battery is charged for several hours before you pick up your bike.

This initial charge your new battery should have is called bulk, or initialization, charging and not all chargers are capable of performing this function. The charger used to initialize a new battery must be capable of reaching 12.8 volts. Yuasa, Kisan, and Optimate battery chargers are all capable of performing this job. A battery is properly initialized if the open circuit voltage reaches a minimum of 12.8 volts and does not exceed 13.8 volts. This range will work for conventional and maintenance-free types of batteries. Open circuit voltage should be checked after the battery has been disconnected from the charger for about an hour. This will avoid a false reading of the battery's surface charge.

Before testing a battery, perform a visual inspection. For conventional batteries, check for the correct acid level by looking at the side of the case. Upper and lower electrolyte levels should be indicated. If the battery you are testing has a translucent case you'll be able to see extensive sediment buildup that may indicate extreme sulfation. This condition, which appears as a white, crusty substance, can also be observed by looking inside the cells with the filler caps removed. If the battery has been sitting unused for a long time, it can become sulfated. Some smart chargers can recover a sulfated battery. The next step in testing is to fully charge the battery. See Figure 4-9 for charging times. Once the battery is fully charged, it should be tested for state of charge, using a digital voltmeter.

Battery Charging Time in Hours

State of Charge	Battery Amp-Hours								
	10AH		14AH		18AH		20AH		
75%	3	6	4	8	6	10	6	11	Hours
50%	6	11	9	14	11	18	13	20	"
25%	9	15	13	20	17	26	19	28	"
0%	13	20	18	27	23	34	25	37	"

1 amp taper charger
1 amp constant current charger

Fig 4-9—Battery charging time is determined by battery amp hours. Taper, or trickle, chargers charge at about one-half the rate of constant current types of battery chargers. Courtesy Yuasa Battery, Inc.

This hydrometer is specifically designed for testing state of charge on conventional powersports batteries. Instead of reading specific gravity, it uses colored balls to indicate state of charge. After sucking up enough electrolyte to cover the balls, the balls that float are counted. One floating ball equals 25 percent charge; 2 balls—50 percent; 3 balls—75 percent; and 4 balls indicate 100 percent state of charge.

BATTERY TESTING

There are several methods available for testing a battery, and the tools for doing so range from expensive, professional-grade test equipment to a multimeter and the engine's starter motor. All of these tests, with one exception, require the battery to be fully charged. If the battery is a conventional type, the filler caps can be removed and a hydrometer test used to determine state of charge by measuring specific gravity. Some auto parts stores still carry hydrometers, but since they are gradually being phased out of use. Most batteries used today are maintenance-free types, which have no filler caps for hydrometer testing. However, instead of measuring specific gravity, an open circuit voltage test can determine state of charge on both conventional and maintenance-free batteries.

OPEN CIRCUIT VOLTAGE TEST (STATE OF CHARGE)

The open circuit voltage test determines the battery's state of charge. Results of the test will indicate only two aspects of battery performance: the battery's ability to be charged to 100 percent capacity, and if any of the cells are bad (shorted or open). This test is not conclusive, and it is possible for a battery can pass the open circuit voltage test and still be no good. Perform the open circuit test using the following steps.

Step 1, remove the surface charge on the battery. The surface charge needs to be removed before an accurate open circuit voltage test can be performed. To remove the surface charge, turn on the ignition key so the headlight(s) come on for about three minutes. Now let the battery sit for about 10 minutes. Connect a digital voltmeter to the battery, red lead to positive and black lead to the negative terminal. Open circuit voltage indicates what percent of charge the battery has reached after charging.

A digital voltmeter is used to determine state of charge of maintenance-free batteries. At 13.00 volts, this battery is 100 percent charged. Less than 12.5 volts is only 75 percent charged and below 11.5 volts is between 25 and 0 percent charged. Courtesy Fluke Corporation

Consult Figure 4-10, Battery Open Circuit Voltage. If the open circuit voltage indicates that the battery is less than 75 percent charged, the battery is probably no good. Before you condemn the battery, try charging it again. If the battery is still not close to 100 percent charged, it's junk and unfortunately, it's time for a new battery. The open circuit voltage test is not conclusive. It is possible to have a 100 percent charged battery that will not start your motorcycle reliably. A load test must be done to determine actual battery performance.

DYNAMIC BATTERY LOAD TESTING

Once the battery is charged and passes the open circuit voltage test, it's time to see if the battery can really perform its main job—starting the engine. Now, it might seem obvious that you could simply press the start button and if the engine starts, the battery must be okay. While a marginal battery might start your engine a few times, will it start

Battery Open Circuit Voltage

State of Charge	Battery Type		
	AGM (Maint.free)	Conventional	6 Volt
100%	12.8v - 13.0v +	12.6v +	6.32v
75% - 100%	12.5v - 12.8v	12.4v -12.6V	6.21v
50% - 75%	12.0v -12.5v	12.1v - 12.4V	6.12v
25% - 50%	11.5v - 12.0v	12.0v - 12.2V	6.02v
0% - 25%	11.5 or less	11.5 or less	5.93 or less

Fig 4-10—Measuring open circuit voltage is an accurate method for determining a battery's state of charge. Make sure to remove the surface charge and turn off all electrical loads when performing the test. Courtesy Yuasa Battery, Inc.

tomorrow morning or the day after that? To find out if you have a reliable battery, the cranking voltage must be measured. Low cranking voltage will indicate that the battery is getting tired and should be replaced. Here's a quick way to do a battery load test using a digital voltmeter.

Connect a digital voltmeter to the battery, red lead to the positive terminal and black lead to negative. While watching the voltmeter, press the start button and start the engine. Just before the engine starts, note the voltmeter reading. As the starter motor places an electrical load across the battery's terminals, battery voltage will normally drop. If battery voltage drops to 9.5 volts (at 70 degrees F) or less, the battery is junk and needs to be replaced. If you're performing the test in cold conditions (around 40 degrees F) voltage can drop to 9.3 or less. If the battery barely cranks the engine over, don't forget to perform a voltage drop test before replacing the battery (see Chapter 2).

HAND-HELD BATTERY TESTERS

Hand-held battery load testers are becoming more widely available and can now be found in most auto parts stores. Even the largest motorcycle battery is generally smaller than the smallest automotive battery. Because the hand-held battery load tester was designed for the automotive market, some limitations and common sense should be applied before using one to test a motorcycle battery. Using a fixed resistor, these testers can electrically load a battery to

Automotive type, hand-held battery testers will work for testing motorcycle batteries but you have to use caution. Press the load button on this OTC Stinger Battery Tester (Part No. 3180) for no more than five seconds to keep from cooking the battery. Also, don't try to test batteries with an amp hour rating of less than 14 AH. Courtesy SPX/OTC Service Solutions, Yuasa Battery, Inc.

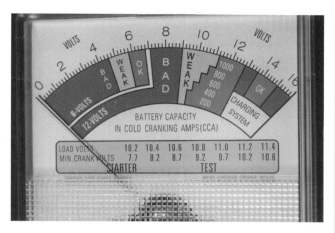

Depending on CCA, loaded voltage above 9.0 indicates a good 12-volt battery. The OTC No. 3180 battery tester can also test 6-volt batteries using a different scale on the meter's face. Courtesy SPX/OTC Service Solutions

100 amps or more—more than enough to fry even a large motorcycle battery if applied for too long. Only use these load testers on motorcycle batteries that have an amp hour rating of 14 AH (over 200 cold cranking amps) or higher. When you perform the test, place the load on the battery for between 3 and 5 seconds—NO LONGER.

To use the Stinger battery tester, connect the red and black cable clamps to the positive and negative battery terminals, respectively. Determine the cold cranking amps of the battery being tested. If CCA is not printed on the battery case see Figure 4-8 (on page 54) for a chart to convert amp hours to CCA The switch located on the tester triggers a relay that connects an internal resistor to the battery's terminals. This places a 100-amp load across the battery. While watching the meter, depress the load switch on the tester for no more than 5 seconds—3 seconds is probably enough. Just be sure as you release the test button you read the voltage on the tester. If the needle is in the green area, the battery is good. A steady needle reading in the yellow area means the battery may need to be charged or it could cause starting problems in the future, especially in cold weather. If the needle drops like a rock, the battery is bad and needs to be replaced.

The previous battery testing methods required that a battery be fully charged before testing. However, there is a professional grade battery tester that will test a battery even if it's dead. These digital testers measure a battery's internal resistance regardless of its state of charge. Internal resistance is an indication of a battery's ability to deliver current. The more capacity a battery has to produce amperage, the lower its internal resistance. A digital capacitance battery tester uses single load dynamic resistance technology to calculate

battery performance. These testers use a modified DC load test to apply a small, momentary load to the battery while measuring instantaneous voltage drop across all of its cells. The load is then removed and voltage across the cells is measured again after a recovery period. These analog measurements are converted into digital information—the tester calculates the dynamic internal resistance in order to evaluate overall condition. The entire process takes about two seconds and current drain on the battery is minimal. The tester provides information on open circuit voltage, state of charge, and battery health and condition. This tester can also test a partially charged or fully discharged battery, whether on or off the vehicle. The only drawback is the price—at $300 and up, these testers are not cheap and are mostly used by professional technicians.

To use the BTY01 tester, connect it to the battery. When the connection is made, battery voltage will be displayed. The next step is to program what type of battery you are testing—valve regulated lead acid/maintenance free/absorbent glass mat/sealed lead acid (VRLA/MF/AGM/SLA) or starting, lighting and ignition (SLI) conventional batteries. "SET CAPACITY" is displayed and arrow keys are used to select the amp hour rating of the battery being tested. Testing begins when you press ENTER, and takes less than two seconds. Open circuit voltage is displayed with each test result that includes: Good & Pass, Good & Recharge, Recharge & Retest, Bad & Replace, and Bad Cell & Replace. After testing, pressing the up/down arrow keys displays state of charge and battery health, both listed as a percentage.

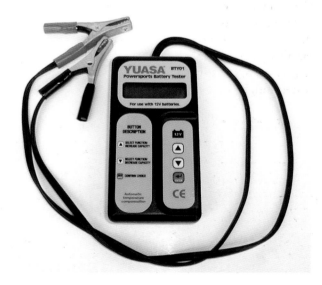

Yuasa's BTY01 battery tester provides information on open circuit voltage, state of charge, and battery health and condition. The unit can test a partially charged or discharged battery. Courtesy Yuasa Battery, Inc.

CHAPTER 5
CHARGING AND STARTING SYSTEMS

CHARGING SYSTEMS

Chapter 4 focused on the storage battery and battery chargers in general. In this chapter, the focus shifts to the motorcycle's on-board battery charger, more commonly known as the charging system. The charging system is the heart and soul of a motorcycle's electrical system. Without a reliable charging system, anything on your bike requiring electricity will not work for long.

In the early 1900s, before batteries were used in motorcycles or cars, only ignition systems required electricity in order to operate. These early vehicles used a magneto—a small generator capable of producing only enough energy to charge an ignition coil. Once electric lights, and eventually starters, were introduced for use on motorcycles, storage batteries were added as well. With the addition of a battery, there had to be some way to keep it charged.

Early motorcycles used DC generators in their charging systems. In the 1960s, these were replaced with AC charging systems that came in two flavors: the three-piece, permanent-magnet system consisting of a stator, rotor, and rectifier, and the alternator. Both types of AC charging systems represented new technology in the 1960s, made possible only because of then new solid state electronics such as transistors and diodes. Both generators and AC charging systems convert AC into DC volts, which can be used by the battery and ignition systems on a motorcycle. The diode proved to be an economical means of converting AC to DC volts for alternators. The DC generator mechanically converts AC voltage into DC without the use for diodes.

A motorcycle charging system has only two purposes: (1) to charge the battery; and (2) to power all the electrical components used on a motorcycle once the engine starts. The charging system must have enough capacity to meet all the electrical demands of the bike—including any accessories added by the owner—and charge the battery at the same time. The charging system's output and electrical requirements of the motorcycle must be matched and coordinated. Both DC generators and alternators are rated by

Above: *Pictured is an alternator from a Honda Gold Wing. Unlike three-piece separate charging systems that use a stator, rotor, and separate rectifier, this alternator uses internal diodes and voltage regulator forming a complete charging system. Alternators are far superior to three-piece charging systems because they can produce more electrical power and are more reliable—the downside is they're heavy, take up lots of space, and if you ever have to replace one, bring your wallet.* Courtesy Twigg Cycles

Left: *The components that make up charging and starting systems can be expensive when purchased from a dealer, especially for an older motorcycle. Rick's Motorsport Electrics Inc. remanufactures both starters and charging systems for most Japanese motorcycles.* Courtesy Rick's Motorsport Electrics, Inc.

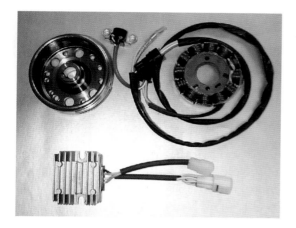

The most common type of motorcycle charging system consists of three components: rotor (left) stator (right) and rectifier. In general these systems are reliable unless overworked by the owner adding too many electrical accessories. Courtesy Rick's Motorsport Electrics, Inc.

since some charging systems are close to overload even without the addition of electrical accessories.

For example, a motorcycle with a total electrical power requirement of 450 watts would typically have a charging system capable of producing 500 watts or more. However, if a bike's electrical system requires more than what the charging system is capable of producing, the storage battery makes up the difference until it goes dead. This process is accelerated if the charging system has a problem and cannot produce full output. In such cases, the charging system probably won't be able to keep up with the normal demands of the electrical system, and the battery won't get charged at all.

the amount of current they are capable of producing. While automobiles are rated in amps, motorcycle charging system capacities and electrical accessories are usually rated in watts. For reliability, manufacturers design charging systems so they don't operate at maximum-rated power output for long periods of time. Charging systems are typically designed to have a slightly larger capacity than the requirements of the motorcycle's electrical system, that way riders can add accessories and the charging system won't be taxed to the extreme. However, this isn't always the case,

DC GENERATORS

Generators used in both motorcycles and cars produce electricity by means of a magnet and rotating coils of wire. All magnets have north and south poles. These poles create an invisible magnetic field around the magnet. If a coil of wire is rotated between two magnets, voltage is induced into the wire; alternatively, the magnets can be moved and the coil of wire held stationary with the same results. This process of rotating either wire coils or magnets is called magnetic induction. In a simple generator, two magnets are placed inverted, so that the north pole of one faces the south pole of the other. The magnets are separated by an air gap. The magnetic lines of force from one magnet bridge the air gap and extend to the other. When a coil of wire is placed between the two stationary magnets and rotated,

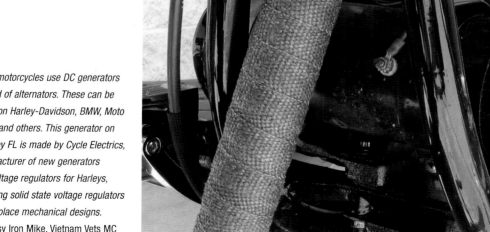

Older motorcycles use DC generators instead of alternators. These can be found on Harley-Davidson, BMW, Moto Guzzi, and others. This generator on a Harley FL is made by Cycle Electrics, manufacturer of new generators and voltage regulators for Harleys, including solid state voltage regulators that replace mechanical designs. Courtesy Iron Mike, Vietnam Vets MC

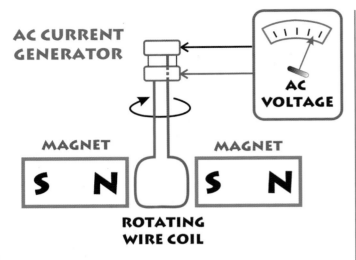

AC CURRENT GENERATOR

AC VOLTAGE

MAGNET

S N

MAGNET

S N

ROTATING WIRE COIL

Fig 5-1—Both generators and alternators work in a similar manner—a coil of wire is rotated between two magnets. As the invisible lines of magnetic force are cut, voltage and current are induced into the coil of wire.

the magnetic lines of force are intermittently cut. Each time the magnetic lines of force are interrupted, voltage and current are induced into the coil of wire. When the coil of wire is rotated 180 degrees, the lines of force are cut in the opposite direction, causing the induced voltage and current to reverse. The current travels first in one direction and then reverses and goes in the other direction. This back and forth reversal of current and voltage is known as alternating current, or AC. Both DC generators and AC generators (alternators) produce AC voltage and current. However, motorcycle electrical systems can only use DC

current (direct current) and voltage. AC output from either a generator or an alternator must be converted into DC current. Alternators and generators accomplish the conversion of AC to DC current in different ways.

A DC generator produces electrical current when coils of wire rotate around a stationary field coil, which acts like a magnet. The multiple coils of wire are wrapped around a laminated iron core called an armature, which is rotated by the engine's crankshaft. The circular ends of each coil of wire (loops) are isolated from each other and connected to copper commutator bars. These copper bars are located at the end of the armature and are positioned in a circle around the armature shaft. The stationary field coils, which act like magnets inside a generator, are actually electromagnets in the form of coils of wire wrapped around iron-pole shoes, which are energized by the battery when the ignition key is turned on. Once the engine is running, the generator self-powers the field coils. As the armature turns, AC voltage is produced and converted into DC current via two carbon-based generator brushes that touch the rotating commutator bars (acting like a mechanical switch). The generator brushes are mounted 180 degrees apart, allowing them to contact only one armature wire loop at a time. As each wire loop rotates past the brushes, small amounts of voltage passes into the brush and then into the motorcycle's electrical system. Because the commutator bars rotate rapidly across the brushes, voltage output is constant. Since the commutator bars have to carry the generator's output, it limits the amount of current that 12- or 6-volt DC generators can produce. Most DC generators only output between 10 and 20 amps (135 and 270 watts).

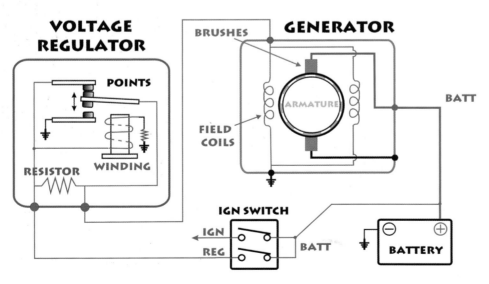

VOLTAGE REGULATOR

POINTS

WINDING

RESISTOR

GENERATOR

BRUSHES

ARMATURE

FIELD COILS

BATT

IGN SWITCH

IGN

REG

BATT

BATTERY

Fig 5-2—This simple mechanical voltage regulator illustrates how a generator's output is controlled by switching its field coils on and off. When charging voltage reaches a set level, the winding inside the regulator becomes an electromagnet and pulls the contacts down to ground the field coils inside the generator, turning the field coils off. When the battery needs charging and system voltage drops, the winding releases the contact points and the field coils are turned back on and charging resumes. The voltage regulator's contact points cycle on and off rapidly to control voltage output at a steady rate.

MECHANICAL VOLTAGE REGULATORS

As a DC generator rotates, its voltage output and current increase; if unchecked, it would keep doing so until it self-destructs. Consequently, DC generators are equipped with an external mechanical voltage regulator that controls current and voltage. When output voltage gets too high, the voltage regulator switches off the field coils inside the generator. Inside the voltage regulator is a calibrated electromagnet that moves a set of contact points (similar to those used in older ignition systems) open and closed—these turn the field coils on and off at a rate of about 200 times per second. With no current going to the field coils, no magnetic lines of force are cut inside the generator, and it stops producing current. As voltage in the electrical system drops, the regulator switches the field coils back on. By turning the field coils inside the generator on and off, a voltage regulator can set voltage at a constant rate even though the vehicle's electrical loads may vary.

If the battery is discharged, or there are excessive electrical loads placed on the charging system, the voltage regulator keeps the generator's field coils constantly energized in an attempt to keep up with the electrical loads. In addition to controlling voltage, the voltage regulator also limits the amount of current the generator produces. The current regulator circuit (within the voltage regulator) works in a similar manner as the voltage regulator—as amperage flow increases from the generator, an electromagnetic coil pulls open a second set of contact points and turns off the field coils (which limits generator current output). One additional component makes up a voltage regulator—the cutout relay. The cutout relay prevents the battery from discharging back into the generator's field coils when the ignition is off. Without the cutout relay, the generator would always be on and the battery would go dead with the engine not running. Some older voltage regulators could be adjusted for voltage output by bending the metal tabs that hold the springs for the contact points.

TRANSISTORIZED ELECTRONIC VOLTAGE REGULATORS

Transistorized electronic voltage regulators basically perform the same functions as a mechanical regulator. However, a transistor takes the place of coils of wire and moveable contact points. Nearly all external electronic voltage regulators control an alternator's or generator's field current by switching the circuit on and off. Because solid state electronics (transistors) are used, the switching rate is around 7,000 times per second. Compared to a mechanical

This Cycle Electric solid state voltage regulator introduces modern technology to a generator-type charging system on this vintage Harley-Davidson. The regulator senses the temperature of the armature, and when cold (after cold engine startup) it allows more current to be produced by the generator to help charge the battery. After the generator has been operating for a while, current is limited to keep from overworking the generator. Courtesy Iron Mike, Vietnam Vets MC and Cycle Electric Inc.

This BMW mechanical voltage regulator is used with an alternator but is similar to those used for control of DC generators. It functions by controlling the alternator's field coils to regulate output voltage. Courtesy Bob's BMW

Left: *Honda Gold Wings and Valkyries, and some BMWs, use an alternator (left) similar to those used on automobiles. The diodes used convert AC to DC volts and regulator are contained inside. A rectifier, top, right, and stator are pictured. This style of AC charging system can't produce the power that the single alternator can, but they are smaller and more compact. The stator fits inside the engine cases and the rectifier can be mounted almost anywhere on the frame.* Courtesy Twigg Cycles

Below: *This Honda Gold Wing alternator uses internal diodes to convert AC voltage to DC volts. The diodes are located under the black plastic cover with the bolts protruding through it.* Courtesy Twigg Cycles

Bottom: *The diodes for this BMW alternator charging system are not built into the alternator. Instead they are housed in a metal box located inside the front engine cover along with the alternator.* Courtesy Bob's BMW

voltage regulator's contact points switch rate of 200 times per second, an electronic regulator provides much better control—and all without any moving parts!

Internal regulators manufactured by Cycle Electric, Inc. use a current-limiting circuit that senses armature temperature and then limits the current in an amount inversely proportional to the temperature. As armature temperature goes up, amperage output goes down. This provides higher amperage output right after the engine is started to recharge the battery. As the engine and generator heat up, charging current is lowered to keep the generator from overheating.

ONE-PIECE ALTERNATORS

The development of a solid state device called a diode led to the wide use of alternators in automobiles in the early 1960s. By the 1970s most motorcycles used either a single alternator or three-piece alternator charging system. Diodes are the key to these systems' ability to convert AC voltage and current to DC. A diode is an electrical one-way valve that allows current to pass in one direction, but not the other. The diodes are used in motorcycle rectifiers and alternators to convert AC current and voltage into DC current and voltage by means of a process called rectification.

An alternator produces AC current in the same manner as a DC generator—by use of electromagnets and coils of wire. However, a major difference between DC generators and alternators is the relative positions of the magnets and coils of wire. An alternator has a rotating magnet and stationary coils, while a DC generator uses rotating coils

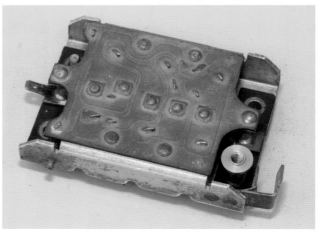

with stationary magnets or field coils. The rotor inside an alternator takes the place of an armature; it consists of an iron core mounted on a shaft with a coil of wire wrapped around it. The coil is enclosed between two pole pieces that are also made of iron. The two ends of the coil connect to copper slip rings at one end of the rotor shaft. These slip rings are in contact with two carbon brushes; one is grounded and the other is connected through the alternator's field terminal to the voltage regulator (internal or external). Unlike the segmented commutator bars in a DC generator, slip rings on an alternator are continuous, so brush wear is minimal. The amount of current passing through the slip rings is far lower than what passes through the brushes in a DC generator. The high current instead is produced in the stationary stator coils. Unlike generator brushes, alternator brushes usually last the life of the alternator; typically, other internal components, such as bearings and diodes, fail before the slip ring brushes.

Modern motorcycle charging systems use three coils of wire incorporated into the windings on a stator. The stator coils are fitted inside the alternator and surround the rotor. As the rotor turns, its magnetic field induces voltage into the stator coils. Three coils make up the stator, each producing its own voltage. The stator output is AC voltage that swings up and down from negative to positive in repeating cycles.

THREE-PIECE ALTERNATORS

By far the most common type of motorcycle charging system is the three-piece alternator. It operates by the same principles as the single alternator. The stator is made up of laminated steel core stacks, with a wound copper coil of wire winding around each stack. These stacks are located around the circumference of the stator. There are three

Top: *With the rotor removed on this Gold Wing alternator, the brushes can be seen. They are made from carbon and are spring-loaded so they will make contact with the rotating slip rings when the alternator operates. An internal voltage regulator (finned box at bottom) is used to control voltage output.* Courtesy Twigg Cycles

Center: *A coil-type spring exerts pressure on the alternator slip ring brushes in this BMW alternator. In general, slip ring brushes won't wear out before other alternator components such as bearings and diodes fail.* Courtesy Bob's BMW

Bottom: *The alternator's stator is made up of three separate coils. The rotor spins inside the stator, inducing voltage and current into the stator windings.* Courtesy Twigg Cycles

wires that come from the stator coils because the charging system has three phases of output. This component is usually located at the end of the engine's crankshaft. Surrounding the stator is a round metal drum called a rotor, which has magnets cast into it. When the engine turns, the rotor spins it around the stator. With the magnets whirling around the stator, AC current and voltage are produced in the stator's windings.

The key to making either alternator function is the diode. Both single and three-piece alternators must convert AC output to DC in order to power the motorcycle's DC electrical system. Diodes are solid state devices containing no moving parts. They are used to block only negative voltage produced by the stator coils. One end of each stator coil is connected to both a positive and negative diode. The other ends of the coils are connected together and form a triangular Delta arrangement. Not all alternators are designed this way, but most are. For purposes of testing or mode of operation, they all function in the same manner. By using the diode's one-way current flow attributes, the negative voltage output from each coil is blocked—only positive voltage is allowed to reach the vehicle's electrical system. Both types of alternators have a three-phase output because three coils are used in the stator. These three phases overlap each other, producing a more or less even DC current and voltage output. This process is also known as AC voltage rectification

An alternator's rotor consists of a coil of wire and two iron pole pieces. The slip rings that transfer power to the rotor coil are located at the end of the rotor shaft next to the bearing. An internal cooling fan is mounted between the slip rings and rotor in this alternator. Courtesy Twigg Cycles

The most common type of charging system used on motorcycles today is often referred to as a three-piece charging system, as it consists of a stator (right), rectifier, and rotor (not pictured). When permanent magnets imbedded in a rotor (not pictured) are rotated around the stator, it produces AC voltage and current. The rectifier changes AC to DC current and voltage that is used to charge the battery and power the bike's electrical system. Courtesy Twigg Cycles

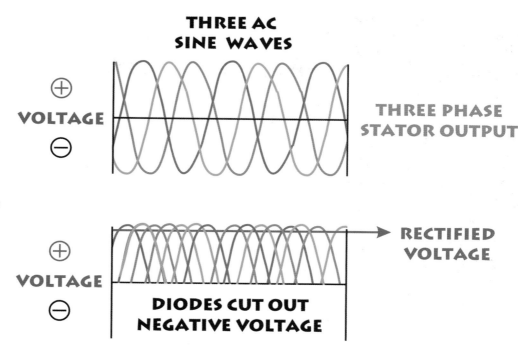

THREE AC SINE WAVES

⊕
VOLTAGE
⊖

THREE PHASE STATOR OUTPUT

⊕
VOLTAGE
⊖

RECTIFIED VOLTAGE

DIODES CUT OUT NEGATIVE VOLTAGE

Fig 5-3—The graph at the top represents the voltage output from the three stator coils. Voltage for each coil (a single phase) transitions between positive and negative. The lower diagram shows the effect of the presence of negative voltage blocking diodes in the stator circuit. The negative part of the stator coil's voltage output is "flipped" up to produce a positive output. The resulting voltage and current are changed, or rectified into DC voltage and current.

Six diodes are used in a single alternator—two for each output phase or stator coil. Each diode is mounted at the slip ring end of the alternator housing. The three negative diodes are attached to the alternator's frame, while the three positive diodes are insulated from ground and mounted in a heat sink. Because the diodes get hot, an internal or external fan is used to create airflow inside the alternator to cool things off.

The diodes for a three-piece alternator are remotely located inside the rectifier, which is connected to the stator via three wires. The rectifier performs three functions: conversion of AC input to DC output, voltage regulation, and current regulation. There are six diodes within the rectifier that work in the same manner as an alternator to convert AC voltage to DC voltage. The diodes only allow positive current to reach the battery by blocking negative voltage from the stator. Current and voltage regulation is controlled by three thyristors and a voltage-sensing integrated circuit.

A thyristor is a semiconductor device that acts as an on-off switch triggered by a signal from the voltage sensing circuit. When DC voltage reaches a preset level (usually between 13.5 and 14.5 volts), the voltage sensor sends a signal to the thyristors. When the thyristors are triggered, they turn on, connecting the stator windings to ground—effectively short-circuiting them and shutting off any current production from the stator. As soon as the DC voltage level drops below a preset voltage level, the thyristors are

Fig 5-4—This drawing illustrates how each stator coil's output voltage connects between a pair of diodes inside the rectifier. Only positive voltage is allowed to reach the battery, as it passes through the three positive (red) diodes. The negative diodes block the negative voltage. The voltage regulator keeps charging voltage below 14.5 on most bikes by sending excess current to ground through three thyristors (in blue).

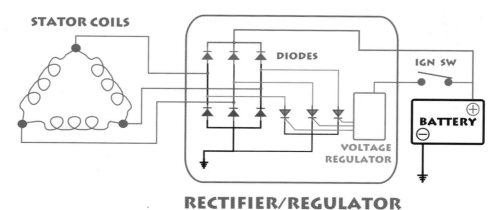

STATOR COILS

DIODES

IGN SW

BATTERY
⊕
⊖

VOLTAGE REGULATOR

RECTIFIER/REGULATOR

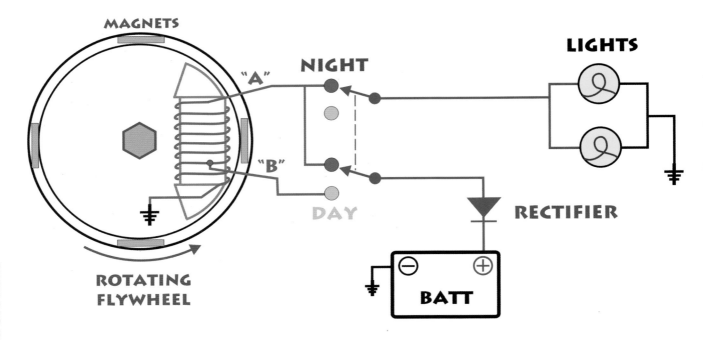

Fig 5-5—Off-road motorcycles and some older, smaller street bikes use a variation of the three-piece charging system, the flywheel alternator. As the flywheel rotates, current is generated in the charging coil. For daytime operation, the battery is charged using the B terminal of the charging coil. At night when more current is required to operate the lights, the A terminal is used for power. The A and B terminals provide different amounts of power due to the length of wire in each—more wire/coils in A and less in B. A simple diode serves as a rectifier to change the AC current to DC before charging the battery.

switched off, and the charging process begins again. This switching process takes place thousands of times per second. Another effect of dumping the stator's charging voltage to ground, as it is sometimes referred to, is that the thyristors and diodes get hot. That's why motorcycle rectifiers are made of aluminum and have heat fins—just like an air-cooled motorcycle engine.

FLYWHEEL ALTERNATORS FOR SMALL MOTORCYCLES

Off-road and smaller motorcycles use a variation of the three-piece charging system often called a flywheel alternator charging system. These systems have been around for years and have some variations but basically operate on the same principles. The engine's flywheel has magnets cast into it just like the typical three-piece charging system. Instead of a stator, a laminated pole shoe is used and wound with a coil of wire. As the rotating magnets pass in over the coil of wire on the pole shoe, AC voltage is generated.

Many charging coils have three wires. One end of the coil is grounded and the other two are voltage outputs. The two outputs are for modes of operation that function with and without the running lights. With the running lights

off, only battery charging occurs and less current is needed. Terminal B is used for daytime operation as it is only about one-half of the charging coil's length of wire, and therefore only produces enough current to charge the battery (see Figure 5-5). At night when the lighting system is on, terminal A is used because it uses the entire charging coil to produce more power. (The ignition system uses a separate charging coil for power not shown in figure 5-5.)

The AC voltage and current must still be converted to DC for use in the bike's electrical system. The same type of voltage rectifier used in the three-piece charging system is used with flywheel alternators. Modern systems use a solid state integrated circuit for rectification and voltage regulation and are similar to the system in Figure 5-4 (on page 67). Some early systems used a Zener diode to regulate voltage. The Zener diode works like a pressure relief valve. When electrical pressure (voltage) is below 14 volts, the Zener diode does not allow current to pass to ground. Consequently, all the charging current goes to the battery and electrical system. As charging voltage rises to 15 volts, the Zener diode passes most of the charging current to ground and almost none reaches the battery. This is a primitive method of voltage regulation and is not used today.

The Heads-UP Voltage Indicator can be mounted almost anywhere on your motorcycle. The single LED gives the rider warning should the charging system malfunction. The LED shows a steady green light if everything's normal; flashing green indicates overcharging (above 15 volts). A steady amber light indicates system voltage is between 11 and 12 volts, and a flashing red means that charging system voltage is below 10 volts. Courtesy Signal Dynamics

CHARGE INDICATORS

Charge indicator lights are used only on older (vintage) motorcycles. Charge light indicators are usually connected between the ignition switch and voltage regulator. When the ignition is turned to ON, battery voltage gets supplied to one side of the charge indicator light; the other side is connected to the voltage regulator that provides a ground for the light when the engine is not running. As soon as the engine starts, and the generator turns, voltage increases on the ground side of the charge light. As voltage builds, the charge light has less and less of a ground and goes dim,

eventually turning off. If anything in the charging system goes wrong and causes the system voltage to drop, the charge indicator light receives a ground from the voltage regulator and comes on. On some Harley-Davidsons, it's common for the charge light to be dim at idle and then shut off when engine and generator speed increase. Charge indicator lights are not generally used in motorcycles with alternators or three-piece charging systems. If the charging system malfunctions on older bikes, the rider is only informed of this fact when the engine quits and the battery is dead.

Fig 5-6—A charge light indicator receives power from the ignition switch and a ground from the voltage regulator. When the generator starts turning, the ground for the light builds voltage until the charge indicator light eventually has no ground (12 volts on each side of the light) and goes out. Unfortunately, charge indicators are a thing of the past and are not used on modern motorcycles.

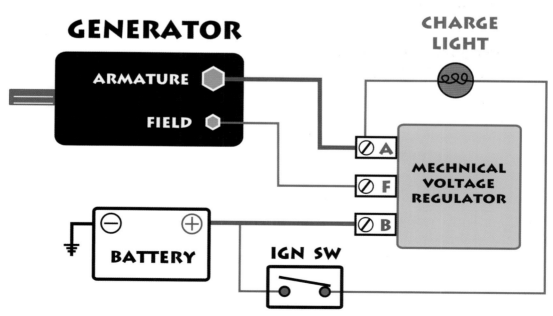

CHARGING SYSTEM TESTING

If your battery dies after riding several miles or the acid gets cooked out of it, the bike's charging system is probably at fault. Charging systems are usually reliable on modern motorcycles. In fact, most charging system problems are typically caused by something "stupid," rather than as a result of a component malfunction. To eliminate needless hours of electrical testing, the following common problems should be eliminated first as the most likely source of a charging system malfunction. They are listed in order of the most common problem first: (1) Battery condition; (2) loose or poor electrical connections; and (3) fuses or circuit breakers.

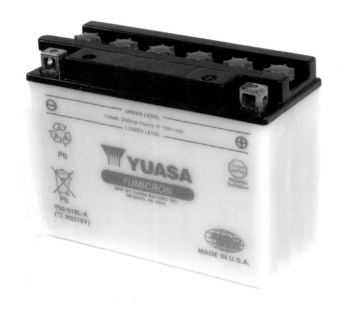

Before blaming the charging system for a dead battery, make sure that the battery is good. A shorted battery cell or an old, tired battery that can't take a charge may damage the charging system by burning out the stator or rectifier, or both. Test the battery before diagnosing the charging system for a problem. Courtesy Yuasa Batteries, Inc.

BATTERY CONDITION

If a motorcycle's battery keeps going dead overnight, or in only a few hours, replacing charging system components won't necessarily fix the problem. This may seem obvious, but unfortunately, NOT testing the battery first is the cause of more needless charging system component replacements. Even if the battery is fairly new, it doesn't necessarily mean it's good. Test it to make sure, and don't forget to check for loose battery cable connections while you're at it. (See Chapter 4 for battery testing procedures.)

Don't forget, the battery should be fully charged *BEFORE* testing or installing charging system components. Jump starting a bike with a dead battery and newly installed stator or rectifier may damage these components as a result of the initial heavy electrical load being placed on them. In addition, if the battery is dead (less than 5 volts of open circuit voltage), the charging system may not recognize it as part of the circuit since the end result is the same as if the battery was disconnected from the motorcycle. Alternators and three-piece charging systems must balance their voltage output against the battery's internal resistance. With no battery seemingly present in the electrical system to push against, charging system voltage increases, and could exceed 20 volts. With 20 volts in the electrical system, other electrical components such as on-board computers, ignition modules, etc., may not survive. Do *NOT* disconnect the battery on any motorcycle while the engine is running—it will put a severely large dent in your wallet. Disconnecting the battery with the engine running was a questionable charging system test even for vintage motorcycles equipped with DC generators; however those bikes didn't have solid state electronics, which are easily damaged by such a procedure.

WIRES, FUSES AND CONNECTORS

Always make sure to check for loose wires or connectors at the alternator, stator, voltage rectifier and battery before assuming an alternator is faulty. Look for connectors that are not plugged into stator wires coming out of the engine case, since you never know who might have worked on the charging system last and forgot to plug them in. Even though a connector may appear tight, and might not feel loose, doesn't mean it's actually working electrically. A voltage drop test is the fastest way to determine the strength and solidity of the connection between the wires coming from the stator, voltage rectifier, and positive battery terminal. (See "Voltage Drop Testing" in Chapter 2.) Basically, a voltage drop test will help determine if voltage produced at the alternator is actually getting to the battery.

To perform a voltage drop test on the charging system, connect the red lead of a voltmeter to the "power" wire at the rectifier (or back of the alternator) and the black meter lead to the positive battery terminal. Start the engine. Hold engine speed at 4,000 rpm (check the service manual for your motorcycle's specific charging system test procedures). The voltage drop should measure between 0.2 volts for alternators with voltage output capacity of around 30 amps, and 0.7 volts for alternators with output capacity closer to 100 amps (the greater the amperage, the greater the range of acceptable voltage drop). However, if voltage

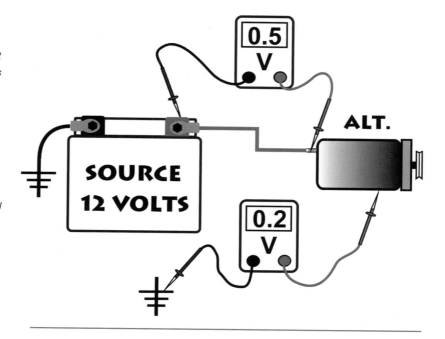

Right: *Fig 5-7—This alternator is putting out 60 amps at 2,000 rpm. The drop of 0.5 volts between the alternator's output terminal and the battery is acceptable for this application. The ground side voltage drop is 0.2 volts, so the ground return is good as well.*

Below: *Fig 5-8—Voltage drop tests for both power and ground sides of a three-piece charging system on a small motorcycle should be around 0.2 volts. On many bikes, the rectifier is bolted to the frame but could still have a bad connection due to corrosion on mounting bolts and surfaces.*

drop is higher than it should be, there's a problem with the alternator/rectifier wire going to the battery or its connections. Perform the same test on the ground side of the alternator or rectifier. Connect the red voltmeter lead to the alternator's case and the black lead to the negative battery terminal. Voltage drop should not exceed 0.2 volts. If the voltage reading is higher, there's probably a bad connection at the point where the negative battery cable attaches to the engine case or the mounting bolts for the rectifier.

GENERIC CHARGING SYSTEM TESTING

The first step before testing any charging system is to ascertain how much electrical current has to be produced. Connect an inductive ammeter probe to the positive or negative battery cable. Switch the ignition to ON and check if the meter's reading is a negative or positive number. If it's negative, the ammeter is connected correctly; if it's positive, unclamp the probe, turn it 180 degrees, and reconnect it. With the ignition key on, but with the engine *not* running, switch the headlight to high beam and operate the brake to get the brake light to come on. If you have a late-model fuel-injected bike, the fuel pump should run for about two seconds once the ignition is turned on. In addition, running any electrical accessories such as CB radio, CD player,

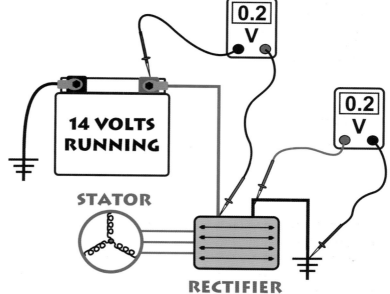

GPS, any electric clothing, heated seats, heated grips or anything else, turns them on as well.

Record the highest amperage reading displayed on the meter—this is the total amount of amperage from all the electrical loads. (Well, almost all. On some EFI bikes, the ignition system won't operate unless the engine is running.) The meter should display a negative number, because it's measuring current coming out of the battery. Shut off all electrical loads. Now start the engine and hold the rpm steady above 4,000 (3,000 on a Harley-Davidson). Once

This BMW alternator is located under the front engine cover. The diodes are not part of the alternator and can be seen at the far right. A mechanical voltage regulator is used in this older system. Courtesy Bob's BMW

the engine is running, the charging system must produce the same number of positive amps in order to break even. However, the alternator has to produce additional amperage to keep the battery charged. The final number is the amount of amperage the alternator must produce in order to both power the accessories and charge the battery. You should see a positive amperage number on your meter between 1 and 5 amps. This number represents the amount of current that is available to charge the battery.

Next, add the negative amperage number recorded with all the loads on and the engine *not* running to the positive amperage number recorded when the engine speed was above 4,000 rpm. The result should be within 10 percent of the rated overall output capacity for the charging system.

For example, assume all of the electrical loads on a motorcycle total—30 amps as measured at the battery (loads on, engine off). With the engine running, and all the loads turned on, the ammeter should read a positive 3 amps. These two readings need to be added together.

The math for this hypothetical alternator's total amperage output looks like this: +30 amps (to match the total output from the battery for all the loads) plus an additional 3 amps (to charge the battery) equals a total of 33 amps. Motorcycle charging systems are rated in watts so multiply 33 amps times 14.5 volts for a total of 478.5 watts. Because this motorcycle's charging system is rated at 500 watts and the 478.5 you measured is within 10 percent of the rated output, the charging system is operating as it should (10 percent of 500 is 50 watts, so any output above 450 watts is considered good).

In addition to testing for charging amperage, charging voltage should be checked as well. Be sure to do this test with all loads on and the engine holding steady above 4,000 rpm (refer to a service manual for your motorcycle). Charging system output voltage should be at least 1 volt over the battery's open-circuit voltage—usually somewhere between 13.5 and 14.5 volts. See a service manual for specific voltage output numbers. If the only testing equipment available is a voltmeter, only charging voltage can be read.

Right: Charging system voltage should be at least 1 volt over open circuit battery voltage. On most motorcycles it should be between 13.5 and 14.5 volts. Engine rpm has a substantial effect on charging system voltage. Engine speeds above 4,000 rpm may be required for maximum charging system output. See a service manual to find out what charging voltage should be at any given engine rpm for your motorcycle. Courtesy Fluke Corporation

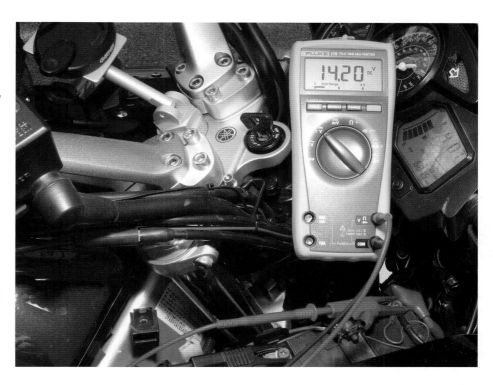

Below: Generally reliable motorcycle charging system stators can sometimes malfunction. The coils of wire that make up the stator can short together or to ground, or become open. This stator has been "cooked" as evidenced by the two melted coils (top right). Courtesy Twigg Cycles

As long as charging voltage is above open-circuit battery voltage, the voltmeter will confirm the alternator is producing some current, but not how much. Consequently, this test is inconclusive. Unfortunately, without the ability to read amperage, you can only guess (and hope!) that the charging system is okay.

STATOR AND RECTIFIER TESTING

Most stators are simple in construction and easy to test. Two common problems typically occur: electrical opens, and shorts. Shorts can exist between stator windings or from one of the windings to ground. Opens occur when a stator coil has a break in its windings. Using an ohmmeter to check for opens and shorts is not the best way to diagnose a bad stator. While the theory of checking for opens and shorts using a meter is okay, the reality is the stator may pass an ohmmeter test but not produce enough AC voltage to charge the motorcycle's battery. Dynamic testing is the best way to determine if a stator is working.

Shorts between windings can be tested with a digital voltmeter and shorts to ground can be tested using a test light. To test the stator, unplug its connector from the rectifier and start the engine. All three wires from the stator should produce AC voltage. A service manual will provide specific stator AC voltage output values at specific engine rpm. If you don't have a service manual, watch for increases in AC voltage as engine rpm rises. A good rule of thumb is divide the system charging output (watts) by four. The result is a good estimate of what the three stator wires should collectively produce in AC volts. For example if a charging system is rated at 400 watts, then the AC voltage output from the stator should be 100 volts AC (400 ÷ 4 = 100 volts). An open stator winding will not produce AC voltage.

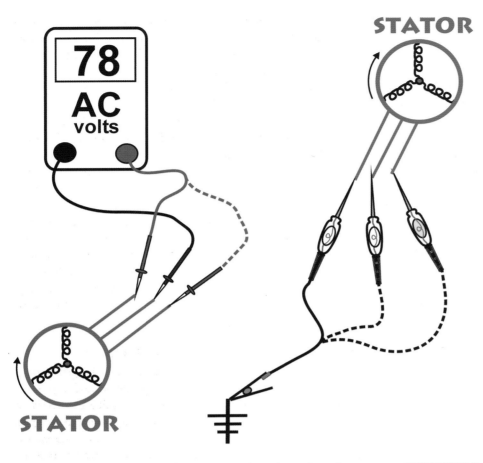

Fig 5-9—Testing a stator dynamically with the engine running is the best way to see if it's working. First unplug the stator from the rectifier and connect a multimeter to two of the stator wires. The AC voltmeter should read AC voltage from each of the three-stator wires with the engine running. To test for a grounded stator coil, the test light should NOT light when touched to any of the three wires. The stator wire to the far right is shorted to ground, causing the test light to glow—the stator needs to be replaced.

Use a test light to check for stator winding shorted to ground. With the stator unplugged and the engine running, use a grounded test light to touch each of the three stator wires. If any wire causes the test light to light up or glow, that winding is shorted to ground. If this is the result, the stator is junk and needs to be replaced.

Voltage rectifier testing is a little trickier than testing the stator. The rectifier has three jobs: to convert—rectify—AC to DC volts, to control charging system voltage, and to prevent the battery from discharging through the stator when the engine is off. Testing rectifiers using an ohmmeter and following a factory procedure is inconclusive and wastes time. Rectifier testing is best done using the process of elimination. If the stator's AC voltage output is good, and the battery checks out OK, the only suspect left that could be responsible for poor or no charging is the rectifier. With the engine running, voltage at the battery should be above 13.5 volts but below 15.0 volts (see a service manual or specific voltages). If charging voltage is outside that range *and* there are no excessive loads on the electrical system, the rectifier is probably bad. (This method assumes that all wires and connectors are plugged in and in good condition.)

CHECKING FOR BAD DIODES

In addition to converting AC voltage into DC, diodes inside the rectifier (or alternator) prevent the battery from discharging back through the rectifier when the engine is not running. By measuring a charging system's maximum output, you are also testing all the diodes indirectly. If one diode is bad, charging output will be decreased. In addition, a bad diode can drain a battery with the engine off. This phenomenon is known as parasitic amp draw. (More information on this symptom can be found in Chapter 9, Troubleshooting Electrical Systems.) To test for this condition, clamp your ammeter probe around the positive battery cable or use a series ammeter. With the ignition in the OFF position, and all accessories turned off, amperage flow between the battery and the rectifier should be less than 0.050 amps (50 milliamps). If the ammeter indicates more amperage, one of the rectifier's diodes could be bad (or an electrical load is still on).

Another diode test uses a voltmeter to measure AC voltage "leaking" from a diode about to go bad. To perform the test, connect the voltmeter leads directly to the battery. Set the scale on the voltmeter to read AC millivolts (mV). AC voltage should not exceed 55mV AC with the engine running and several accessories turned on. If

AC voltage is greater than 55mV, one or more diodes could be about to malfunction.

DC GENERATOR AND REGULATOR TESTING

Even though DC generators are old school, countless collectors and vintage motorcycle enthusiasts will sooner or later need to test these systems. DC generators with voltage regulators can be full field tested by following the same general procedure. Voltage regulators used in conjunction with DC generators have only three wires. The terminals are typically labeled F (goes to generator's field wire); BATT (goes to the battery's positive terminal); and A (goes to the armature in the generator). Connect an inductive amp probe around the wire at the A terminal of the voltage regulator. DC generators can be full fielded to test maximum output. Full fielding simply bypasses the voltage regulator and causes the generator to produce maximum current. Before performing a full field test, check the service manual for your motorcycle. Some DC generator systems may have specific procedures for generator and regulator testing.

To full field a generator, start the engine and hold rpm at 2,000. Connect an inductive amp probe around the wire at terminal A of the voltage regulator. Disconnect the F terminal at the voltage regulator and touch the wire to ground for only a second, while watching the ammeter. The generator should output maximum amperage with the field wire grounded. If it still won't full field, try the same test directly at the generator—if it full fields now, repair the field wire to the regulator—if it doesn't full field, try polarizing the generator (see next section on "Generator Polarizing") before getting a new one. Be sure to check the three wires at the regulator and generator to be certain they're connected properly. Consult a wiring diagram to identify the wires.

The voltage regulator should regulate voltage between 13.5 and 14.5 volts (6-volt systems should be approximately half of 12-volt readings) once the engine has been running for a few minutes. If voltage is too high or low, but the generator full fields, the voltage regulator is probably bad. Before purchasing a new regulator, make sure it's the correct one for the motorcycle. In addition, also try polarizing the generator. Pay attention to the regulator's working voltage—6 or 12 volts depending upon application. You may be able to use an electronic regulator as better replacement for a mechanical one.

GENERATOR POLARIZING

If a new or rebuilt generator is installed, it must be polarized before it can produce current. Polarizing establishes the correct polarity for the magnets inside the generator.

Here is a general procedure for DC generator polarizing: Disconnect the field wire at the voltage regulator. Connect a test light to the field wire and touch the end to battery positive. If the test light lights up, remove it and momentarily touch the field wire directly to the battery terminal on the regulator to polarize the generator. When you touch the field wire to the BATT terminal, a good-sized spark should be produced—this is normal. However, if the test light does not light up when touching battery positive, touch it to the negative battery terminal instead. If it now lights up, reconnect the field wire to the regulator and remove the A (armature) wire from the regulator. Momentarily touch the armature wire to the battery terminal on the regulator to polarize the generator—a good-sized spark should again be produced. Again, this is normal. However, if the test light fails to light up while touching both positive and negative terminals on the battery, the field circuit inside the generator is open and needs to be repaired.

STARTER MOTORS

A DC starter motor operates much like a DC generator—only in reverse. It uses current to operate, instead of producing current when it spins. However, just like a generator, a starter motor uses field coils to create a magnetic field around an armature. Most modern motorcycle starters use permanent magnets instead of field coils, because they are lightweight and more compact. The armature is a series of wire loops connected at a commutator. When the starter

This is a typical starter motor from a Japanese motorcycle. The only electrical connection is a large terminal for the battery cable. The starter's drive gear turns an overrunning clutch that drives the engine's crankshaft when the starter motor operates. Courtesy Twigg Cycles

Left: *Looking very much like it really belongs in a car, this BMW starter uses the solenoid to push the starter's pinion gear into the flywheel to start the engine. Modern motorcycles don't use this design.* Courtesy Bob's BMW

Bottom left: *Pictured is an armature and commutator bars (lower right). Resistance for the armature coils should be around 20 to 50 ohms, depending on manufacture. There should be no continuity between any of the commutator bars and the iron core of the armature. Open armature coils or any short from one of the coils to ground (the armature) will cause the starter to be weak or not operate at all.* Courtesy Twigg Cycles

Bottom right: *Pictured are the commutator and four starter brushes. With four starter brushes, each pair of brushes will energize armature coils opposite each other, or 180 degrees apart. The brushes are spring loaded against the commutator and will eventually wear out—usually the motorcycle wears out first.* Courtesy Twigg Cycles

motor is operating, current from the battery energizes the field coils, causing them to produce a strong magnetic field. At the same time, battery current is also applied to the commutator brushes that carry current from the battery to the armature. The armature rotates because the opposing magnetic lines of force between the field coils or permanent magnets and the armature repel each other, and since the armature has multiple wire loops, it continues to rotate. Starter motors may use as many as four commutator brushes. Older motorcycles that don't use permanent magnets may have two to four field coils.

On older starters, the armature and field coils are in series. This design causes a very high torque output from the starter. With the field windings and armature in series, any increase in current will produce an increase in field strength. As starter load increases, torque also increases. Under a no-load condition, such as during starter bench-testing, or when a starter's pinion gear doesn't engage the engine's drive gear or flywheel, starter speed will continue to increase until centrifugal force destroys the starter. It then makes a big loud noise, like a big bang, followed by a shower of sparks.

Clockwise, from above: *Instead of field coils, this starter uses four permanent magnets that surround the armature. This design allows all the battery's current to go to the armature. Permanent magnets take up less room than field coils and allow the starter's overall dimensions to be more compact.* Courtesy Twigg Cycles

Because of the expense of purchasing a new starter for a used motorcycle, starter rebuild kits are sometimes more practical. New starter brushes can add new life to a tired starter, and they cost a fraction of a new replacement. Courtesy Ricks Motorsport Electrics, Inc.

A starter solenoid (left) is just an overgrown relay, and its job is to connect the battery directly to the starter. A typical relay is shown at right. The two large copper terminals on top of the solenoid go to the battery's positive cable and the starter motor. One of the smaller wires is ground and the other will eventually end up at the start button. When the start button is pressed, the solenoid's low-amperage coil electromagnetically moves a plunger that connects the two large terminals and starts the engine. Courtesy Twigg Cycles

STARTER SOLENOIDS

Starter solenoids perform two functions: connecting the battery directly to the starter and (on some starters) engaging the pinion gear with the engine's flywheel. Solenoids can be mounted either directly on the starter case (older BMWs) or remotely. Starter solenoids are really nothing more than overgrown relays that use a small amount of current to energize a coil of wire, producing a magnetic field.

The strength of the magnetic field pulls the solenoid's plunger into contact with two terminals—one from battery positive and the other to the starter (see page 78). Positive engagement starters use a shift fork or lever that's connected to the solenoid mounted directly onto the starter. When the starter receives battery voltage, the solenoid moves the lever, causing the starter to engage the engine's flywheel.

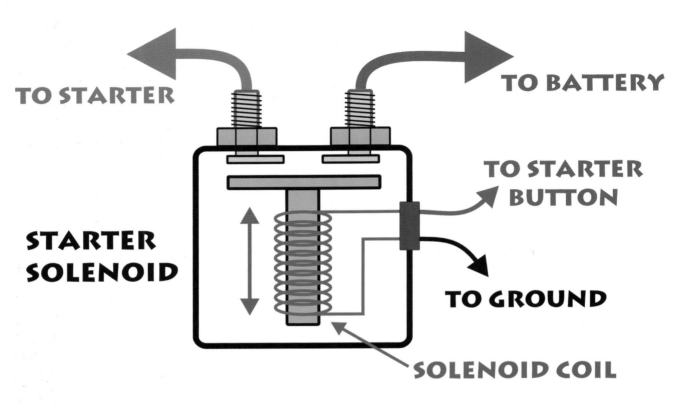

TO STARTER

TO BATTERY

TO STARTER BUTTON

STARTER SOLENOID

TO GROUND

SOLENOID COIL

A starter solenoid is just an overgrown relay. When the start button is pressed, the low-amperage solenoid coil is energized and pushes a plunger up that contacts both high-amperage terminals of the solenoid. This provides a direct connection from battery positive to the starter motor. In general only two things usually go wrong with a solenoid. The high-amperage contacts become corroded or dirty and not enough amps flow to the starter, or the solenoid coil opens or shorts out and the solenoid won't operate.

STARTER TESTING

Before testing a starter motor, the vehicle's battery must be fully charged and load tested. There's simply no point in trying to figure out which part of the starter circuit is bad if the battery doesn't have enough energy to crank the engine. (See Chapter 4, Storage Batteries, for testing and/or charging procedures.) The only real reason to test a starter is because it's cranking the engine too slowly to start it or it won't crank at all. On some motorcycles, the starter motor is difficult to remove (to say the least). By contrast, performing basic starter testing takes only a few minutes and is more productive than spending six hours to change out a starter only to find out the problem was really a bad battery cable. In fact, rather than testing the starter, it's even easier to test everything else. If the wires, cables, connections, and solenoid are good, the starter is the only thing left to replace.

The test that provides the most information with the least amount of work is a starter current draw test. To perform this test, connect an inductive ammeter to the positive battery cable. Turn the headlights on, and read the ammeter—if it reads negative, the probe is connected correctly; if it reads positive, turn the amp probe 180 degrees and turn off the headlights. Then get ready to do the next step—disabling the ignition system.

DISABLE THE IGNITION SYSTEM

The next step is to prevent the ignition or fuel injection system from allowing the engine to start when the starter motor is cranked. On some bikes where the ignition coil is accessible it can simply be unplugged to prevent an ignition spark. If the spark plugs are accessible, remove the spark plug wire(s) and use a jumper wire to ground the plug wire. This will prevent the engine from starting, because the spark from the coil will bypass the spark plugs and go directly to ground. On dual plug style coils, connect the spark plug wires together to prevent a spark from starting the engine. Don't just remove the spark plug wires and leave them dangling in the air—the high-energy spark from the coil has to go somewhere and since it can't get to

Both high-voltage coil wires from this dual plug coil have been grounded by connecting them together using a jumper wire. This prevents the engine from starting and provides enough time to take an amp meter reading when cranking the starter motor. Courtesy Iron Mike, Vietnam Vets MC

the spark plug it may find its way to ground through the ignition box/module or the ECM on a fuel-injected bike. Some EFI motorcycles have an ignition fuse or ECM fuse that will disable the ignition system without affecting starter motor operation.

NORMAL STARTER AMPERAGE DRAW

Before you can recognize abnormal starter amp draw, you first need to know what "normal" looks like. Small motorcycle engines between 250 and 500 cc should draw between 40 and 80 amps; 600 to 800 cc around 80 to 120; and large displacement engines between 1,000 and 2,000 cc could be as high as 200 amps. Some service manuals will provide more specific numbers, but these ranges will work most of the time for testing purposes. Gear-reduction and permanent magnet type starters yield slightly different

results—be sure to check service manuals for starter draw specifications for these starters.

SLOW TURNING STARTER, HIGH AMPERAGE

Although a slow-turning starter with high amperage is not a commonly encountered problem, it does occur occasionally, so follow the next procedure carefully in order to diagnose this condition. With an ammeter connected to the positive battery cable turn the ignition on, push the start button to crank the engine over (do this even if it won't crank at all), and check the ammeter reading. If the amp reading is excessively high (see "Normal Starter Amperage Draw") and the engine is turning too slowly, or not at all, there could be a mechanical problem with the starter motor or engine.

An inductive ammeter is clamped around the battery cable going to the starter motor on this Moto Guzzi. With the ignition disabled and the starter cranking, amperage can be measured. The most common problem is low amperage, and it is usually due to poor connections at the starter or battery. Courtesy Bob's BMW

To eliminate the engine as the cause of a slow-turning starter, place the transmission in fourth or fifth gear and use the rear wheel to turn the engine. Even with spark plugs installed, the engine should rotate with relatively little force. If the engine won't turn by rotating the rear wheel with the bike on its center stand or after pushing it with the transmission in gear (if your bike doesn't have a center stand) a bad starter is the least of your problems. The engine could have a mechanical problem like high-viscosity oil in cold weather (colder than 20 degrees Fahrenheit) or carbon buildup in the cylinders (full of fuel from a leaking petcock), or no oil in the engine (causing the crankshaft to overheat and weld itself to the connecting rods), which could causing other mechanical problems.

On the other hand, if the engine turns okay, get a new starter because the presence of high amperage flowing into the starter circuit indicates a "shorted" starter armature or field coil and *not* an engine problem. The high amperage also indicates that the battery cable connections and battery are good.

SLOW TURNING STARTER, LOW AMPERAGE

On the other hand, if an ammeter reading is low (see "Normal Starter Amperage Draw"), and the starter is turning slowly or not at all, the starter circuit has high resistance caused by either a poor battery cable connection or a bad solenoid. High resistance is, by far, the most common reason for low starter circuit amperage. It can't possibly be a battery problem since the battery has already been tested and charged beforehand. Right? Consequently, a voltage drop test is the ideal test to locate the source of unwanted high resistance in the starter circuit.

The positive side of the starter circuit should be tested first, as it is the most likely place to find a problem. Connect the red lead of a voltmeter to the positive battery terminal (*not* the battery cable). Connect the black meter lead to the starter terminal where the battery cable is attached. Crank the engine over, while watching the voltmeter. If the voltage drop is less than 0.5 volts (less than 0.2 for smaller engine sizes), the positive side of the starter circuit doesn't have high resistance. Perform the same test on the ground side of the starter circuit. Connect the red voltmeter lead to the starter case, the black lead to the negative terminal on the battery, and then crank the engine. The voltage drop should not exceed 0.4 volts (0.2 volts on smaller engines). If either the positive or negative side of the starter circuit exceeds the maximum voltage drop (see chart in Chapter 2, Voltage Drop Testing), the point of high resistance can be located by performing a voltage drop test across individual connections. This can be accomplished by disconnecting the black voltmeter lead and moving it back along the circuit toward the red meter lead. There should be no more than 0.2 volts lost across any connection. Fortunately, cleaning a bad connection is oftentimes all that is required to get the starter to spin faster. Performing a voltage drop test on the starter and solenoid is generally easier than removing the starter and replacing it only to find that a bad or loose connection was the cause of the slow turning starter—and it's a lot less expensive.

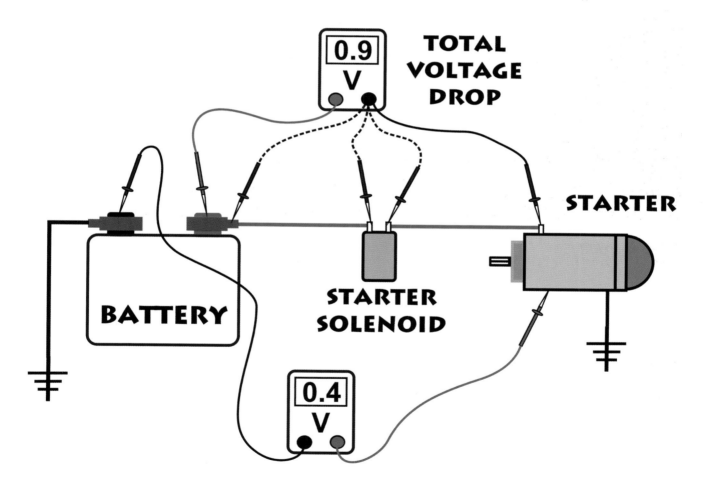

Fig 5-11—*Ground side resistance in this starter circuit is okay, because the voltage drop is only 0.4 volts. The positive side also has a voltage drop of 0.9 volts caused by high resistance. By moving the black meter lead along the positive side of the circuit, the point of high resistance can be located.*

CHAPTER 6
IGNITION SYSTEMS

Ignition-related problems, whether real or only perceived, are the cause of more needless parts' replacement than any other system on a motorcycle. In the past, engine stalling, missing, and "no starts" were most often blamed on carburetors, which could be taken apart and visually inspected—mechanics and owners felt comfortable doing this, so that's what they did. Ignition malfunctions were often fixed by simple replacement of points, condenser, ignition coils, wires, and spark plugs. In the early 1970s, that method of "repair by replacing" changed with the introduction of electronic ignition systems, since they were far too costly to replace in hopes of fixing the problem.

Today, ignitions systems on motorcycles are all solid state and can come in the form of a dedicated ignition system only, or as part of a motorcycle's electronic engine management (fuel injection) system. Consequently, it's much more cost-effective to test ignition components before throwing them in the trash and replacing them with new parts. Modern ignition systems are not as difficult to diagnose as you might think, as there are a great number of similarities between conventional, points-type ignition systems and electronic ignition systems. A basic understanding of how primary and secondary ignition circuits operate goes a long way toward figuring out if you have a bad pickup coil, hall-effect switch, or electronic ignition module. Let's start by taking a look back at conventional ignition systems, which haven't changed much in the past hundred years.

HOW TO GET FROM 12 VOLTS TO 100,000 VOLTS

An ignition system has two jobs: spark production and spark distribution. Spark distribution consists of several designs of ignition coils that provide a spark to single or pairs of spark plugs. Spark production on both points-type and electronic ignition systems is basically the same; the only difference is the manner in which the ignition coil(s) are controlled. Ignition coils on both types of systems operate in the same manner by simply "stepping-up" electrical voltage within the systems from 14.5 volts (charging voltage) to 20,000 volts in points-type ignition systems and to as much as 60,000 volts in electronic systems. The reason high voltages are required is the high resistance of the air gap on the spark plug that serves as the load device in the secondary ignition circuit. Without high voltage, the spark cannot overcome the air gap's resistance, so no spark can occur.

Both conventional and electronic ignition systems have two circuits—primary and secondary. The primary circuit is the first step in the process that causes voltage to

Old and new ignition coils from BMW motorcycles. The conventional coil (left) can only produce about 20,000 volts at the spark plug. By contrast this late-model coil-over-plug weighs about one-quarter as much as the conventional coil and can output more than 60,000 volts. Courtesy Bob's BMW

step up, or increase, in the ignition system. Charging system voltage is increased from 14.5 to between 300 and 500 volts. The primary ignition circuit is made up of one-half of the ignition coil, points, and a condenser (in older motorcycles), or an electronic ignition module or computer (in newer bikes). The secondary circuit raises voltage a step farther. The secondary circuit consists of the other half of the ignition coil, plug wires, and spark plug(s). Thus, every ignition coil contains both primary and secondary circuits and operates in a similar manner on both points-type and electronic ignition systems.

IGNITION COILS

There are two basic designs of ignition coils: conventional and dual-plug. Both coil types produce a spark but have different internal circuit designs. Conventional coils can be used on single-cylinder engines or sometimes on multicylinders with one coil per cylinder. Some late-model bikes use coil-over-plug systems fitted with individual coils for each cylinder and no spark plug wires. Conventional coils have three terminals—a power source for the primary circuit, a ground for the primary circuit, and a high-voltage terminal connected to the spark plug(s) via high-voltage plug wire. Power for an ignition coil's primary circuit is supplied from the ignition switch. A set of mechanical points or a transistor controls the coil's primary circuit by switching the ground side of the primary

circuit on or off. When the primary circuit is switched off, a spark is produced.

Ignition coils also have two internal windings—primary and secondary. The primary winding is made up of about 200 turns of heavy gauge wire. Secondary windings are constructed of lighter wire and more than 20,000 turns of wire wound around an iron core that concentrates the coil's magnetic field. Primary windings surround the secondary windings and iron core. When current from the battery flows through the primary windings, a magnetic field is produced inside the coil. The primary circuit is controlled either by a mechanical switch (points) or a transistor in electronic systems. When the primary winding's power is switched off, the magnetic field inside the coil collapses. This collapsing field produces as much as 400 volts and induces current into the secondary windings. Because the secondary windings have more turns of wire than the primary circuit, voltage is stepped up—as much as 60,000 volts on a late-model ignition system.

A conventional coil's primary circuit is connected internally to the secondary circuit at the negative coil terminal. Power for the secondary circuit comes from the primary circuit's collapsing magnetic field, which produces about 300 to 500 volts. Voltage is stepped up in the secondary circuit, causing current to pass through the high-voltage tower in the center of the coil, then onto the spark plug, and finally returning to battery ground. (See Figure 6-1.)

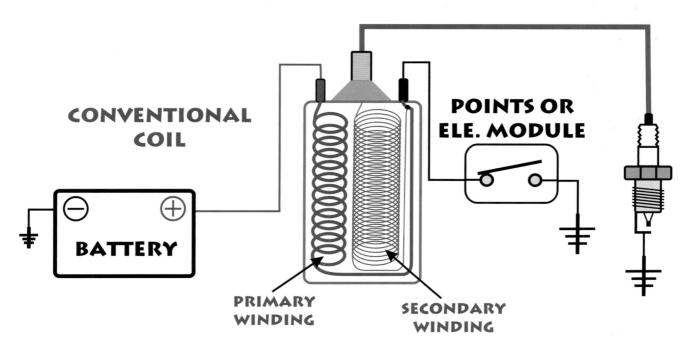

CONVENTIONAL COIL

POINTS OR ELE. MODULE

BATTERY

PRIMARY WINDING

SECONDARY WINDING

Fig 6-1—In this conventional ignition coil, the primary windings actually surround the secondary windings (the drawing separates the two in order to illustrate how they're internally connected). An ignition module or points switch the coil's ground circuit on and off.

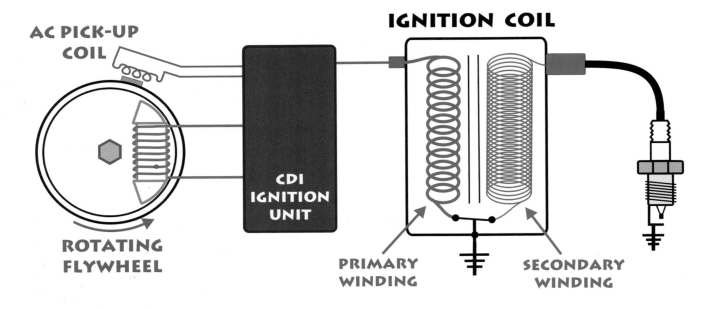

Fig 6-2—There is a variation of the single ignition coil that's used on off-road or smaller motorcycles. The coil is similar to a conventional single-plug coil except the primary circuit is not switched to ground to fire the spark plug. Instead the capacitor discharge ignition (CDI) box charges a large capacitor that discharges through the primary ignition circuit. The secondary windings inside the ignition coil then step up this voltage to fire the spark plug. The CDI unit gets power from a charge coil on the flywheel, and the AC pickup coil provides the trigger signal for the CDI ignition.

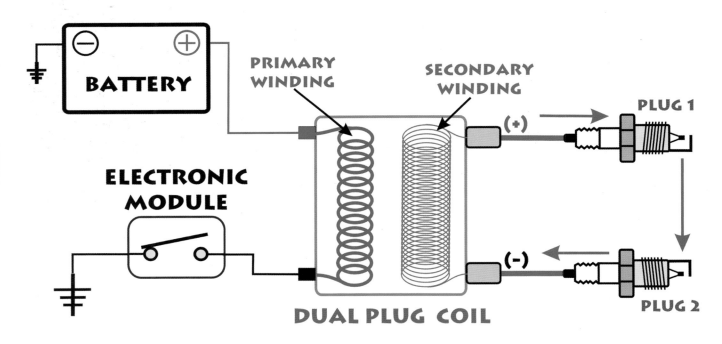

Fig 6-3—There is no internal connection between the primary and secondary windings on a dual spark plug coil. The high-voltage path starts at the positive side of the secondary windings, onto plug 1, through the cylinder head and plug 2, and back to ground (of the secondary windings). Battery ground and the ground for the secondary windings are not the same ground.

Right: *The difference between the conventional coil (right) and the dual plug coil is that the dual ignition coil's secondary windings are not connected to the primary circuit. This design causes the spark produced by a dual plug coil to go to the first spark plug, across the cylinder head to the other spark plug, and then back to the other side of the secondary side of the dual plug coil. Courtesy Bob's BMW*

Below: *A dual-plug ignition coil on this 1969 Harley-Davidson FL Shovelhead engine is not wired internally in the same manner as a conventional coil. In the mid 1980s these types of ignition systems were introduced for use on automobiles, and they were confusing to many technicians who were used to working with only a single ignition coil and distributor. Courtesy Iron Mike, Vietnam Vets MC*

Two high-voltage terminals are used on the dual plug coil (see figure 6-3), instead of only one used on a conventional coil. Each dual plug coil is connected to a pair of spark plugs. Two-cylinder engines, such as on Harley-Davidson's, use one coil; most four-cylinder engines use two coils. The primary circuit is powered and controlled in the same manner as in a conventional coil, but the major difference between the two is that secondary windings are not connected in any manner to the primary circuit. The dual plug coil's secondary circuit has the same elements as any DC circuit—power, ground, and a load device. One end of the secondary windings is power, the other is ground, and between are the load devices (in this instance, the air gaps of the two spark plugs). When the primary circuit's magnetic field collapses, voltage is induced into the secondary windings. Electrons flow from the positive end of the secondary windings to the first spark plug and across the air gap. The current then passes along the cylinder head—the equivalent of a

This dual-style coil from a 1955 BMW/2 uses screw-type terminals for connection to the spark plug wires. Dual coils found on Harley-Davidson motorcycles are similar and have been used for more than a few years. Courtesy Bob's BMW

Motorcycles that use points and condenser, and some early electronic ignitions, use a mechanical system to provide ignition timing advance. These units consist of weights and springs that rotate along with the crank or camshaft. As rotational speed increases, the weights are thrown to the outside by centrifugal force and a cam advances the ignition timing by moving the breaker points or speed pick up. Solid state electronics have replaced these troublesome mechanisms and calculate ignition advance using engine rpm and, on some models, throttle position. Courtesy Bob's BMW

really big wire—and into the second spark plug's ground electrode, where it jumps the air gap, producing a spark. After jumping the air gap of the second plug, the current returns to the other side of the secondary windings—the ground side of the coil (see page 84, figure 6-3).

To make sense of this type of circuit, think of a dual plug coil's secondary windings as having nothing to do with the motorcycle's battery ground. Each coil fires the spark plugs in two cylinders simultaneously. A dual plug coil fires on spark plug in the normal direction, and the other plug in reverse. One cylinder is on its compression stroke and the spark ignites the air/fuel mixture. The other "companion" cylinder is at the end of its exhaust stroke and its spark has no effect, because there is nothing to burn inside the combustion chamber. Most of the coil's energy goes to the spark plug that is igniting the air and fuel mixture. Because that cylinder is on its compression stroke, there is high resistance across the plug's air gap. The companion cylinder is on its exhaust stroke and because the exhaust valve is open, there is no compression in that cylinder. Without the high-pressure air surrounding the air gap, it takes relatively little voltage to overcome the plug's resistance.

GENERIC COIL TESTING

Both types of coils can be checked for "opens" or shorts using an ohmmeter. To check resistance on a conventional coil, connect one ohmmeter lead to the negative side of the coil and the other to the positive. Primary resistance should read between 1.5 and 3.5 ohms. Resistance in the secondary circuit can be measured by connecting one ohmmeter lead to the negative coil terminal and the other to the high-voltage tower. Resistance should be between 7,000 and 25,000 ohms. Remember, the primary and secondary windings are not connected inside a dual plug coil. Primary resistance should measure between 0.5 and 3.0 ohms, while secondary resistance should be between 5,000 and 10,000 ohms. A service manual will provide specific resistance values, but the numbers provided here are close enough to tell if there is a problem with the coil's windings. Measuring ignition coil resistance is not a conclusive test for determining whether a coil is bad. An ignition coil can

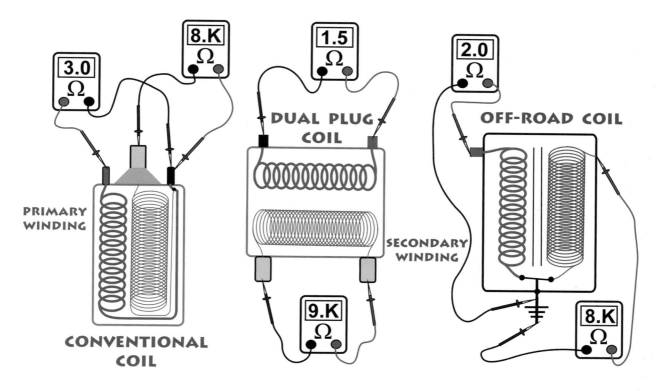

Fig 6-4—An ohmmeter will only tell you if the windings are open, or shorted. The coil may check out okay, but still may not produce a spark. A good method to find an open or shorted winding is to beat on the coil with a screwdriver handle, or heat it with a hair dryer, while watching the resistance reading. If the reading changes, the winding is bad and the coil should be replaced.

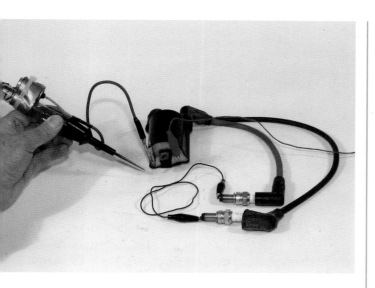

This dual plug ignition coil is being bench-tested using a homemade coil tester. The red wire is 12 volts and the wire coming out of the coil tester goes to ground. When the pointed end of the coil tester is tapped on the negative coil terminal, a spark is produced at both plugs (spark plug grounds are connected together using a jumper wire). The tester will work on almost any type of ignition coil.

check out okay with an ohmmeter but still not produce a spark when electrically loaded.

Here are a couple of additional things you can do to try to find out if you are dealing with a bad coil: With the ohmmeter connected to the coil's primary or secondary windings, try tapping on the coil with a screwdriver handle, or try heating it with a hair dryer. If the ohmmeter's readings change, the internal coil windings are broken.

You can make an inexpensive universal ignition coil tester with an old condenser and some jumper wires. Make sure the condenser is good by testing it on a known good coil. To use the tester, disconnect the negative side of the coil. Connect the condenser wire to the negative coil terminal and ground the condenser's mount tab using a jumper wire. Connect a second jumper wire to ground and turn the ignition on. Now tap the grounded jumper wire to the negative side of the coil. It should produce a spark between the high-voltage terminal and ground on a conventional coil, or between high-voltage terminals on a dual-plug coil. If you don't get a spark, check for battery voltage at the coil and good connections on all jumper wires. Be careful doing this on a dual-plug or stick type of coil—the spark

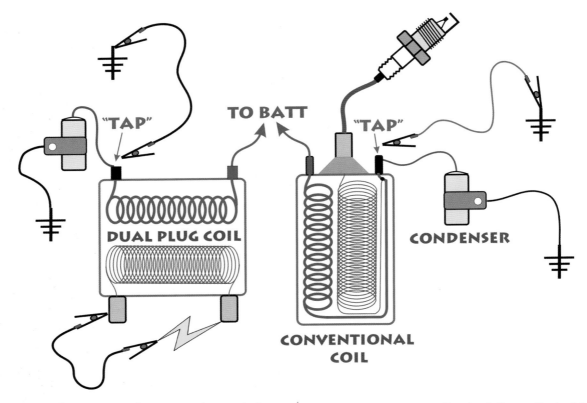

"TAP" TO BATT "TAP"

DUAL PLUG COIL

CONVENTIONAL COIL

CONDENSER

produced can really "zap" you if you get in the way (refer to above figure). More information regarding coil testers can be found in Chapter 3, Electronic Testing Tools.

Conventional ignition coils with threaded or spade terminals can be mistakenly connected backward, causing reverse polarity and a weak spark. A coil with reverse polarity will start and keep an engine running, but could misfire under load because the coil produces about 15 percent less voltage when connected backward. Most coil terminals are marked, but if you're working on one that isn't, you can check coil polarity using a lead pencil. Remove one spark plug wire and hold it close to the spark plug. Place a lead pencil point in the path of the spark and crank the engine. The spark will flare as it contacts the pencil point. A flare in the direction of the spark plug indicates correct coil polarity, but if the spark flares toward the spark plug wire, the coil has reverse polarity and the coil's primary circuit is connected backward.

POINTS AND CONDENSER

The contact points in a conventional ignition system cause an ignition coil to switch on and off. When the points are closed, ground is supplied to the coil's primary circuit. When the points are open, the primary circuit loses its ground and the magnetic field inside the coil collapses, causing the secondary windings to produce a spark. The points open and close according to engine rpm and are

Above: *A homemade coil tester will work on both conventional and dual-plug types of coils. Be careful using it on a dual-plug coil as the spark can really zap you. If you are testing an ignition coil on a motorcycle that doesn't have a 12-volt battery, the coil test won't work.*

Contact points have been in use for nearly 80 years in motorcycles. These simple mechanical switches are subject to wear and have to be adjusted every 3,000 miles or so. Motorcycles fitted with points ignition systems were hard to start when cold, and sometimes impossible when it rained. Consequently, they can't provide the reliability needed to meet the requirements of modern ignition systems. Courtesy Bob's BMW

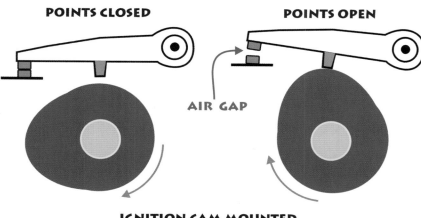

POINTS CLOSED **POINTS OPEN**

AIR GAP

IGNITION CAM MOUNTED
TO END OF CAMSHAFT

Right: *Fig 6-6—Ignition dwell or ignition coil charge time is not measured on motorcycles. Points are adjusted by changing the air gap between the contacts. This distance varies between manufacturers and model years of motorcycles. See a service manual for the correct adjustment.*

Below: *The test light—the universal tool for testing primary ignition coil switching. The flashing test light provides visual confirmation that the points or ignition module is turning the coil on and off. Simply connect one end of the test light to one end of the coil primary terminals and touch the pointed end to the other. Crank the engine and watch for the test light to flash, indicating primary switching.*
Courtesy Iron Mike, Vietnam Vets MC

timed via a cam on the end of the crankshaft. The closed or on time is called ignition dwell. The longer the dwell time, the more the coil gets charged or saturated, creating a larger magnetic field; thus, longer dwell time equals higher resulting secondary voltage. Dwell time is adjustable by changing the air gap between the contact points. Though dwell meters are not generally used on motorcycles, changing the resulting air gap when the points are open changes dwell. The wider the gap, the longer

the dwell time. Conversely, a smaller gap results in decreased dwell time. Consult a service manual for the correct point gap for specific motorcycles.

All points type ignition systems use a condenser as part of the primary circuit. The condenser (or capacitor) is connected across the points and reduces arcing between the contact points as they open and close. Without the condenser, an electric arc would occur at the points instead of at the spark plugs, causing the points to quickly burn out.

If you think you might be facing a "no spark" problem, pull the high-voltage wire off of a spark plug and insert a pocket screwdriver into the plug boot. Hold the metal shank of the screwdriver near ground. Crank the engine and watch for a spark to jump between the screwdriver and ground. If you don't get a spark, checking primary ignition switching is the next step. A quick way to check the operation of the points or ignition module is to use a test light connected across the primary circuit of the ignition coil. Connect the alligator clip of the test light to the negative side of the coil and touch the test light's probe to the positive coil terminal. With the test light "looped" across the coil, crank the engine over. The test light should flash if primary switching is taking place. The test light is simply taking the place of the ignition coil and will provide you with visual confirmation if the coil is being turned on and off. If the test light doesn't flash, check the following:

(1) power to the coil; (2) the wire between coil negative and the ignition points or module; and (3) the points—to see if they are opening/closing as the engine turns.

ELECTRONIC IGNITION AND COMPUTER CONTROLS

The primary reason automotive manufacturers switched over from points type ignition systems to electronic ignition systems is because they were forced to as a result of stricter government-mandated emissions standards. Lean air/fuel mixtures and the mandatory use of exhaust gas recirculation (EGR) required an increase in spark plug firing voltages above the levels found in older points type ignitions. The motorcycle industry, while not subject to early environmental/clean air standards, did feel competitive to provide more reliable designs to expand sales of motorcycles, thus the migration toward the use of electronic ignition systems.

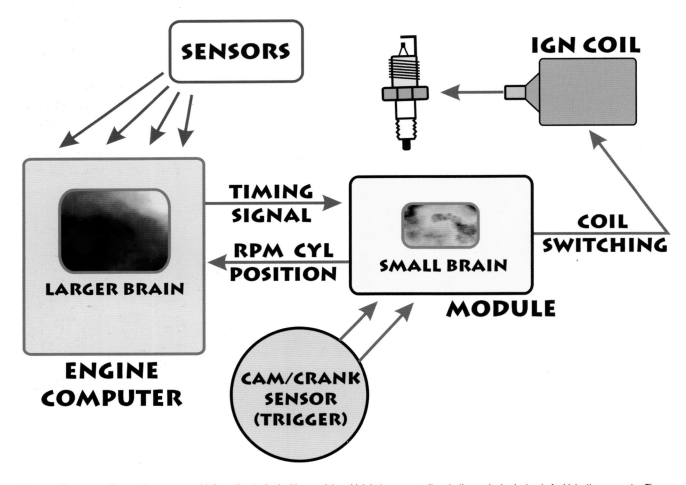

Fig 6-7—The cam and/or crank sensors send information to the ignition module, which in turn passes it on to the engine's electronic fuel injection computer. The computer calculates the ideal spark timing signal and sends it back to the module, which then fires the coil. On some EFI motorcycles the ignition module and fuel injection computer are one in the same.

I have often heard it said that before the 1980s if you wanted to own a motorcycle, you had better want (and be able) to repair it yourself. The introduction of solid state electronics, including ignition, charging, and eventually fuel injection, would provide machines that mechanically challenged riders could own and not have to pick up a wrench (or voltmeter) to keep on the road.

Conventional contact point ignition systems on motorcycles usually had to be adjusted every 3,000 miles or sooner. If a condenser went bad, the points would promptly burn out, and you and your motorcycle would be left by the side of the road. Many owners carried an extra set of points in a jacket pocket along with spare spark plugs and master-link for the drive chain. By contrast, electronic ignition systems contain no moving parts and consequently are usually able to last the life of the motorcycle. The only maintenance items typically are spark plugs and ignition wires. In fact, maintenance intervals on late-model coil-over-plug systems (with no spark plug wires) are oftentimes as high as 16,000 miles, and the maintenance usually amounts to nothing more than spark plug changes. As more manufacturers continue to expand their use of electronic fuel injection, the standalone electronic ignition system is going by the wayside as technology improves and it is replaced with on-board computer-controlled EFI ignition systems.

Today, street and some off-road motorcycles are equipped with ignition modules or engine management systems that are quite sophisticated. Information about engine rpm, cylinder identification, crankshaft position, and throttle position are sent to the electronic control module (ECM), where the ideal ignition timing is calculated. Some EFI system use additional sensor information to calculate timing, including engine and intake air temperature, engine load, knock or ping, barometric pressure, and transmission gear selection. The on-board computer crunches the numbers from the various digital inputs and sends a modified timing signal to the module, which then fires the ignition coil(s). The basic input to any electronic ignition system is the trigger signal from the engine's rotating crankshaft, and that's where we'll start our discussion of electronic ignition.

TRIGGERS

For more than 80 years, a set of points served as the trigger in conventional ignition systems. The points triggered or turned the coil on and off. Today, both electronic and computer-controlled ignitions use a transistor to switch current on or off to the ignition coil. A transistor requires a signal, or trigger, in order to switch an ignition coil on or off.

There are only three types of triggers currently in use in motorcycles: an AC pickup coil, a hall-effect switch, and an optical sensor. Whatever trigger is used is connected to the engine's crank or camshaft where it produces a signal indicating engine speed and position, which is sent to the ignition module. In addition, some triggers are capable of providing crankshaft or camshaft position and cylinder identification. Following is an explanation of how each of the various triggers works and how to test their operation.

AC PICKUP COIL

By far the most common trigger used on motorcycles is the AC pickup coil. Whenever a wiring diagram shows an engine speed sensor with only two wires coming out of it, it's an AC pickup coil. AC pickup coils operate in the same manner as an alternator to produce AC voltage. A rotating magnet passes across the pickup coil and produces an AC voltage pulse. As engine speed increases, the number of pulses per second increase. The ignition module or computer counts the number or frequency of the pulses and based on this information, calculates engine rpm, and in some cases, crank or camshaft position. In addition to the increase in pulses per second as engine rpm increases, AC voltage output from the pickup coil also increases. The increase in AC voltage is ignored by the computer or module, but is a good way for you to verify whether an AC pickup coil is working or not.

AC pickup coils can be tested using a voltmeter, ohmmeter, or logic probe. To test one using a voltmeter, disconnect

This AC pickup coil is located next to the engine's flywheel. Each time a magnet on the flywheel passes the pickup coil, AC voltage is generated and sent to the ignition module, where engine rpm is calculated. AC pickup coils are common on many motorcycles; they are usually reliable and require no maintenance. Courtesy Twigg Cycle

the AC pickup coil and connect the meter leads to the pickup wiring harness. Set the voltmeter to read AC voltage and crank the engine. As the engine turns, AC voltage should be produced—generally between 0.5 and 3 volts AC. A logic probe can also be used to test a pickup coil just as easily and effectively. Connect the logic probe to the vehicle's battery. Leave the AC pickup coil connected and back probe one of the two wires coming from the pickup coil with the logic probe. Crank the engine and watch for a pulse on the LED display of the logic probe. If no AC voltage is present, or if the logic probe doesn't show a pulse, you can always check a pickup coil's resistance using an ohmmeter. Resistance will vary depending on the pickup coil manufacturer, but a resistance reading somewhere in the 150 to 1,200 ohm range is generally okay. Also, always check for broken wires leading to the pickup coil, metal filings between the coil and magnet, a loose coil, or too large an air gap between the coil and magnet. The service manual for your bike will provide you with the air gap measurement, if applicable, as well as pickup coil resistance.

HALL-EFFECT SWITCH

The Hall-effect switch consists of a sensor, magnet, rotating shutter blade, and three-wire connector (the latter will distinguish it from an AC pickup coil or other speed sensor on a wiring diagram). The three-wire connector has a power, ground, and signal wire that goes to the computer or ignition module.

Hall-effect switches are powered by a reference voltage that is sent by the computer or module. Each Hall-effect switch is equipped with a magnet situated opposite the switch; between them is a series of rotating shutters or blades—one for each cylinder. As the blades rotate between the sensor and magnet, the magnet's magnetic field is interrupted and voltage at the sensor drops. The output signal from the Hall-effect switch is a square wave or series of on-and-off pulses. These pulses are sent to the vehicle's computer or ignition module, which then uses them to calculate engine rpm and crankshaft position.

To test a Hall-effect switch, turn the ignition on and back probe each of its three wires with a voltmeter. A process of elimination will help you identify what each wire is used for. The voltmeter display should indicate one wire is reference voltage—it should have between 2.5 and 12 volts, depending on year, make, and model of the motorcycle. Another wire is the ground wire, and it has no voltage. The third wire is a signal output wire from the Hall-effect switch and it will show either reference voltage or something less than reference voltage, depending upon whether or not a shutter blade has stopped rotating between the

Dual Hall-effect switches from a BMW use a rotating metal disk with shutter blades that pass between the Hall sensor and permanent magnets. As the magnetic field is broken by the shutter blades, a square wave is generated and sent to the motorcycle's ignition computer to trigger the ignition coil. Hall-effect switches are very reliable and don't require any maintenance. Courtesy Bob's BMW

This Newtronic optical ignition kit is a good way for older motorcycles to use modern electronics. Pictured are two optical sensors and a sensor plate. As the plate rotates, it breaks a beam of light and triggers the ignition module. These kits are available for a range of older bikes from Motorcycle-Ignition.com located in Sheffield, Australia. Owner Shayn Harkness sent in this photo of his 1973 Suzuki T500K, a 500-cc two-stroke twin cylinder—a wild ride to be sure. Courtesy Motorcycle-Ignition.com

Hall-effect switch and magnet. Turn the engine over by hand and watch the signal wire. If the Hall switch is working, voltage will switch from reference voltage to a lower voltage (sometimes 0 volts) and back. If a signal is not present, try the other wire that had voltage on it, since you might have been reading the reference wire by mistake.

In addition to testing a Hall-effect switch with a voltmeter, a logic probe can also be used. Connect the logic probe to the vehicle's battery. Leave the Hall-effefct switch connected and back probe the signal wire. Crank the engine using the starter and watch the LED on the logic probe. It should indicate a pulse. If it doesn't, check to make sure there are both power (reference voltage) and a ground source to the Hall-effect switch, as well as for broken wires or loose connections.

OPTICAL SENSORS

An optical sensor is another form of trigger for the ignition module. An optical sensor typically consists of an LED, a phototransistor, and a rotating metal or plastic disk. (Some optical conversion kits designed to replace a set of points have a plastic shutter instead of a metal disk.) These sensors provide trigger signals for ignition switching and generally can be distinguished from other speed sensors on a wiring diagram by the presence of four wires. The signal output from the optical sensor's computer takes the form of a square wave made up of ON-and-OFF pulses (similar to a Hall-effect switch).

When in use, a beam of light from the LED is projected through the holes in the disk onto the phototransistor.

As the disk rotates, the spaces between the holes interrupt the light beam. Each time the light beam is interrupted, a pulse is generated by the sensor's processor (computer). Some optical sensors are really two sensors in one: One measures crankshaft angle (position); the other measures camshaft position and identifies which cylinder is the number one cylinder in the engine's firing order.

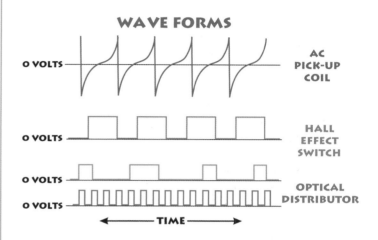

Fig 6-8—An AC pickup coil's wave form shows AC voltage transitioning between negative and positive as the sensor is rotated. Both the Hall-effect switch and optical sensor produce a square wave. The optical sensor has two signals, one for engine rpm (lower wave form) and the other for cylinder identification.

Pictured is the Spyke Acculight Ignition System. It uses an optical trigger with phototransistor and LEDs (left) and a slotted disc that rotates with the crankshaft. This unit has four preset ignition advance curves as well as programmable ignition advance. It also features a triple-spark ignition that fires the spark up to three times on the engine's compression stroke and can be set to dual- or single-fire modes. Courtesy MCAdvantages

While various ignition modules might look different, they all perform the same function—switching the coil on and off. All ignition modules have to have power, ground, and receive a trigger signal (engine rpm) to function. Some newer modules also receive throttle position and engine temperature inputs as well. Courtesy Twigg Cycles

To test an optical sensor, use a voltmeter to measure voltage on all the wires going to the sensor. With the ignition key on, one wire should read 12 volts, the ground wire should read 0 volts. However, it is difficult to determine if the two signal wires are both working properly using only a voltmeter. A logic probe is the better tool for detecting the presence of pulses at each signal wire. With the logic probe connected to the battery, back probe each signal wire and crank the engine. There should be a pulse on each wire. If there is no pulse, check for oil or dirt blocking the holes on the metal plate and make sure the sensor has both power and ground. See a service manual for specific procedures on checking optical triggers.

IGNITION MODULES

In its most simplistic form, an electronic ignition module is simply a modern replacement for a set of points. Points receive engine rotational speed information by direct mechanical means—they open and close, turning the ignition coil on and off. An ignition module performs the exact same function, but it uses a trigger signal. Once a trigger signal (or wave form) is produced by the engine's speed sensor, the ignition module processes it and then fires the coil. Later model vehicles use on-board computers in conjunction with ignition modules to control coil switching. Either way, the basic operation of an ignition module is equivalent to a set of points.

GENERIC IGNITION MODULE TESTING

When electronic ignitions were first introduced, many technicians had trouble diagnosing no-spark problems. Without any moving parts to check, it was visually impossible to determine if primary coil switching was occurring. Fortunately, today, even though you can't see a transistor operating, you are able to see the results of primary switching—just like on a set of points. The first step in the process of determining if an ignition module is operational is a testing procedure originally used on conventional ignition systems—just connect a test light across the ignition coil's primary wires and crank the engine. A flashing/flickering test light tells you three things—(1) the ignition module is switching the coil on and off, (2) the trigger is sending a signal to the module, and (3) the ignition coil has power. This test works regardless of the type of ignition box, module, or engine computer management system used.

However, if the test light doesn't flash because no primary switching is occurring, you need to check the ignition module for power, ground, and trigger input(s). Because each year, make, and model of motorcycle is different, consult a wiring diagram to determine module inputs/outputs and wire colors. Powers and grounds can be checked using a digital voltmeter. Make sure ground voltage is close to 0 volts

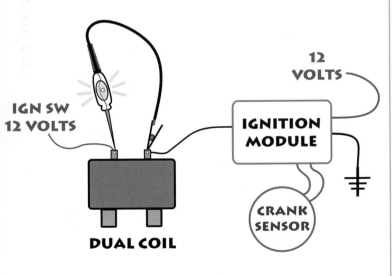

Fig 6-9—The test light provides visual confirmation that the module is sending a primary switching signal to the ignition coil. This test will work on both dual-plug and single coils. The test will not work on bikes that only use a magneto and have no battery. Not enough current may be available at the coil primary terminals (even if everything's working) to light the test light.

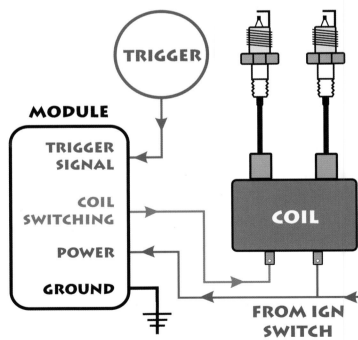

Fig 6-10—A generic ignition module requires the presence of four things in order to fire the ignition coil: power, ground, trigger input, and coil switching. On a specific motorcycle, a wiring diagram will identify what each of the wires at the ignition module is used for. These should be checked before replacing the module.

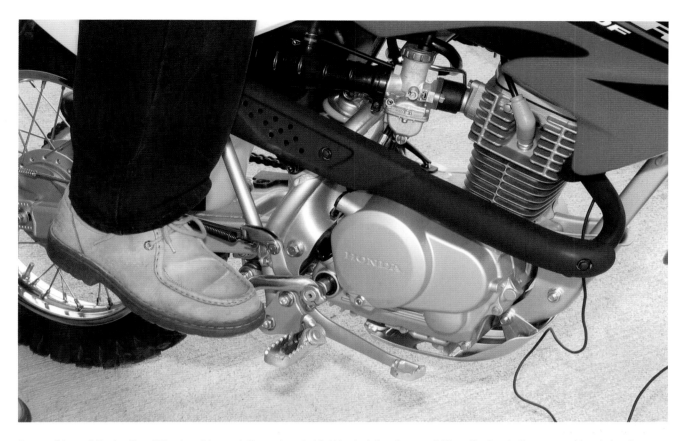

Because this small Honda off-road bike doesn't have a battery, using a test light to check for primary switching will not work. The energy produced when the engine is kicked over won't light the test light. Instead a voltmeter set to read DC volts can indicate the presence of primary switching at the ignition coil. Around 0.2 volts is produced at the coil primary when the engine is kicked over. Courtesy Twigg Cycles

and the power wires have battery voltage. Check for power and grounds with the ignition switch on. Then be sure to recheck them with the engine cranking, especially the grounds since some ground voltages that checked out okay with the ignition on may increase once the starter is turning. The trigger signal will either come directly from the trigger (Hall-effect switch or AC pickup coil), or on some bikes, from the computer. If any of the module's wires don't have correct electrical values for voltage, grounds, or trigger signals, be sure to repair them before further testing. However, if all the wires going to the ignition module have correct values, the module needs to be replaced.

IGNITION MODULE TAP TESTING

Another useful method for testing an ignition module is to provide a substitute trigger signal in order to determine if the coil can produce a spark. This method is called a tap test since a grounded (or powered) test light is used in place of a trigger to tap on the trigger inputs to the ignition module. If the module is okay, and all the power and ground

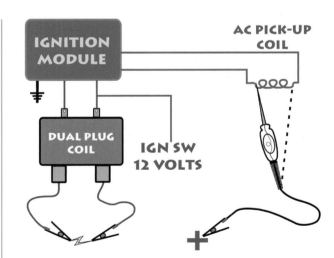

Fig 6-11—To perform a tap test on an ignition system using an AC pick-up coil, leave all connectors plugged in. Use jumper wires connected to the high-voltage terminals of the ignition coil. (This is where you'll look for a spark.) Turn the ignition key on. Using a "hot" test light (connected to battery positive), or grounded test light, tap back and forth between the module terminals where the pickup coil is plugged in. If the module is good, the coil should produce a spark.

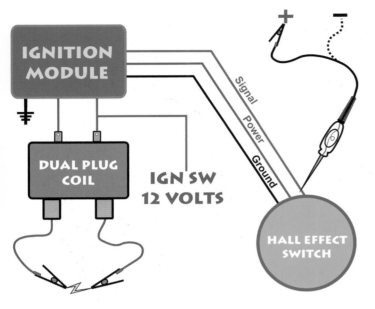

wires going to it are also good, it should fire the coil. If you don't get a spark after performing a tap test, always check for the presence of power and a good ground at the module, or for a bad ignition coil. Also, make sure the test light you use to perform the tap test has a resistance value of less than 10 ohms, since test lights with bulbs that have more resistance may not pass enough current to make a tap test work (see Chapter 3, Electronic Testing Tools). Never use a jumper wire to perform a tap test—it could fry the ignition module.

SECONDARY IGNITION CIRCUIT

So far we've dealt only with primary ignition switching. The focus now shifts to the secondary ignition circuit. When a spark is produced at the ignition coil, it goes from there to the spark plug. Spark plug wires are not used in coil-over-plug systems, since the coils are directly connected to the spark plug.

Voltage at the spark plugs must overcome the high resistance of the plug's air gap between the center and ground electrodes. When the engine's cylinder is on its

Fig 6-12—To perform a tap test for ignition systems that use a Hall-effect switch trigger leave everything plugged in. Use jumper wires connected to the high-voltage terminals of the ignition coil—this is where you'll look for a spark. Make sure that the Hall-effect switch has power and ground. Turn the ignition key on. Using a test light connected to battery positive, tap on the signal terminal from the Hall switch to the ignition module. If a spark is produced at the ignition coil, the ignition module is good. If you don't get a spark, try tapping using a test light connected to battery negative. If that doesn't work, the ignition module is probably no good.

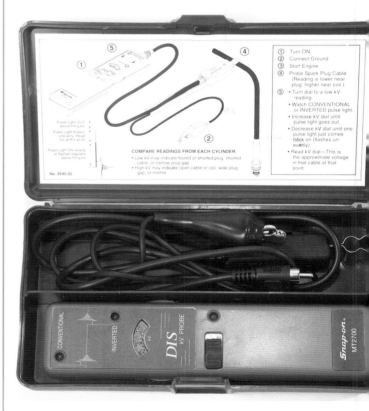

Because of the high voltage produced at the ignition coil, secondary ignition wires have to use high-resistance insulation to prevent the spark from taking the path of least resistance and going to ground before it reaches the spark plug's air gap. Secondary spark plug wires should be inspected for damage periodically, along with spark plug boots. Courtesy Twigg Cycle

This Snap-on MT2500 kV Spark Tester can be used on both conventional and dual-plug ignition systems. Flashing LEDs and a rotary dial indicate spark voltage levels.

An inductive timing light clamped around the ignition coil's high-voltage wire going to a spark plug can serve as a poor man's ignition scope. The human eye can detect an ignition misfire on this Moto Guzzi. Courtesy Bob's BMW

compression stroke, the resistance of the air gap is increased; consequently, even more voltage is required for the spark to jump the gap. Older motorcycles with points type ignition systems required as much as 15,000 to 20,000 volts to fire a spark plug with the throttle open, and about 7,000 volts at idle. On late-model bikes featuring electronic fuel injection and three-way catalytic converters, the air/fuel mixtures are leaner, causing spark plug firing voltage to be even higher. This combustion chamber environment increases the spark plug's air gap resistance well beyond what older ignition systems were capable of providing, since firing voltage may reach 50,000 or more on some late-model systems.

As a result of high ignition voltage requirements, secondary voltage will try to make its way to battery ground via a path of least resistance. The secondary plug wires

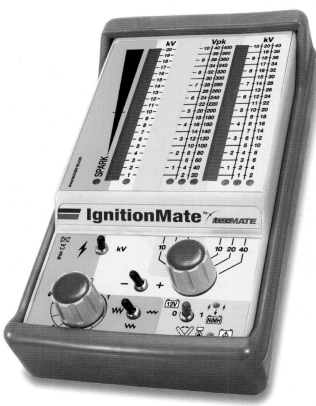

The IgnitionMate can measure high voltage in the secondary ignition system—up to 40,000 volts. Consistency of the voltage signal can be observed to determine if a cylinder is misfiring. Two columns of LEDs show a comparison between ignition signals. A stick coil adapter comes with the IgnitionMate and can be used on coil-over-plug systems to measure peak firing voltages. Courtesy TecMate

eventually wear out with age and must be inspected periodically for damage and/or arcing caused by voltage leaks. Ignition coils should be checked for corrosion where the spark plug wires are connected. Secondary wires should be visually inspected for cracks, brittle insulation, or loose connections at the ignition coil or spark plug boots. High-voltage spark plug wires can also be checked using an ohmmeter, but resistance values vary widely between manufacturers, so be sure to consult a service manual for specific ohms per inch/foot values. Keep in mind that using an ohmmeter for resistance checking has limited value. When the throttle is twisted open, engine compression increases to its maximum. The added resistance of high compression may cause a bad wire to leak voltage to ground (without going to the spark plug first).

There are several low-dollar methods for diagnosing secondary ignition misfires. An inductive timing light clamped around one end of the spark plug wires can serve as a poor man's ignition scope. To check for ignition misfires, connect the timing light to the spark plug wire and start the engine. Point the timing light at your face and snap the throttle open. The human eye is quick enough to observe the results of an ignition misfire by watching the flashing timing light. If the flashing light skips a few flashes, the misfire could be caused by either a bad spark plug wire or primary switching problem. If no misfire is detected with a timing light, but the engine is obviously misfiring, move the inductive clamp of the timing light to each individual ignition wire and repeat the test. This will help isolate the bad spark plug wire. On coil-over-plug systems, the coil must be removed and a temporary plug wire installed between the coil and plug in order to provide a place to connect the timing light for the test.

Another method for finding bad ignition wires requires a grounded test light and water. Using a spray bottle filled with water, get the ignition wires really wet. The water helps magnify a spark plug boot or wire that's leaking voltage. Connect a test light to ground and start the engine. Move the tip of the test light along all the ignition wires while listening to the engine. When the test light is placed close to a bad section of wire, secondary voltage will jump to the sharp tip of the test light, causing the engine to misfire. If it's dark outside when you do this test, you can see as well as hear where the problem is occurring.

After spraying secondary ignition wires with water, a grounded test light can be used to find bad wires or spark plug boots. When placed close to the leaky wire, the tip of the test light will attract the high-voltage spark and that cylinder will misfire.

CHAPTER 7
FUEL INJECTION SYSTEMS

With a final gasp of breath, the use of carburetors for fuel delivery on motorcycles for U.S. sales will die on or about 2010. First introduced by BMW, and then followed by Japanese manufacturers, Harley-Davidson, Ducati, and Moto Guzzi, electronic fuel injection (EFI) is here to stay. Why electronic fuel injection? Just like automobiles and light trucks, motorcycles must face ever-tightening emissions standards. Three-way catalytic converters used on bikes to clean up the exhaust emissions must have precise fuel delivery control to function; EFI is the only technology that currently accomplishes this task.

In addition to motorcycles, other power sports applications are currently experiencing a transition phase from carburetion to EFI, including watercraft, ATVs, scooters, and even lawn tractors. Today the professional technician or home mechanic working on an EFI-equipped motorcycle who doesn't have an understanding of how these systems work is severely limited in ability to perform even basic electronics diagnostics and repair.

This electronic control module (ECM) is out of a late-model BMW motorcycle. The combination of government-mandated emissions and cheap computers has caused motorcycle manufacturers to follow the automotive industry to make the switch from carburetors to electronic fuel injection systems.
Courtesy Bob's BMW

However, working on an EFI system does not have to be as complex as many people think. Just like electronic ignition systems, different EFI designs share many similarities—once a technician understands the basics of EFI operation, most types are relatively easy to understand. Before we get into EFI, a review of just what a carburetor does will make EFI easier to digest.

CARBURETORS

All gasoline-powered engines need only two basic ingredients to run—the correct amount of fuel for any given rpm and throttle opening, and a spark from the ignition coil at the right time. Motorcycles have used electronic ignition systems for some time, but carburetors are still found on smaller, less expensive models.

A carburetor's fuel-delivery system is made up of separate fuel circuits, each with a specific job to perform. Take a look at how a stock CV (constant velocity) carburetor's fuel delivery circuits work (page 100, figure 7-1). When your bike hasn't been started for a while, the engine is cold and the choke lever or knob is pulled out to open several holes in the carburetor to add extra fuel and air. The additional fuel provides the engine with a rich mixture required for cold starting. Increased air flowing into the carburetor raises the idle speed to keep the engine from stalling until it's warmed up. Once the engine is warmed up, the choke is turned off, closing the choke circuit. At idle, just as the throttle is opened, the idle mixture circuit and transfer port circuits provide enough fuel to match airflow for operating conditions. As the throttle continues to open, the main jet and jet needle take over fuel delivery. As airflow increases into the engine, the diaphragm and slide pull the jet needle out of the main jet, adding more fuel to the incoming air stream. The main circuit provides fuel delivery at throttle openings from one-quarter to full throttle. If the throttle is opened suddenly, the accelerator pump circuit squirts fuel directly into the intake manifold. This is necessary because air is 400 times lighter than gasoline and without the accelerator pump, the air would get to the intake valve and into the cylinder ahead of the fuel, causing a flat spot and possible backfire during acceleration.

CV Carburetor Circuits

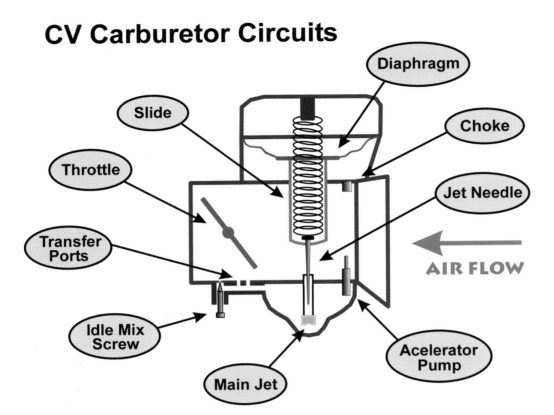

Slide

Diaphragm

Choke

Throttle

Jet Needle

Transfer Ports

AIR FLOW

Idle Mix Screw

Acelerator Pump

Main Jet

Fig 7-1—While this typical constant velocity (CV) carburetor provides reasonable power and fuel economy, it can't lower emissions to a level to keep the federal government happy. After all, a carburetor is just a hunk of aluminum with some holes drilled in it. Modern motorcycles require a fuel delivery system with brains— electronic fuel injection, or EFI.

This 2005 Yamaha FJR1300 EFI system provides better performance, more reliability, cleaner emissions, and better fuel mileage than the carbureted motorcycles of the past. Courtesy Twigg Cycles

Although carburetors have been providing fuel delivery services for well over a hundred years, and have basically always worked pretty well, there are some things they just can't handle. A carburetor is basically a hunk of aluminum with a bunch of holes drilled in it. As air pressure changes within the carburetor, it regulates the amount of fuel flowing through the various holes in the carburetor and into the engine. However, a carburetor's ability to deal with constantly changing operating environments is limited with regard to reactions to changes in altitude, compensation for engine temperature, lack of precise fuel control for emissions purposes, and overall use of excessive fuel during steady-state engine operation and acceleration. In a word, carburetors are just plain too "dumb" to continue delivering accurate air/fuel mixtures in modern motorcycles. What is needed is a fuel delivery system with some brains.

ELECTRONIC FUEL INJECTION

In addition to performing all the functions of a carburetor, EFI systems also control engine idle speed and ignition timing system functions. EFI systems regulate fuel delivery using electromagnetic valves (fuel injectors) that turn on electronically for varying lengths of time. Once activated, the fuel injectors spray fuel into the engine. The amount of on time is called injector pulse width, and the longer this is, the greater the amount of fuel-injected into the engine.

While all EFI systems use fuel injectors, which operate in the same manner, there are several different EFI designs and computer strategies found in use today on motorcycles today.

Port fuel injection (PFI) engines use individual injectors for each cylinder. Unlike a carburetored system, fuel is sprayed directly at the back of the engine's intake valves; it has less distance to travel before getting to the combustion chamber, resulting in more precise fuel delivery. Most motorcycle EFI systems use sequential port fuel injection (SPFI). The injectors on these systems are pulsed in accordance with the engine's sequential firing order—just like spark plugs. These systems provide accurate fuel delivery, which in turn reduces exhaust emissions and increases fuel mileage. Some sport bikes use two injectors per cylinder with one injector taking care of fuel delivery at idle and midrange engine operation, and the other high-mount injector for high-rpm operation.

TAKING EFI FOR A TEST RIDE

In order for an electronic control module (ECM) to control the injectors and ignition timing, it must receive information about engine rpm, engine temperature, altitude, air temperature, rider demand, and other inputs. This information is passed along to the ECM via its sensors. The ECM uses this information for overall engine fuel and ignition management. How a fuel injection system operates is worth a closer look. Taking a virtual test ride onboard a modern fuel-injected motorcycle with all the latest sensor technology will illustrate how an EFI system functions. In reality, not all EFI systems use all of these sensors, and many will differ in their fuel delivery strategies as well.

STARTING

Imagine yourself on a nice fall day sitting on your new motorcycle, which is, naturally, equipped with the latest-greatest

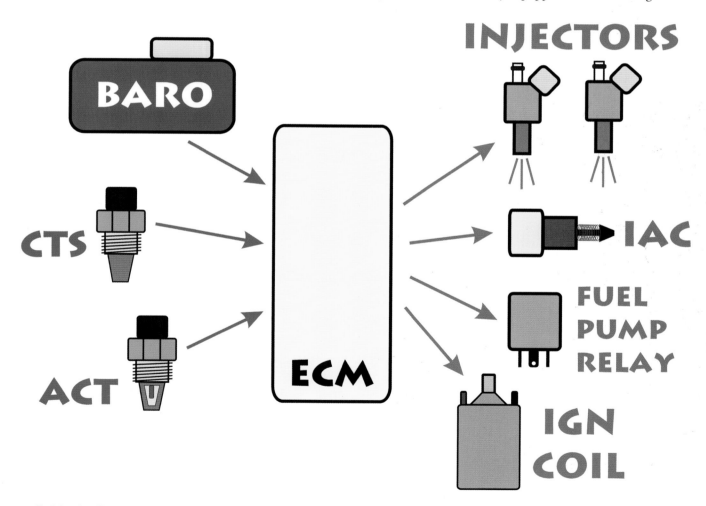

Fig 7-2 —Just like a fast idle cam and choke circuit on a carburetor, coolant and air temperature sensors, the ECM, and injectors now serve to provide a rich fuel mixture for cold starting. The idle air controller adds extra air, increasing engine idle speed during cold start-up so the engine won't stall.

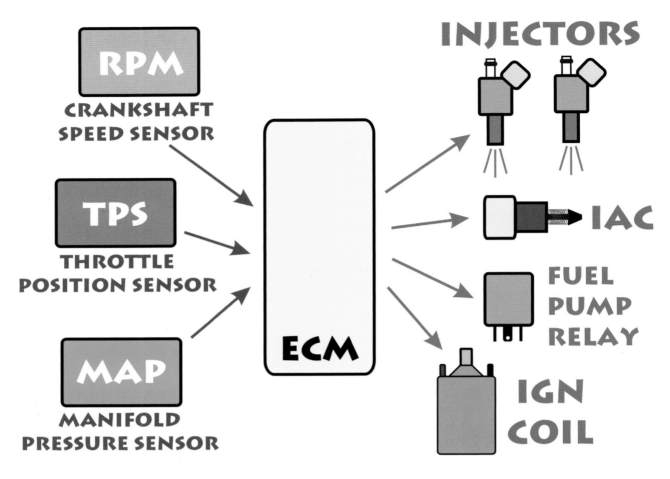

Fig 7-3—Three basic inputs—engine rpm, throttle position, and engine load—determine the base injector pulse width (on time) and ignition timing. The MAP sensor works like an electronic vacuum gauge in effect telling the ECM how hard the engine is working. The TPS sensor sends the ECM rider demand information—how hard the throttle being twisted.

EFI system. When the ignition key is turned to the ON position, the ECM turns the fuel pump on for two seconds to pressurize the fuel system. The reason the fuel pump doesn't keep running is that the engine has not started. As soon as the ECM detects an rpm signal, it will keep the pump running. The ECM then checks in with the sensors for engine coolant/oil temperature, air temperature, and barometric pressure. These sensors report the outside ambient temperature as cool (50 degrees Fahrenheit), and because the bike has been sitting overnight, the engine coolant and oil temperature are also 50 degrees Fahrenheit. Since your imaginary motorcycle was parked near the beach, the barometric pressure (BARO) sensor indicates to the ECM that barometric pressure is at sea level. When you push the start button, the ECM goes into start mode. Because the engine temperature is cold, the ECM adjusts the injector's initial pulse width, or on time, in accordance with its internal program to produce a rich fuel mixture for

cold starting. The ECM also opens an idle air controller that allows extra air to enter the engine, causing a fast idle. This keeps the engine from stalling until it warms up. These functions take the place of the manual choke lever that your old carbureted bike had.

With the engine cranking, the ECM receives a signal from the crankshaft and camshaft position sensors to start firing spark plugs. The crankshaft sensor sends an engine rpm signal, and the camshaft sensor identifies which cylinder is next in the firing order. The ECM pulses the injectors (turning them on, then off) to start the engine. As the fuel injectors operate, they atomize the high-pressure fuel stored in the fuel rail as it's squirted into the intake manifold. During cold startup, the ECM pulses all of the injectors during every crankshaft revolution to help provide extra fuel for cold startup. However, once the engine warms up, the injectors will get pulsed in the same sequence as the engine's firing order—just like spark plugs.

This Harley-Davidson crank sensor (left) and cam sensor provide the ECM with engine speed and cylinder identification information. The cam sensor is used for the sequential fuel injection, as it identifies which cylinder is approaching top dead center on its compression stroke. This allows the ECM to pulse only that injector just before the intake valve opens. Courtesy Harley-Davidson of Frederick

Each injector is switched on just before the intake valve opens for that cylinder. This fuel delivery strategy is called sequential port fuel injection. Sequential injection decreases exhaust emissions while increasing horsepower and helps out in the fuel economy department as well.

WARMING UP AND DRIVING

As the engine warms up, the fuel mixture must be leaned out, creating a mixture with less fuel and more air. Based on the engine's coolant or oil temperature, the ECM turns on—pulses—the injectors a shorter amount of time. Also, the ECM lowers engine idle speed by closing down the idle air control valve. Once you're ready to head out on the road, you pull in the clutch and using the shift lever put the transmission into first gear. As you twist the throttle, the ECM immediately changes ignition timing by advancing it. When the throttle is twisted more, the ECM checks several inputs to determine injector pulse width and ignition timing, including the throttle position sensor (TPS), manifold absolute pressure (MAP) sensor, and crankshaft speed sensor.

The TPS senses how far and how fast the throttle opens. A MAP sensor is used to measure engine vacuum, an indication of engine load or how hard the engine is working. The ECM uses TPS and MAP sensor inputs, as well as engine rpm, to determine injector pulse width and ignition timing. The ECM does this by consulting

its computerized internal dictionary or look up tables to calculate all of its outputs. These tables contain information about how long to keep the injectors on under specific operating conditions. For example, if the throttle is opened at a moderate rate, causing engine rpm to increase slowly, the ECM increases the injector on time gradually. If the throttle is twisted rapidly, the ECM momentarily increases injector pulse width to provide an extra shot of fuel, similar to a carburetor's accelerator pump.

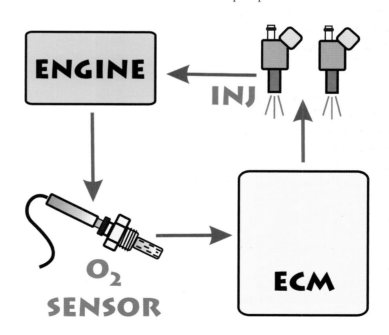

Fig 7-4—The informational loop of inject-sense-control works to maintain the correct air/fuel ratio required by the motorcycle's catalytic converter. Since the loop is endless, it's often referred to as a closed loop or feedback loop.

NORMAL OPERATING TEMPERATURE AND DRIVING

As you ride down a scenic country road, the engine is at normal operating temperature, and you're holding the throttle steady. The ECM goes into what is known as closed loop operation. The interaction between ECM, fuel injectors, and oxygen (O_2) sensor is often called a feedback loop—also commonly referred to as closed loop or closed loop control. During closed loop operations, the ECM pulses the injectors to inject specific amounts of fuel in order to maintain a precise air/fuel ratio. As fuel and air are burned in the engine's combustion chamber, the resulting exhaust gases travel through the exhaust system, where any unburned exhaust gas oxygen is measured by the O_2 sensor. The O_2 sensor sends a signal voltage to the ECM, which then modifies the injector pulse width to maintain a 14.7:1 air/fuel ratio. This air/fuel ratio is considered ideal for the exhaust gases to be processed by the three-way catalytic converter. The sequence of inject-combust-sense-control creates a feedback loop (see page 103, figure 7-4).

The ECM adjusts fuel delivery based on outside air temperature and altitude. You decide to take a side road that leads up into the mountains. As you gain altitude, the BARO or ambient air pressure (AAP) sensor changes the signal it sends to the ECM. As you rider higher, the surrounding air density decreases (less oxygen) so the ECM leans the air/fuel mixture by decreasing the injectors' on time. The ECM matches fuel delivery to the lower air density found at higher-than-sea level altitudes. At sea level or 8,000 feet. This technology allows EFI bikes to run smoothly with optimum air/fuel ratios. Both BARO and outside air temperature sensors are used as a trim adjustment by the ECM and have only a small effect on injector pulse width.

In addition to regulating fuel control, the ECM is also continually adjusting ignition timing advance. Depending on engine rpm and TPS and MAP values, the engine's ignition timing may be advanced or retarded. For example, if a light throttle is used in conjunction with moderate rpm, ignition timing will advance to promote fuel economy. However, if the throttle is wide open but engine rpm is low, timing will retard to prevent engine ping or knock. As engine speed increases, the timing is advanced to its optimum setting for maximum power. With a straight section of road ahead, you decide to "whack" the throttle wide open. A knock sensor "hears" the engine starting to knock and send s a signal to the ECM. The ECM retards the ignition timing for the cylinder that's detonating or knocking. (See "Knock Sensors" for more information.)

After your ride through the mountains, you travel along a country road and approach a quaint little town

The oxygen sensor is the key to keeping the air/fuel ratio at 14.7:1 (14 parts air to 1 part fuel). This mixture allows the three-way catalytic converter to clean up what's coming out of the engine's exhaust.

near where you live. A group of kids are crossing the street so you slow your bike and come to a stop. As you roll off the throttle, the ECM recognizes the TPS signal for a closed throttle. The crank sensor indicates that the engine rpm is also decreasing. These operating conditions cause the ECM to shut off the fuel injectors, causing a fuel cut (as it is sometimes called). Cutting off the fuel to the engine reduces exhaust emissions during deceleration.

Heading out of town, you pull alongside a shiny, new 600-cc sport bike waiting at the stoplight. The road in front of you is straight and passes through open fields. As he glances over at you he revs his engine. The light turns green, and you take off before he can react, twisting the throttle three-fourths open on your 1,300-cc, sport-touring motorcycle and accelerate through first gear. When the throttle is opened suddenly, the TPS signal voltage goes up instantly and the injectors are given a long on time, but only for an instant. This squirt of extra fuel is the same provided by a carburetor's accelerator pump and causes just the right amount of fuel to be available at the intake valves when they get hit by the big blast of air from the wide-open throttle. You reach 60 miles per hour, shift into second gear, and open the throttle all the way. The ECM looks at TPS, MAP, and RPM signals to determine the pulse width for its four injectors.

Meanwhile, onboard the sport bike, other technology is at work. Lighter motorcycles (especially 600-cc crotch rockets) are prone to lofting the front wheel during acceleration in lower gears if too much throttle is applied. To keep overenthusiastic riders from flipping over backward, the EFI system limits power delivery to the rear wheel at low

Three components—an ECM, injector, and oxygen sensor—make up a closed loop fuel-control system. The informational loop of sense-compare-correct takes place at part throttle on most motorcycles and provides cleaner emissions. Courtesy Bob's BMW

speeds in first and second gear. To accomplish this, two throttle plates are used per cylinder. The rider operates one set of throttles and a stepper motor controlled by the ECM actuates a second set. Instead of going round-and-round, a stepper motor rotates in steps controlled by pulses it receives from the ECM. Two TPSs are used to measure both the manually operated throttle and the computer-controlled throttle.

When the clutch is let out in first gear, the ECM looks at a signal from the vehicle speed sensor (VSS) attached to the front sprocket cover. By comparing engine rpm to rear wheel speed via the rotation of the drive chain's counter sprocket, the ECM can determine if the engine's speed,

throttle opening, and rear wheel speed are all in line, preventing the bike from pulling a major wheelie. The ECM delays the opening of the secondary throttle plates via the stepper motor to limit engine power output. As vehicle speed increases, the stepper motor opens the secondary throttle all the way.

You've finally reached your destination—home. You pull into your driveway and turn off the ignition key. The ECM on your motorcycle goes into sleep mode and remains this way until you start the process over again by turning the key on. During our virtual ride, the operation of the ECM, its various sensors, fuel injectors, and ignition system operation were depicted in real time. In reality, all

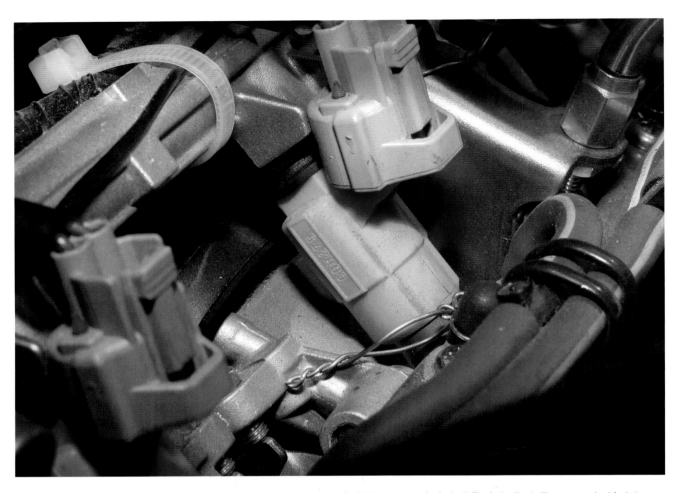

One of four injectors on a Yamaha FJR1300. Each injector is sandwiched between the intake runner and a fuel rail. The fuel rail acts like a pressurized fuel storage tank. Excess fuel is returned to the fuel tank via the fuel pressure regulator. Courtesy Twigg Cycles

of this interconnected electronic communication and decision-making happens in the blink of an eye.

Sensor inputs to the ECM are processed at an amazing rate of more than 1 million times per second. However, the rate at which ECM outputs change is much slower, only about 80 times per second. Because a rider can't open the throttle, accelerate, or change gears faster than the EFI system can process information, the operation of the engine management system is seamless and not noticed by the rider.

Motorcycles that use computerized engine management systems have "good manners" when it comes to engine operation. Typically, EFI engines start and run well either cold or hot, accelerate smoothly, get good fuel mileage, and don't pollute. As a result, electronically fuel-injected motorcycles offer better overall performance while exhaust gases coming from the tailpipe(s) are often cleaner than the surrounding air, especially in large cities (can you say smog?) during summer months.

TPS sensors come in different shapes and configurations. Most are variable resistors and provide throttle angle, or position, to the motorcycle's electronic fuel injection computer. On some bikes adjustment is critical, and a service manual should be consulted for the proper procedure. Courtesy Bob's BMW

Honda's 599 EFI motorcycle uses a TPS to relay rider demand as the throttle is twisted open. The ECM not only knows how far the throttle is opened but how fast it's opening and can adjust fuel delivery accordingly. Courtesy Twigg Cycles

Fig 7-5—This is a typical throttle position sensor/ECM circuit. A TPS is simply a variable resistor. As the throttle is opened, the TPS signal voltage gets closer to the reference voltage of 5 volts. This increasing voltage indicates to the ECM that it should add fuel accordingly as the vehicle accelerates. If voltage increases rapidly, additional fuel is injected into the intake manifold.

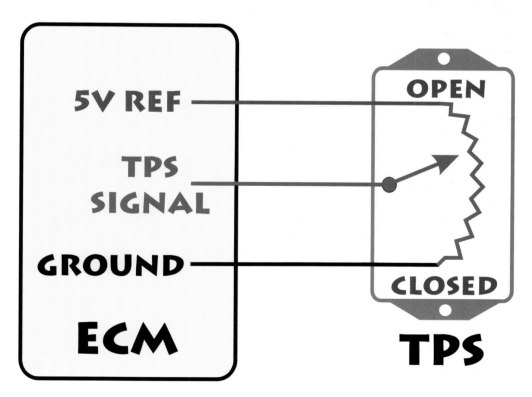

THROTTLE POSITION SENSOR (TPS)

Most motorcycle TPSs have three wires: power (5 volts), ground, and signal. A TPS can be tested in two ways: (1) by measuring varying voltage; (2) measuring resistance. Measuring TPS voltage is the more accurate method for testing this sensor, because the ECM reads voltage instead of resistance from the TPS.

To check for the presence of a TPS signal, turn the ignition key to the ON position. Leave the TPS plugged in. Back probe each wire with a digital voltmeter. The three wires tested should have readings as follows:

5-volt reference wire—The ECM sends 5 volts to the TPS as a reference voltage. If none of the wires at the TPS have 5 volts, check the fuse(s) that power the ECM. If the fuses are good, and the TPS wires to the ECM are also okay, there may be a bad power supply within the ECM.

Ground wire—The TPS ground comes directly from the ECM. This wire should read close to 0 volts. If it's higher than 0.02 volts the ECM may have a bad ground wire. If this is the case, perform a voltage drop test on the ECM ground wire(s).

Signal wire—The TPS sends a varying voltage signal to the ECM via the signal wire. With the throttle closed, voltage should be around 0.5 volts. As the throttle opens, voltage should gradually increase until it reaches around 4.5 volts at wide open throttle. Inside the TPS is a variable resistor that changes resistance in relation to

throttle angle (opening). This resistor can eventually wear out over many miles of engine operation. Open the throttle slowly while checking the voltmeter reading—a steady increase in voltage without any skipping or jumping around indicates a good TPS. Digital voltmeters with bar graphs make it much easier to recognize a bad TPS, since the bar graph has a faster display rate than the digital display.

TEMPERATURE SENSORS

Depending on manufacturer, temperature sensors are also referred to as ECT (engine coolant temperature), ET (engine temperature), CT (coolant temperature), and

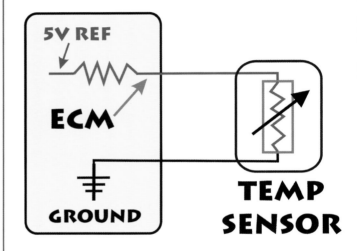

Fig 7-6—The ECM reads voltage at a point on the temp sensor's signal wire located just before the internal resistor (blue arrow). Depending on the sensor (air, coolant, or oil), this variable voltage signal is interpreted by the ECM as temperature—the higher the temperature, the lower the sensor voltage output.

Air temperature sensors work in a similar manner to coolant or oil temp sensors. The difference is the sensor's probe may have holes or cutouts to allow airflow to come in direct contact with the sensor. The motorcycle's ECM uses intake air temperature to trim and fine-tune fuel delivery.

The Harley-Davidson (left) and BMW oil temperature sensors provide engine temperature information to the on-board computer. As engine temperature increases, injection pulse width is decreased by the ECM, resulting in a lean fuel mixture. Both sensors send a varying voltage to the ECM. Courtesy Harley-Davidson of Frederick and Bob's BMW

CHT (cylinder head temperature) on air-cooled engines. Intake manifold temperature sensors operate in a similar manner and can be called: ACT (air charge temperature), IAT (intake air temperature), or MAT (manifold air temperature) sensors. Both coolant and intake manifold temperature sensors can be tested in the same manner. Temperature sensors are negative temperature coefficient (NTC) thermistors. An NTC thermistor changes resistance as the temperature changes—resistance decreases as temperature increases. The ECM sends a 5-volt reference signal to the temperature sensor. As the sensor's resistance changes, the voltage that the ECM reads changes as well. High voltage (more than 3.5 volts) is interpreted as low temperature—low voltage (close to 0.5 volts) is for normal engine operating, or high temperatures.

Temperature sensors are typically equipped with two wires. To check a two-wire coolant or air temp sensor, turn the ignition key to ON and back probe both wires using a DVOM. One wire should read close to 0 volts since it is the temp sensor ground; the other wire should have between 0.1 and 4.5 volts depending on manufacturer and sensor temperature. On a cold engine, voltage should be approximately 3.0 volts or higher. Start the engine and

Oxygen sensors without internal heaters are usually located as close to the engine as possible. This keeps the sensor hot enough to produce an exhaust gas oxygen content signal that is sent to the on-board computer. Courtesy Bob's BMW

This Moto Guzzi uses a cylinder head temperature sensor. The sensor's probe is located inside an oil galley and uses oil temperature as an indication of engine temperature. Courtesy Bob's BMW

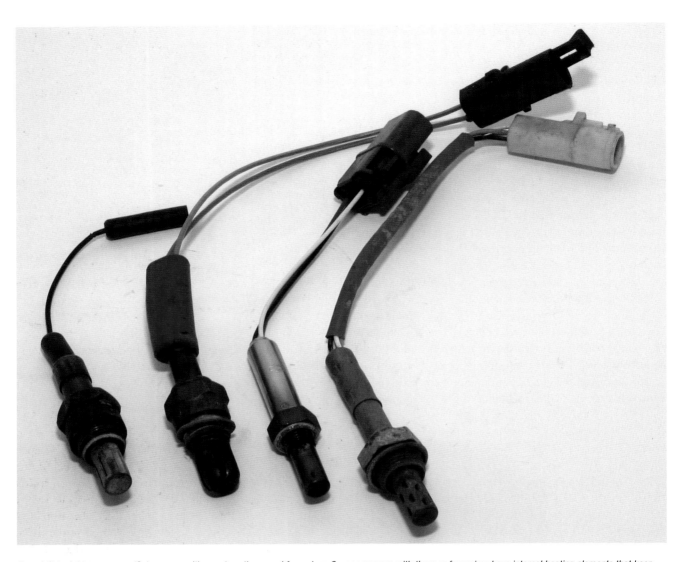

From left to right are oxygen (O₂) sensors with one, two, three, and four wires. Oxygen sensors with three or four wires have internal heating elements that keep the sensors at operating temperature (more than 600 degrees Fahrenheit), even if the exhaust gas temperature is low due to prolonged engine idling. The use of an internal heater allows the placement of the O₂ sensor to be farther away from the cylinder head. This provides a more accurate sample of exhaust gas oxygen for the sensor to measure.

watch the voltmeter reading as the engine warms up. Voltage should gradually start dropping to around 1 or 2 volts depending on manufacturer. If signal voltage drops fast or skips around, the coolant/air temp sensor is probably bad. Engine or air temperature sensors can also be tested for internal resistance by unplugging the coolant/air temp sensor and using an ohmmeter. Measuring internal resistance is one indicator of proper functioning. In general, resistance should be high (thousands of ohms) when it's cold outside and lower (less than 2,000 ohms) when hot. See a service manual for exact resistance values versus temperatures for a specific motorcycle.

OXYGEN (O₂) SENSORS

The key to making all closed loop feedback systems work is the oxygen sensor. The function of an O₂ sensor is to measure the oxygen content of exhaust gas. There are two types of O₂ sensors commonly used—zirconia and titania.

A zirconia dioxide sensor acts as a galvanic battery, generating a small DC voltage by comparing oxygen content inside the exhaust to the surrounding atmosphere. When the oxygen content is low (rich mixture), the difference between exhaust gas oxygen and the oxygen in the atmosphere is high, causing the sensor to produce a high voltage—between 0.5 and 0.9 volts. Conversely, when

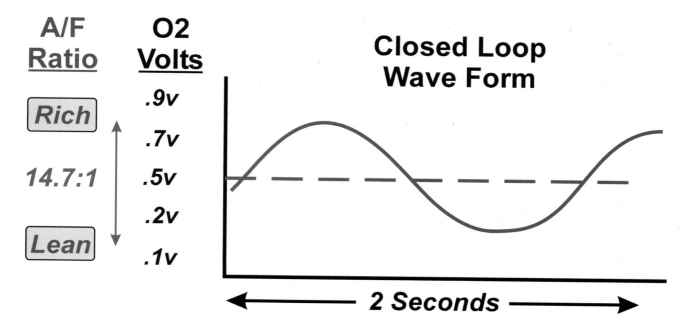

A/F Ratio	O2 Volts	Closed Loop Wave Form
Rich	.9v	
	.7v	
14.7:1	.5v	
	.2v	
Lean	.1v	

2 Seconds

Fig 7-7—This lab scope wave form shows an O_2 sensor switching between rich and lean air/fuel mixtures. Rich mixtures are indicated by sensor voltage readings above 0.5 volts, while readings below 0.5 volts are for lean air/fuel ratios. The switching voltage indicates that the fuel management system is in closed loop.

the O_2 sensor detects high exhaust gas oxygen content (lean mixture), and compares it to the outside air, the difference is that smaller and lower voltages are generated (0.1 to 0.4 volts).

A titania O_2 sensor operates somewhat differently from a zirconia sensor, but the end results are the same. Instead of producing voltage, a titania O_2 sensor uses a reference voltage from the ECM and changes its internal resistance based on the oxygen content found in the exhaust gas. A titania sensor's resulting voltages are the same as those of a zirconia sensor. Both sensor types have to be hot (600 degrees Fahrenheit) before they can function. Some sensors use an electric heating element that keeps them from cooling down at idle (when engine exhaust gas temperature is low) and facilitates a quicker sensor warm-up time during cold starting.

Unlike other sensors, O_2 sensors can have one, two, three, or even four wires. To test an O_2 sensor, the engine should be warmed up to normal operating temperature. To do this, don't just let the engine idle in your garage for a few minutes, go for a short ride. Gaining access to the O_2 sensor's wires is usually easier at the ECM wiring harness connector than at the O_2 sensor itself. Using the positive lead of a digital voltmeter, back probe the O_2 sensor's signal wire at the ECM. Connect the meter's negative lead to a good ground. Start the engine and maintain speed at 2,000 rpm for 60 seconds. If the O_2 voltage starts switching back

and forth somewhere between 0.2 and 0.8 volts, the EFI system is in closed loop mode. (For purposes of this test, it doesn't really matter if the system is in closed loop or open loop.) Next, while watching the voltmeter, snap the throttle open. The O_2 voltage should immediately go up to 0.9 volts, indicating a rich mixture. Hold engine speed steady again, and then quickly close the throttle. This time, O_2 voltage should drop to 0.1 volts or less, because the ECM has cut off fuel to the engine, creating a lean mixture. How fast the O_2 sensor responds to the changes in exhaust gas oxygen, as well as the range of voltage displayed (0.1 to 0.9 volts), indicates whether the sensor is good or bad. A good sensor should be able to make voltage transitions instantly, while a lazy or worn-out O_2 sensor makes voltage transitions only slowly and won't be able to reach 0.9 volts, no matter how rich the engine is running.

MAP AND BARO SENSORS

As mentioned before, a MAP sensor is nothing more than an electronic vacuum gauge connected to a vacuum source at the intake manifold. MAP sensors can be bolted directly to a manifold or a remote mounting location (if a vacuum hose is used). A MAP sensor provides the ECM with engine load information, letting the ECM know when the engine is working hard. Most MAP sensors send a variable voltage to the ECM. Whenever the engine is idling, the negative pressure inside the intake manifold is high—

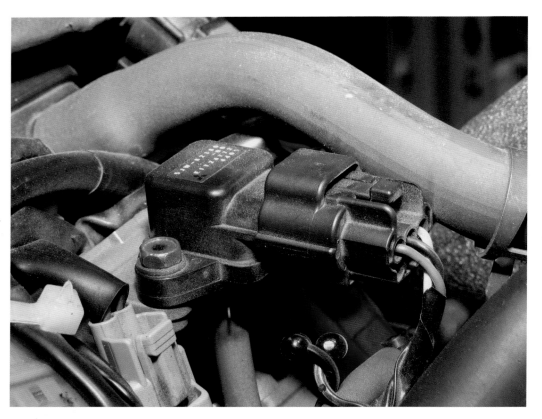

All MAP sensors are basically electronic vacuum gauges. They have three wires—power (5-volts), ground, and a signal wire that indicates intake manifold pressure. Some MAP sensors are mounted remotely from the engine, and others can be directly attached to the intake manifold (pictured). Some are located inside the motorcycle's ECM. Courtesy Twigg Cycles

around 20 inches of mercury. Once the throttle is opened, the negative pressure (vacuum) drops until, at wide-open throttle, engine vacuum is at 0 Hg. The MAP sensor senses the engine vacuum, outputs a voltage signal, then sends it to the ECM for processing.

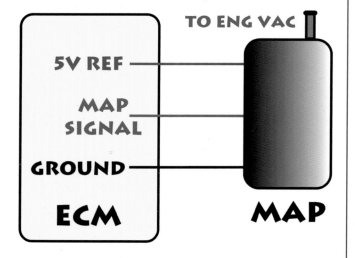

Fig 7-8—MAP and BARO sensors have three wires: (1) power [5-volt reference], (2) ground, and (3) signal. Some MAP sensors have a nipple fitting to accept a vacuum hose in order to connect the sensor to the intake manifold.

Similar in operation to a MAP sensor, a BARO sensor measures ambient air pressure (altitude) and then sends a signal to the ECM. Motorcycle manufacturers may use different names for a BARO sensors including ambient air pressure (AAP), intake air pressure (IAP), or throttle inlet pressure (TIP). Often these sensors are located in the intake air box, where inlet air pressure increases with speed (ram air) on some bikes. The ECM changes the fuel and ignition timing parameters depending on altitude or pressure inside the intake plenum (air box). Mountain driving requires a leaner fuel mixture, so the ECM changes the injector pulse width accordingly. Both of these sensors have three wires: power (5 volts), ground, and signal.

To test both MAP and BARO sensors, turn the ignition key to ON. Using a DVOM, back probe all three wires. One wire should have 5 volts, one should be close to 0 volts (ground), and the last should be the signal wire. If there is no 5-volt reference at the sensor, check the wires going to the ECM. Use a hand vacuum pump to test MAP sensors. As you vary the vacuum pressure to the sensor, the voltage should change as well. MAP sensor voltage must be compensated for when testing at, or above, sea level, since voltage readings will be slightly lower—about 0.2 volts for every 1,000 feet above sea level. BARO sensors won't have a vacuum nipple, so testing

Some early electronic fuel-injected BMW and Kawasaki motorcycles used a flapper-style mass airflow sensor. This design of MAF uses a mechanical valve or door that swings open as engine airflow increases. They are sensitive to engine vibration and too large to fit in the tight confines of a motorcycle engine compartment, and are no longer in use. Courtesy Bob's BMW

is just a matter of reading voltage with the ignition on. Consult a service manual for voltage versus altitude readings for a specific motorcycle.

MASS AIRFLOW (MAF) SENSORS

Mass airflow (MAF) sensors measure the volume of air entering the engine. In addition, air density and temperature are also calculated and the resulting signal is sent to the ECM. Mass airflow sensors are not used on modern motorcycles, but older model BMWs and Kawasakis used a flapper type MAF. Manufactured by Bosch, These sensors use a mechanical door that opens in direct proportion to engine airflow. Air temperature sensors were usually located just inside the door; they were used to calculate, along with airflow, the total air volume required by the engine. These sensors were prone to failure due to motorcycle engine vibration—not much of an issue on automobiles, which these sensors were originally designed to be used in. In addition, flapper-type MAF sensors are rather large and don't fit well into the tight spaces on a motorcycle. To test this type of MAF, simply find which wire is the signal wire to the ECM (see a service manual) and connect a digital voltmeter to it. With the ignition on, move the door with a screwdriver or your finger, and watch the voltage. A good MAF sensor will show a steady increase in voltage as the door is pushed open, similar to a TPS signal.

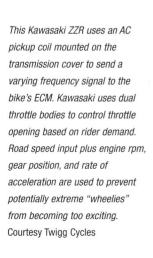

This Kawasaki ZZR uses an AC pickup coil mounted on the transmission cover to send a varying frequency signal to the bike's ECM. Kawasaki uses dual throttle bodies to control throttle opening based on rider demand. Road speed input plus engine rpm, gear position, and rate of acceleration are used to prevent potentially extreme "wheelies" from becoming too exciting. Courtesy Twigg Cycles

KNOCK SENSOR (KS)

The knock sensor, or detonation sensor as it is sometimes called, has a piezoelectric crystal that generates voltage when subjected to mechanical stress. This crystal produces an electrical signal with a unique signature based upon engine knock or ping. Knock sensors operate similar to an electronic lighter for a gas refrigerator or BBQ, except they does not spark, but rather, only produce voltage. When an engine knocks or pings under heavy acceleration, the knock sensor sends a signal to the vehicle's ECM. The ECM then retards the ignition timing in an effort to stop the knocking—a safety feature designed to prevent damage to pistons and rings. The use of a knock sensor to help control ignition timing also allows for the use of different gasoline grades without the consequence of engine damage or poor performance.

Following is a general diagnostic test for knock sensors; however, a service manual should be consulted for specific tests, as these sensors can vary in output. To test the knock sensor, disconnect it and probe the sensor wire with

This Harley-Davidson vehicle speed sensor is located on the transmission. It provides a signal to indicate road speed for the electronic speedometer and fuel injection management system. The sensor, an AC pickup coil, produces AC voltage and a varying frequency. Courtesy Harley-Davidson of Frederick

An idle air controller (IAC) receives a signal from a vehicle's ECM and adjusts engine idle speed. This IAC on a late-model Harley-Davidson is a stepper motor that is pulsed and opens a plunger in small increments. The pulses move a plunger that bypasses air around the throttle plates to increase engine idle. Courtesy Harley-Davidson of Frederick

The idle air controller can be seen mounted on top of the left cylinder's intake manifold. This stepper motor can precisely control the amount of air bypassing the throttle plate to control engine idle speed. The TPS is also visible on the outside of the intake runner. Courtesy Bob's BMW

a DVOM. Set the multimeter to read AC mV (millivolts). Take a small hammer and tap on the engine case (near the sensor) while watching the voltmeter. The sensor should produce a small amount of AC voltage, usually less than 4 volts AC.

VEHICLE SPEED SENSORS (VSS)

A vehicle speed sensor (VSS) provides a signal to the ECM to monitor the road speed of the motorcycle. The ECM uses this information to control ignition timing and, on some motorcycles, to operate secondary throttle plates. There are two types of VSSs: (1) an AC pickup coil; and (2) a Hall-effect switch. Both of these speed sensors operate in the same manner, much like ignition counterparts in ignition systems. (See Chapter 6, Ignition Systems, for an overview of testing methods used on speed sensors.)

IDLE AIR CONTROL

Idle air control (IAC) sensors are not really sensors at all—they are actuators. The ECM controls these devices in order to change engine idle speed. Idle speed is increased by the ECM for cold starting and to help the alternator charge the battery or run accessories. Some IACs use a "stepper motor" to control the amount of air allowed into the engine, while others use a bypass valve. In general, these actuators can be checked for proper resistance, but they are difficult to test for actual operation. Using a computer scan tool (hand-held computer interface) is sometimes the only way to verify if the ECM and IAC sensor are functioning together correctly. Consult a service manual for proper testing procedures for specific motorcycles.

FUEL INJECTORS

Fuel injectors are nothing more than actuators controlled by a vehicle's computer. The ECM controls the amount of fuel injected into the engine by varying the pulse width

BMW was the first motorcycle manufacturer to widely use electronic fuel injection. The fuel injectors on this BMW oil head are located on the top of the intake runner. Courtesy Bob's BMW

While they might look different, all of these fuel injectors operate in the same manner. Each uses a coil of wire that acts like an electromagnet when energized by the ECM. The pulse width—length of on time—determines how long the injector remains opens and, consequently, how much fuel is injected into the engine.

of the injectors. How long the injectors are open (allowing fuel to be injected) is a function of the corresponding length of time the injector pulse width lasts.

All fuel injectors are solenoids consisting of a coil of wire and a moveable electromagnetic valve. When energized, the coil of wire acts like a magnet, causing the valve to open.

A fuel injector's resistance can be measured using an ohmmeter. However, resistance readings only confirm the injector's internal coil is not shorted or open. Because resistance values vary widely between injector manufacturers, consulting a service manual for specific values is always a good idea. The only way to tell if an injector is actually working electrically is to use a lab scope to monitor the injector's pulse from the ECM. However, there are a number of simple tests that work most of the time to indirectly confirm that an injector is operating. The first four tests verify that the ECM is sending an injector pulse to the injector. The final test checks for mechanical operation.

1. Unplug the injector and connect a test light between the two wires at the injector connector. Crank or start up the engine while watching the test light. If the light flashes, the ECM is sending an injector pulse to that injector. (While a test light will work most of the time for performing this test, it's important to know this test will not work on all motorcycles, because some use a dropping resistor in the injector circuit that limits current going into the injector to keep it from overheating.)

2. Instead of using a test light, use a noid light that is specific to the particular EFI system being tested. A noid light has low enough resistance to flash during the test, even when a dropping resistor is used in the circuit. (See Chapter 3, Electronic Testing Tools, for information about noid lights.)

3. Use an inductive ignition timing light to verify injector pulse. Clamp the timing light's probe around *one* of the wires going to the injector. Start or crank the engine and watch the timing light to see if it flashes—a flashing light provides confirmation that the ECM is sending an injector pulse to that injector.

4. Use a logic probe to verify the presence of an injector pulse signal from the ECM. Connect a logic probe or red and green test light to the motorcycle's battery. (See Chapter 3, Electronic Testing Tools, for more information about logic probes and red and green test

lights.) Touch the probe to one of the injector wires (the injector can be left plugged into its connector). Crank or start the engine and then watch the LED on the logic probe—if it flashes or pulses, the ECM is sending an injector pulse to that injector.

5. For a low-tech testing method, simply take a long screwdriver, touch either end to the fuel injector, and stick the other end in your ear. (No kidding!) If the injector is working, you'll hear a steady clicking from the injector. A wooden dowel or mechanic's stethoscope works just as well!

RELAYS

Relays have been used for years on non-EFI motorcycles. Electronic fuel injection systems use relays to control various functions, including operation of the electronic fuel pump, headlight(s), accessories, and other electronics. A relay uses a relatively small amount of amperage to switch a high-amperage load on and off. All motorcycles equipped with electric starters use a starter relay to accomplish this task, and it works in a similar manner to other smaller relays. The starter relay simply connects the battery to the starter motor when the start button is pressed.

A starter relay has four terminals. The two large terminals are connected to the positive battery terminal and the starter motor. The two smaller terminals control the relay. One of these is connected to ground and the other to the starter button on the handlebars. When the start button is pressed, power is sent to the relay. Inside the relay, a coil of wire is energized so it acts like an electromagnet. The magnet pulls the two high-amperage contacts together, connecting the starter to the battery.

Five-terminal automotive relays (left) are common on motorcycles, even those with carbureted fuel systems. The starter solenoid (right) is just an overgrown relay that controls the high-amperage connection between the battery and starter motor. Both relays can be tested in a similar manner. Courtesy Twigg Cycle

With the cover removed, the relay low-amperage control coil and high-amperage contacts can be seen. The coil pulls the contacts together to complete the high-amperage circuit. Most small relays used on motorcycles can handle up to 30 amps. Starter solenoids (big relays) can operate at several hundred amps.

In addition to normal relay functions, some relays use solid-state electronics to control when the high-amperage contacts operate. This Bosch fuel pump relay must "see" an engine rpm signal before it will allow the high-amperage contacts to close. If the engine stops running, the relay's contacts open and the fuel pump stops running.

Smaller relays work just like a starter relay. On a fuel-injected motorcycle, the fuel pump relay is controlled by the ECM for safety reasons. This keeps the fuel pump from running if the engine can't start or if the motorcycle were to tip over—or worse, crash. When the ignition key is switched on, the fuel pump is turned on for about two seconds to pressurize the fuel system. If the engine is started, the ECM keeps the fuel pump relay energized for normal engine operation. If the motorcycle gets knocked over, a sensor sends a signal to the ECM to shut off the fuel pump relay. These sensors are called tip-over or bank angle sensors. They measure what angle the bike is from side to side (upright versus lying on its side). On some bikes, the ECM also controls the headlight relay. If the key is switched on and the engine does not start, the ECM keeps the headlight off to save the battery. Once the engine starts, the headlight relay's control coil is grounded by the ECM, and the headlight operates normally.

Testing a relay is simple. Most motorcycle relays have four or five terminals. These are often numbered, but not always. Terminal numbers 87A, 87, and 30 are the high-amperage contacts. Terminals 85 and 86 are for the low-amperage relay control coil. Terminal 87A is normally closed while terminal 87 is normally open. To test the relay turn the ignition on and using a grounded test light, touch each of the terminals. If the relay is supposed to be on, terminals 30 and 87 (sometimes 87A) should be hot. Also either terminal 85 or 86 should also be hot. (If one has

The terminal numbers are etched on the cover of this Bosch style relay. Most relays on motorcycles don't use the normally closed terminal (87A) and are used to close, or connect, terminals 87 to 30. Terminal 30 is usually battery power.

power, the other is a ground.) If the relay is supposed to be off, touching the grounded test light to terminal 85 or 86 should make the relay click (energize) and the two high-amperage terminals should both have power. For more details on relay tests, see Chapter 8, Wiring Diagrams.

CHAPTER 8
WIRING DIAGRAMS

Taking a cross-country car trip when you were little may have been your introduction to reading a road map. Your parents might have shown you a road atlas, and said: "We're here now, and after we drive for four days, we'll be there." Reading a wiring diagram is similar to reading a road map. Road maps illustrate how to get from point A to point B. However, instead of connecting interstates, highways, and roads, a wiring diagram shows major electrical systems, subsystems, and individual circuits, all interconnected. When a technician looks at a wiring diagram, the goal is to figure out why a circuit isn't operating, so destination points are replaced with power sources, controls, identification of and routes to load devices, and pathways for ground returns back to the negative battery terminal.

Wiring diagrams and road maps also have another feature in common—layers of detail. For example, if you look at a road atlas of California, you won't be able to locate a street address. You might find a city or town, but you won't find a specific route to an exact address. In order to find the exact location of a particular residence or building, you would need a detailed street map. The same is true (to a lesser extent) of wiring diagrams. On smaller, and older motorcycles, wiring diagrams show the electrical system on one page. As motorcycles grew larger and more complex, wiring diagrams were categorized and separated into major electrical systems and subsystems (instead of one system for an entire bike). This occurred, in part, due to the complexity of late-model motorcycles—with so many electrical components, it was no longer practical to put everything on one wiring diagram on a single page. Honda's Gold Wing is a good example of a large, complex motorcycle with many subsystems such as premium audio, Satellite Linked Navigation, anti-lock brakes, and cold weather comfort package (heated grips, seats, and back rests with individual rider and passenger controls). Honda uses individual wiring diagrams for each specific electrical systems or subsystem. For example, if the heated pillion backrest isn't receiving 12 volts when the control is turned to hot, and you want to find out why, it can take several pages of wiring diagrams to map out exactly the path that power takes from the battery to the control and to eventually the backrest. The diagram for the heated backrest will likely show you how power passes from the control to the heating element, but power to the controller might come from a relay located inside the fairing; consequently, a different wiring diagram might need to be consulted to determine how the relay receives power.

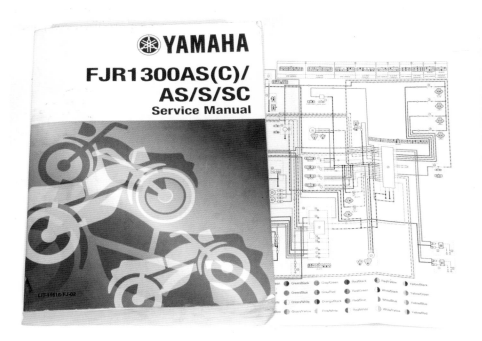

This wiring diagram for a Yamaha FJR1300 is in color to make it easier to identify individual wires. Unfortunately, only numbers are used instead of component labels, and a legend must be referred to often to make any sense of the diagram. In general, automobile wiring diagrams are much easier to read and interpret. Late-model Honda motorcycles are simpler to use than those from other powersports manufacturers—probably because they also make cars.

The secret to reading a particular wiring diagram is not found on the page or chart identifying all the electrical symbols used. While this information is certainly valuable, it does not teach you how to read a wiring diagram. The secret to deciphering a wiring diagram is to understand how a circuit and/or load device operates. If you keep in mind the "Three Things" (introduced in Chapter 1, Ohm's Law) necessary for all 12-volt DC circuits to operate (power, ground, and a load device), cracking the mystery of a complex wiring diagram is much easier.

Every load device (motors, bulbs, relays, solenoids, computers) requires a power source and ground return. In addition, load devices must be controlled. Some load devices are switched on or off via a power source, while others are controlled by switching the ground returns on or off. Load devices may also depend on other load devices in order to operate, and some produce signals used by solid state electronics that trigger other load devices as well. The process of figuring out how load devices are controlled must be determined by using a wiring diagram. This can get complicated, so to make it easier, we'll start out with some basic examples of circuit wiring diagrams and then we'll add layers of complexity as we go. Understanding how these diagrams relate to the circuits they depict will help you when reading more complex motorcycle wiring diagrams.

Figure 8-1 is a simple hypothetical diagram showing a passing lamp lighting circuit in both ON and OFF positions. The circuit consists of a 25-amp fuse (used to protect the circuit), a switch (located on a fairing panel of the bike), and two passing lamps. The red wires have 12 volts, the black wires are ground returns (0 volts), the purple wires represent load devices, and the yellow areas are intended to show the lights operating. With the panel switch in the OFF position (upper circuit), the power wire from the battery to the switch has 12 volts. When the panel switch is in the ON position (lower circuit), the wires going to both driving lights have power and the lights are on. The ground wires at each light are at 0 volts, because all of the available voltage is used by the lights.

Reading the wiring diagram illustrated in Figure 8-1 is easy for two reasons: (1) the passing lamp circuit has been isolated and is not shown as a subcircuit of any other part of the overall lighting system; (2) the wires and load devices are different colors—red for power, black for ground, and purple for load devices (the bulb filaments). Unfortunately, most wiring diagrams do not provide any of these advantages. Even late-model motorcycle diagrams may not isolate passing lights to this extent—more likely they will be part of the overall lighting system. Color, if used at all in a wiring diagram, is used solely for the purpose of identifying individual wires—not to indicate power and ground sides of a circuit. In addition, wiring diagrams will not show the differences between a circuit in on and off states.

Consequently, the circuit depicted in the sample wiring diagram illustrated in Figure 8-1 does not truly the reality of motorcycle wiring diagrams. It is too simplistic, and there is an inherent problem with the circuit's design. However, that design flaw simply solved by the addition of another component—a relay. Here's why: In its present state, the wires and fairing panel switch that control the passing lamps would have to be too heavy gauge to function realistically in a motorcycle in order to work reliably with the amount of current the lights require. These components are large and relatively expensive.

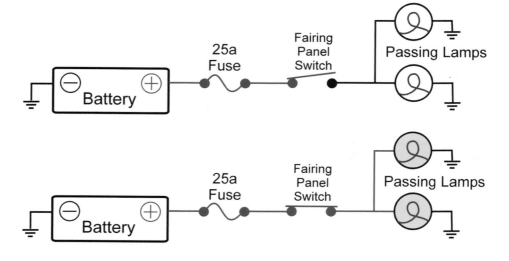

Fig 8-1—This multicolor wiring diagram shows the passing lamp circuit in both on and off conditions. Unfortunately, most manufacturers don't provide the luxury of color diagrams—they are typically black and white only. In addition, they don't usually show a circuit in both on and off states.

However, in a real motorcycle application, a relay would be used instead of the heavy-duty switch and heavy-gauge wires. The relay takes the place of the heavy-duty switch and provides the high-amperage connection between the passing lamps and the battery. A panel switch would still be part of the overall circuit, but now it only has to switch the relay on, instead of the passing lights (a much smaller amperage load—about 0.3 amps). As a result, the wires going to and from the switch, as well as the switch itself, no longer have to be heavy-duty because the relay, instead of the switch, is turning the lights on and off.

In Figure 8-2, a relay has been added to the passing lamp light circuit. The relay connects battery power directly to the passing lights. The relay is switched on and off via the fairing panel switch. Because the control coil inside the relay is low amperage (about 0.3 amps), the wires going to the dash switch and the switch itself don't have to be too heavy gauge, and small wires can be used. The relay contains two circuits: (1) A low-amperage circuit consisting of a single control coil, which when energized causes the relay's contact switch to close; and (2) A high-amperage circuit that acts as a switch to connect the passing lamps directly to the battery's positive terminal. The use of relays in motorcycles is common, so understanding how to figure out if one is working or not will help solve many electrical problems.

To better understand the passing lamp circuit in Figure 8-2, each subcircuit must be identified and then separated out from the larger overall circuit. In this particular diagram there are two separate circuits and control switches: (1) A passing light circuit and high-amperage relay contacts; and (2) A relay control coil circuit and a fairing panel switch. Each individual circuit requires power, a load device, and a ground return. In addition to these standard essential "Three Things," each circuit also has a control.

In this case, the panel switch controls a relay instead of directly controlling the driving lights—a much smaller electrical load. Consequently, the passing lamps are now connected to the battery via contact points inside the relay instead of directly through the panel switch. As a result, the wires going to and from the panel control switch for the passing lamps can now be very small since they will now only carry about 0.3 amps—the amount of energy required to power the relay's control coil. By contrast, the contact switch inside the relay now carries the high-amperage load needed to power the driving lights.

When the panel switch is turned to the ON position, it connects a ground to the relay's control coil (Terminal 4 on the relay in Figure 8-2). The control coil receives power directly from the battery. Since the control coil is now on (it has power and a ground), it develops a magnetic field, which in turn pulls the high-amperage relay contact switch down, causing relay Terminals 1 and 3 to connect. With Terminals 1 and 3 connected, the passing lamps are able to receive battery power and turn on.

To better understand how the relay operates, an examination of the voltage present on the relay's terminals is necessary, with the passing lamp circuit in both an off and on state. Unfortunately, this diagram is typical of real wiring diagrams, in that the voltage values for each wire and relay terminal number must be imagined for the on state. The diagram displayed in Figure 8-2 does not show the same circuit in its on state. This makes using Figure 8-2 a little more challenging than the diagram in Figure 8-1. This wiring diagram is pretty typical of those distributed by motorcycle manufacturers (with the exception of the added feature of colored wires indicating power and ground).

Referencing Figure 8-2 as a working example of a wiring diagram, and using a voltmeter to measure voltage levels at various points in the diagram, the following is the method that would be used to obtain the electrical values present in the circuit. With the fairing panel switch in the OFF, or open, position, voltage at the various relay terminals would be as follows when measured using a voltmeter:

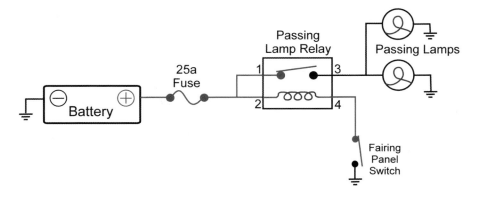

Fig 8-2—A relay has been added to the passing lamp circuit. The relay now controls the high-amperage load that the passing lights need in order to operate (instead of the switch and wires depicted in Figure 8-1). The addition of a relay allows for the use of smaller gauge wires on the panel switch, because it is now only controlling the relay instead of directly controlling the lights. In fact, the switch itself can be made smaller still; as with this design, it doesn't have to contend with a high electrical load any more.

Relays used on motorcycles come in all shapes and sizes, but they all basically operate the same. Some late-model bikes use as many as 20 relays or more.

- Terminals 1, 2, and 4 all have 12 volts.
- Terminal 3 has 0 volts (ground).
- Terminal 4 has 12 volts, because the panel switch is open (not connected).

However, when the panel switch for the passing lamps is in the ON (closed) position, the voltage readings at the same relay terminals change as follows:
- Terminals 1, 2, and 4 remain unchanged at 12 volts.
- Terminal 3 now reads 12 volts (since the passing lamps are on).
- Terminal 4 is now at 0 volts instead of 12, because it is now acting as a ground return for the relay's control coil circuit.

Continuing to reference Figure 8-2 as a hypothetical example of a wiring diagram, and using a voltmeter to solve a typical electrical problem, assume the problem is that the passing lamps don't work. The following sequence of steps should be performed to discover the cause of this problem.

1. With the panel switch in the OFF position, relay Terminals 1 and 2 should each have 12 volts. These readings confirm the 25-amp fuse is good, as well as the associated wires going to the relay.

2. Voltage at relay Terminal 3 should be at 0 volts. (No voltage is expected at Terminal 3 because the panel switch is in the OFF position.)

3. Relay Terminal 4 is a different matter. This terminal should have a reading of 12 volts when the panel switch is in the OFF position, as it is connected directly to the battery through the relay control coil. Instead, Terminal 4 has a reading of 0 volts. This indicates the relay

control coil is open (broken) because there is battery voltage at Terminal 2.

4. Using a jumper wire, connect relay Terminals 1 and 3, causing the passing lights to come on. This connection serves to bypass the relay completely, thus removing it from the circuit. As a result, the passing lights come on. This confirms the power wire from the relay to the lights is okay, and the passing lights ground wire is good as well.

5. The last step is to verify if the panel switch is connected and working. When the red (positive) voltmeter lead is connected to relay Terminal 2, it should have a reading of 12 volts. Then connect the negative lead to relay Terminal 4. Once the switch is moved to the ON position, the meter should display a reading of 12 volts, indicating the switch is good and connected to ground.

As components are added to the imaginary electrical system, the wiring diagram in Figure 8-2 is actually starting to look more like a typical real-life wiring diagram (like those found in a motorcycle service manual).

In Figure 8-2, the addition of a relay solved the design problem of having to use large-gauge wires and a heavy-duty switch in the passing lamp lighting circuit. However, the diagram in Figure 8-2 still has a design flaw. There is no protection against the rider inadvertently leaving the passing lamps on by mistake.

The wiring diagram in Figure 8-3 shows how the addition of another relay (controlled by the motorcycle's ignition switch) will prevent the passing lights from being left on by mistake. The purpose of Relay 1 is to connect power to Relay 2 (the same original relay in Figure 8-2). Relay 2 can only receive 12 volts when the ignition key is in the ACCY (accessory) or RUN positions. If the key is in the LOCK or OFF positions, or removed from the ignition completely, no power is available at Relay 2. This prevents the driving lights from being left on, even if the fairing panel switch is left on.

With new features in our circuit design, here is how the circuit now operates: Pass lamp Relay 2 operates in the same manner as the original relay in the previous wiring diagram in Figure 8-2. As long as it has power, the passing lights can be switched on or off via the panel switch. The ignition switch controls Relay 1. With the ignition switch in the ACCY or RUN positions, Terminal 2 of Relay 1 has power. Terminal 4 of the same relay is a constant ground, and with power at Terminal 2, the relay's high-amperage

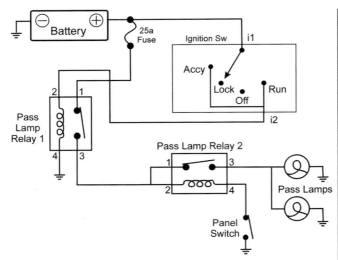

Fig 8-3—Two relays are used in this passing lamp lighting circuit. Relay 1 prevents the passing lamps from staying on even if the dash switch is left on and the ignition switch is in the Lock or OFF position, or even if the key is removed.

contact switch closes. This action connects Terminals 1 and 3 together, sending power to Relay 2. Terminal 1 on Relay 1 receives power directly from the battery via a 25-amp fuse. Finally, Terminal 3 of this same relay is connected to Terminals 1 and 2 on Relay 2, and, as mentioned earlier, this relay operates in the same exact manner as the original relay in Figure 8-2.

The sample wiring diagram in Figure 8-3 is starting to look more like a typical wiring diagram found in a motorcycle service manual (with the exception, again, that none of the wire colors would be used to identify the specific wires shown). To diagnose a problem within this circuit that could result in nonoperational passing lamps, follow the flow of power from the battery to the passing lights.

The following terminals should be hot with the ignition key in the RUN position and the panel switch in the OFF position:

- i1 and i2 (ignition switch).
- Terminals 1, 2, and 3 of driving light Relay 1.
- Terminals 1, 2, and 4 of driving light Relay 2. (All should produce a voltmeter reading of 12 volts.)

When the panel switch is turned to the ON position, the following readings should occur:

- Terminal 4 of Relay 2 should read 0 volts.
- Terminal 3 of Relay 2 should be hot (12 volts).

If the lights still don't operate, there is a possibility of a break in the wire leading from Terminal 3 of Relay 2 to the passing lights, or perhaps the bulbs are burned out, or the ground wire for both lights is broken.

Figure 8-4 is a fairly typical wiring diagram for a motorcycle horn circuit. This is an example of a wiring diagram that has been separated or broken down by systems. In addition, all wires are identified by wire color.

It will take several steps to read this wiring diagram and analyze how the horn circuit works:

1. Starting at the top left portion of the diagram, Fuse F9 is a 15-amp fuse that powers one-half of the horn relay on a red/black wire. The diagram provides additional information about Fuse F9, including its condition (Hot-At-All-Times) and its location (Front Power Distribution Box). If the horns don't work and Fuse F9 isn't receiving power, another diagram would have to be consulted in order to determine the power source for the Front Power Distribution Box.

2. Power for the horn relay control coil comes from the ignition switch via a violet wire. Again, a separate diagram would have to be examined if there was no power present on the violet wire from the ignition switch to the relay. With the key in the RUN, or ACCY positions, horn relay Terminals 6, 8, and 10 should all have 12 volts.

3. The horn switch in this diagram acts as a ground for Terminal 10 of the horn relay via a brown/red wire. When this wire makes contact with a ground, the relay's contacts close, thereby connecting Terminals 6 and 7 and completing the horn circuit.

4. If both horns in the diagram are not working, and you want to bypass the horn relay as a means of eliminating it as the source of an electrical problem, a jumper wire connected between relay Terminal 6 (red/black wire) and Terminal 7 (violet/blue wire) will make them operate—just be sure to hold your hands over your ears to prevent hearing loss!

The most effective way to learn how to read and use a wiring diagram is to practice doing it. With that in mind, the next several wiring diagrams are followed by a series of questions for you to answer. Write your answers on a piece of paper as you look at each diagram. The correct answers to the questions and their analysis can be found at the end of this chapter. You may want to refer back to chapters on charging, ignition, or electronic fuel injection when answering these questions. The questions become progressively more difficult for each wiring diagram. Also, when taking tests in school, some of your teachers probably told you, "There are no trick questions." This is not the case here, as there are a few trick questions designed to make you think! Good luck!

Figure 8-5 (on page 124) is a wiring diagram for an off-road motorcycle. This bike does not use a battery, but instead uses a magneto as a power source for the ignition and lighting systems. The only load devices are a headlight, taillight, and ignition coil. The magneto has two pairs of wires. Each pair connects to a charging coil (not visible in the diagram). One charge coil powers the CDI ignition unit and the other is used for the lighting circuit. The head and taillight can be switched on or off via the lighting switch. The regulator keeps voltage at 12 volts for the lights. The ignition system uses a pickup coil (next to the magneto) to provide an rpm signal to the CDI unit. The CDI unit controls the ignition coil that fires the spark plug. The Engine Stop Button turns off the CDI unit to shut the engine off. Wire colors are listed at the bottom of the diagram and each wire is identified as to its color. Wires marked with two sets of letters have a solid color with a stripe. For example, if a wire's colors are G/W, the wire is green with a white stripe; BK/LB is black with a light blue stripe. Wires that are only one color are marked with one set of letters.

By answering the questions below and reviewing the analysis that follows at the end of the chapter, you will increase your ability to read and understand wiring diagrams.

1. With the engine running, the headlight is working but the taillight is out. How would you determine what is causing the problem?

2. The lighting system doesn't operate, but the engine runs. Using a voltmeter, how would you check the lighting switch? Also, how would you determine if the magneto is functioning?

3. The engine won't start, and there is no spark at the spark plug. The ignition coil has been replaced so assume it's good. How would you check for power to the CDI unit and an rpm signal?

4. In Question 3 the magneto is working as it should, but the ignition coil still won't produce a spark at the spark plug. The only component left to replace is the CDI unit. A new one costs $482. Before replacing it, make sure all the wires going to the CDI unit have the correct readings. What are the correct readings on each wire and how would you check each of them?

As you can see, the wiring diagram for this motorcycle (Figure 8-6 on page 125) is more complex than the off-road bike in the previous wiring diagram and is pretty typical of late 1990s motorcycles. Later model motorcycles sometimes require more than one page to depict all electrical circuits. This bike is carbureted but has electronic ignition that uses a throttle position sensor, in addition to engine rpm, to calculate ignition timing. A one-piece alternator with internal voltage regulator is used for the charging system. Five fuses are used to distribute power to various components. There is only one relay and it's used for the side stand switch. There

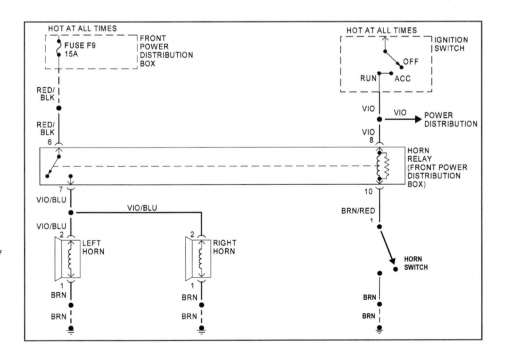

Fig 8-4—This wiring diagram isolates a typical horn circuit. To locate the source of power to the ignition switch and front power distribution box, another diagram would have to be consulted. The diagram also provides locations for the fuse and horn relay.

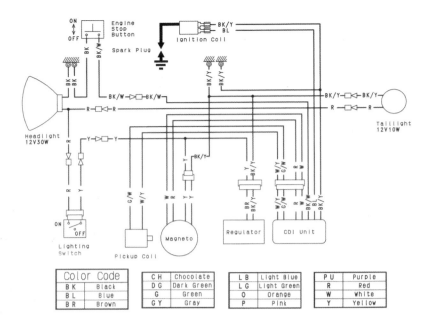

Color Code		C H	Chocolate		L B	Light Blue		P U	Purple
B K	Black	D G	Dark Green		L G	Light Green		R	Red
B L	Blue	G	Green		O	Orange		W	White
B R	Brown	G Y	Gray		P	Pink		Y	Yellow

Fig 8-5—This wiring diagram is typical of off-road motorcycles that don't use a battery as a power source. Instead, a magneto supplies power to the ignition and lighting systems.

is an interlock feature that prevents the engine from starting unless the clutch is pulled in and the side stand is up. Lighting controls are standard except that there is a European-style flash-to-pass switch on the left handle bar control. Instruments are standard and include a speedometer, tachometer, fuel gauge, and indicators for neutral, high beam, and turn signals. Wire colors are indicated by letters. Answering the following wiring diagram related questions will help you apply your wiring diagram reading skills to more complex motorcycles. Good luck again!

1. All four instrument lights are out when the key is in the ON position. The oil pressure light (marked with an "O") works. What fuse powers the instrument lights and what is the wire color at the ignition switch that provides power to the instrument lights?

2. How does the oil pressure warning light work? (The light is located in the tachometer and marked "O.") What is the power source? What is the ground return? What would be the problem if it were stuck on all the time?

3. While trying to diagnose a no-spark problem, you have determined that there is no power at either of the ignition coils (orange/white wires) when the ignition switch is in the ON position. Trace the path that power from the battery takes to get to the ignition coils. What wires (colors) for the fuses/switch/relays are used?

Figure 8-7 (on page 126) is a fuel-injected two-cylinder motorcycle. As you can see, there are no labels used on the wiring diagram, but instead a numbering system is used to identify electrical components, connectors, buttons, switches, and relays. While this makes the diagram less cluttered, it adds another step in reading the diagram, as a legend has to be consulted to make sense of what you're looking at. The ECM is located at the top of the diagram and each terminal, or pin, is numbered. Because the ECM is complex, no circuits are shown in the diagram to indicate its inner workings. The same is true for the speedometer (No. 14). The two fuel injectors (No. 23 and 24) are located at the bottom center of the diagram. This motorcycle uses two spark plugs per cylinder and two dual plug coils (No. 5, top left). Various sensors are scattered through the diagram. Figure 8-8 is the legend for Figure 8-7, where all the components are identified by name and number. Understanding this typical EFI wiring diagram will help you solve EFI related problems. Have fun figuring out the answers to the questions.

1. This EFI system uses two crankshaft sensors. Both sensors are AC pickup coil types of speed sensors. How could you check the operation of both sensors at the ECM? You may want to refer back to Chapter 6, Ignition Systems, to review how these sensors operate.

2. What is each of the four wires at the EFI relay for? Where do they go and how is the relay controlled? What components does the relay provide power to?

3. The motorcycle has no spark. There is power to both ignition coils. When you connect a test light across the coil's primary terminals, there is no primary switching when the engine is cranked over. Both crank sensors produce AC voltage at the ECM—so they are good. Because the

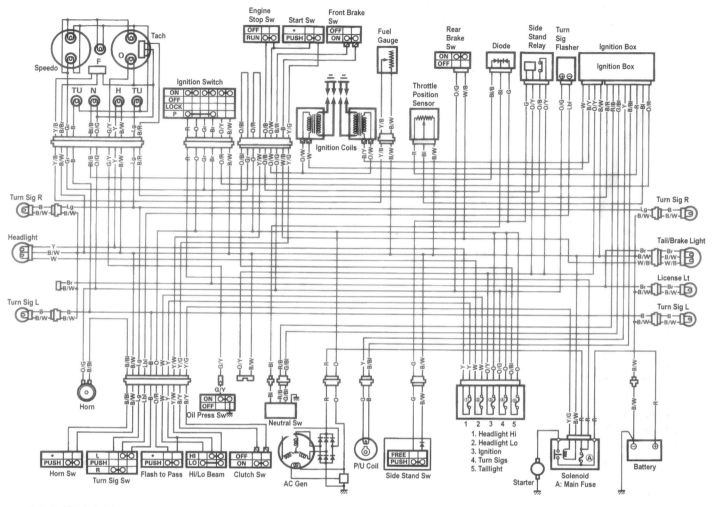

Fig 8-6—This typical Japanese wiring diagram shows a wiring diagram for a complete carbureted motorcycle. The diagram is fairly easy to read, which is, unfortunately, not always the case. Some manufacturers don't label components, but instead use numbers, and the diagrams are so small you need a microscope to actually read one.

ECM not only operates the fuel injectors but also acts as the ignition module, it may be bad. A new one costs—well, suffice it to say it's a lot. Just like the off-road bike in Figure 8-5, the dealer can simply plug in a new ECM and see if that fixes the problem. You don't have that luxury. Before replacing the ECM make sure it has all the power and ground inputs it needs to work. What ECM pins should you check to find all the power and grounds?

ANSWERS TO
WIRING DIAGRAM QUESTIONS

ANSWERS TO QUESTIONS PERTAINING TO THE WIRING DIAGRAM IN FIGURE 8-5.

1. The taillight needs "Three Things" to operate: power, ground, and a functioning load device (a good bulb). If you don't know what I'm referring to, go back to Chapter 1. The black with yellow striped wire is the ground for the taillight. The red wire is power (12 volts), and the bulb is the load device. Take the bulb out and see if the filament is connected—after all, this is an off-road bike and subject to lots of vibration and/or crashing, and the bulb may simply be no good.

If the bulb looks okay, connect the leads of a voltmeter to the two wires going to the taillight. It should read 12 volts with the engine running—instead, it reads zero. One or both of the wires at the taillight may be broken. Because the headlight works, you know the magneto is producing 12 volts. Leave the black voltmeter lead connected to the black/yellow striped wire, and connect the red meter lead to the red wire that goes to the taillight at the headlight. If the voltmeter reads 12 volts, then the black/yellow wire at the taillight is a good ground. The only possibility left is a break in the red power wire going to the taillight.

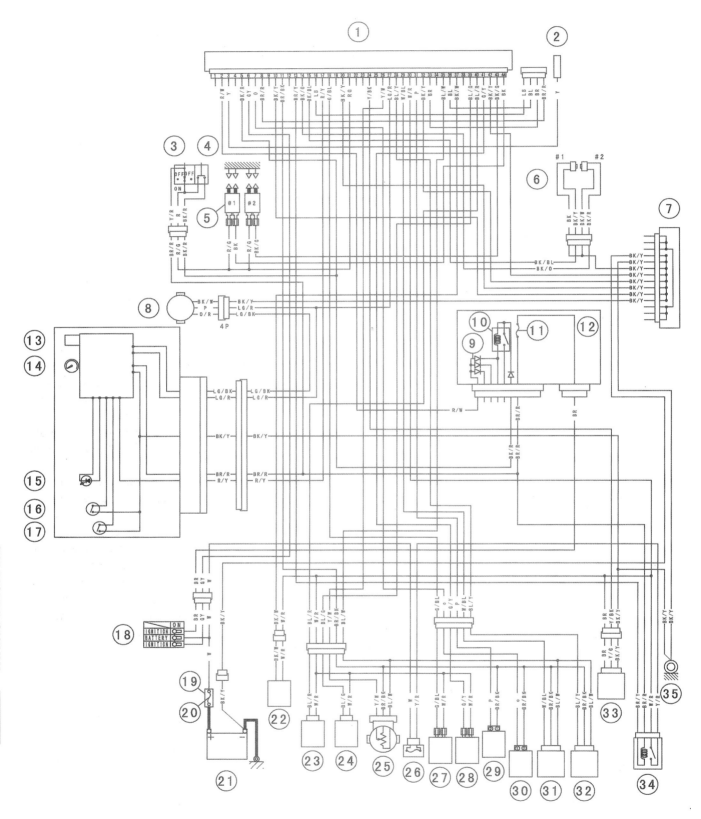

Fig 8-7—This diagram is of an electronic fuel-injected motorcycle. Some manufacturers don't place labels on their diagrams, but instead use numbers. This adds another step in reading and interpreting this type of wiring diagram, as each component has to be identified separately.

EFI Wiring Diagram Legend

Number	Component	Number	Component	Number	Component
1	ECM	13	Instruments	25	TPS
2	Diag Terminal	14	Speedometer	26	EFI Fuse
3	Eng Stop Sw	15	Check Eng Light	27	ISC Valve
4	Start Button	16	Mode Sw	28	ISC Valve
5	Ignition Coils	17	Reste Sw	29	Air Temp Sen
6	Crank Sensor	18	Ignition Switch	30	Eng Temp Sen
7	Connector	19	Starter Relay	31	MAP
8	Road Speed Sen	20	Main Fuse	32	BARO
9	Interlock Diodes	21	Battery	33	Crash Sensor
10	Start Relay	22	Fuel Pump	34	EFI Relay
11	Ignition Fuse	23	Injector	35	Ground
12	Junction Bx	24	Injector		

Fig 8-8—This is the legend for figure 8-7. All components on the wiring diagram are numbered and identified here.

2. To check the lighting switch, first start the engine. Because this motorcycle has no battery, the magneto must be turning for power to be present in the lighting circuit. Connect the black lead of a voltmeter to ground (the engine case is a good place). Turn the lighting switch to the ON position and probe both the red and yellow wires at the switch. If there is no voltage on either, the magneto should be checked next.

Unplug the connector at the magneto with the two yellow wires going to it. Connect both leads from a voltmeter directly to the magneto. Switch the voltmeter to read AC volts. With the engine running the AC voltage reading should go up (at least 30 volts AC) when you rev the engine. Your meter reading is 0, meaning the charging coil inside the magneto for the lighting circuit is open or shorted to ground. Depending on the manufacturer, both charging coils may have to be replaced. You could look up the coil's resistance in a service manual, but a check for AC voltage is a better way to see if it's functioning.

3. The charging coil that powers the CDI unit can be tested in the same manner as the charge coil that powers the lighting system (see the answer to Question 2). When your voltmeter is connected to the white and red wires at the magneto, you get an AC voltage reading when you kick the engine over with the kick starter.

To check for an rpm signal at the pickup coil, back probe the green/white striped wire and the white/yellow striped wire at the pickup coil with a voltmeter. Kick the engine over using the kick starter and watch the voltmeter. If you get no AC voltage reading, the pickup coil is probably open or shorted to ground. You can also check the pickup coil using an ohmmeter. A service manual will provide you with resistance specifications. An AC voltage check is a better way to test the pickup coil as it check to see if the pickup coil is actually producing voltage.

4. At this point you could cough up $482 to buy a new CDI unit and try it. That's what a dealer would do, but they get to try it for free, and if it doesn't solve the problem they can look for a bad wire. Take a good look at the 100-cc bike that you've owned for five years—think about how many times it's been ridden off a cliff or dumped in a river. You might determine that the whole motorcycle isn't worth $482, so checking the wires seems like a better idea.

Starting at the left of the CDI unit, the brown and black/yellow striped wires (from the pickup coil) should have AC voltage when you kick the engine over. They do, as does the red and white wires coming from the magneto charging coil. The black/white striped wire goes to the engine stop switch on the handle bar. Check it for continuity to ground. Even with the engine stop switch in the ON position, the wire is connected to ground. Cut the wire at the CDI unit, kick the engine, and it fires right up. Problem solved—you just have to find where the engine stop switch wire is shorted to ground.

ANSWERS TO QUESTIONS PERTAINING TO THE WIRING DIAGRAM IN FIGURE 8-6.

1. The taillight fuse (No. 5) powers the instrument lights. The wire from the fuse is orange/blue. At the connector located to the right of the ignition switch, the wire changes to green where it goes to the ignition switch. From there it passes through a connector (below the instrument cluster) where it powers the four instrument bulbs.

2. The oil pressure light gets power from the orange/green wire going to the instrument cluster. This is

127

the same wire that also powers the neutral light, tach, and fuel gauge. The orange/green wire goes from the instrument cluster to fuse No. 4, the turn signal fuse. The oil pressure light's ground is the green/yellow wire.

When the engine is off but the ignition switch is on, the oil pressure switch (located at near the bottom left of the diagram) grounds the green/yellow wire to turn on the oil pressure light. When the engine starts, oil pressure opens the oil pressure switch, and the warning light goes out. If the oil pressure light stays on all the time (and the engine has oil pressure), either the oil pressure switch is bad (always closed) or there is a short to ground in the green/yellow wire causing the oil pressure light to be on all the time.

3. Starting at the battery positive terminal, power follows the red wire to the starter solenoid, where it goes through the main fuse. From the fuse power comes out of the solenoid on the red wire that goes to the ignition switch (not the one going to the alternator). When the ignition switch is in the ON position, all the wires at the ignition switch have 12 volts.

That was the easy part. There are now six wires coming out of the ignition switch, all with power. Rather than trace each one, go to the orange/white wire at the ignition coils and work backward to the ignition switch. From the coils, the orange/white wire goes to the engine stop switch. The Run position on the stop switch is an orange/blue wire that goes to the side stand relay (top right of the diagram). The high-amperage contacts inside the relay pass power to the orange/yellow wire where it goes to the No. 3 ignition fuse. Notice that the orange/yellow wire branches out in several directions. This is a clue that this is a power wire that feeds other components/circuits in the diagram. From the ignition fuse (No. 3), the wire color is orange. This wire goes back to the ignition switch and other locations.

The fastest way to diagnose no power at the ignition coils would be to check the ignition fuse (No. 3) first. If the fuse has no power, the orange ignition switch wire should be checked next, followed by the orange/blue wire at the side stand relay.

ANSWERS TO QUESTIONS PERTAINING TO THE WIRING DIAGRAM IN FIGURE 8-7.

1. Checking the crankshaft sensors on this motorcycle at the ECM is less time consuming than taking the engine case off (where the sensors are located) or trying to get to the wiring harness. The crank sensors (No. 6) each have two wires. One from each sensor goes to the connector (No. 7). The connector provides a ground for the crank sensors and other components (No. 35). The other crank sensor wires go to the ECM on Pin 15, a black/blue wire, and Pin 14, a black/orange wire. Notice that the crank sensor wires change colors at the crank sensor connector.

By unplugging the ECM and connecting a digital voltmeter to ground and Pin 14 on the ECM wiring harness, one of the crank sensors can be tested. The voltmeter should be set to read AC volts. When the engine is cranked over, the meter should indicate AC voltage to verify that the sensor is operating. ECM wiring harness Pin 15 would be tested in the same manner for the other crank sensor. Most service manuals provide crank sensor resistance values and sometimes AC voltage specifications.

2. The wires at the EFI relay, No. 34, located at bottom right of the diagram, are brown/yellow (relay control coil); brown/red (relay control coil); white/red (high-amperage contacts); and yellow/red (also high-amperage contacts).

To figure out how the relay is controlled (turned off/on), trace the relay control coil wires. Power for the relay's control coil is on the brown/red wire that comes from the ignition fuse (No. 11) that receives power from the ignition switch (No. 18). To control the relay, the brown/yellow wire receives a ground signal from Pin 13 on the ECM.

The yellow/red wire at the EFI relay is the power wire, which the relay switches on and off. This wire comes from the EFI fuse (No. 26). At the fuse, this wire is white and goes directly to the main fuse (No. 20) located at the battery (No. 21). The EFI relay provides power to the fuel pump, fuel injectors, ECM (pin 24), and ISC valves on the white/red wire.

3. All powers and grounds to the ECM should be checked with the ECM plugged in and the ignition key on. Power to the ECM is on Pin 30 (white/red wire from the ECM relay); Pin 21 (red/green wire) receives power from the engine stop switch (No. 3), which in turn receives power from the ignition fuse (No. 11). Pin 5 should have power when the starter is cranking (No. 10). Pin 6 comes from the ignition switch (No. 18). Pin 11 is the 5-volt reference to some of the sensors and is supplied power by the ECM. ECM grounds are pins 10, 20, 32, and 42, which are all grounds at connecter No. 7. Connector No. 7 is connected at No. 35 and the battery negative terminal.

All the powers and grounds are good and the crank sensors are working, the only thing left as the source of the problem is the ECM. ECM replacement is the only solution to fix the no-spark problem in this scenario.

CHAPTER 9
TROUBLESHOOTING ELECTRICAL SYSTEMS

LOGIC? WHAT LOGIC?

Troubleshooting any complex problem requires a logical approach. While this might seem self-evident, many power sports technicians and home mechanics just don't have a well-thought-out plan of attack when it comes to electrical problems. Oftentimes, they simply start disassembling or replacing components, all the while keeping their fingers crossed and hoping for the best. However, if they would only take the time to carefully analyze an electrical problem and outline the steps required to solve it, they would find that most electrical problems are really pretty basic. (As you will find after reading this book!)

It's helpful to have a routine procedure to follow when troubleshooting electrical problems. A good practice is to do the easiest and fastest electrical tests first. In general, this approach should provide the most information with the least amount of effort. Typically, this practice will either solve the problem or at least narrow down its location. Without a plan, testing wrong circuits and not understanding multimeter readings will only lead to frustration and wasted time.

Even though you can't see current flowing in a circuit, you can use all of your senses to troubleshoot electrical problems. Fortunately, you can observe the effects of a circuit. For example, lights illuminate, motors spin, relays "click," wires get "hot" when amperage flows, and so forth. Touch, sound, and sight testing methods should all be used simultaneously in conjunction with the use of electrical test equipment.

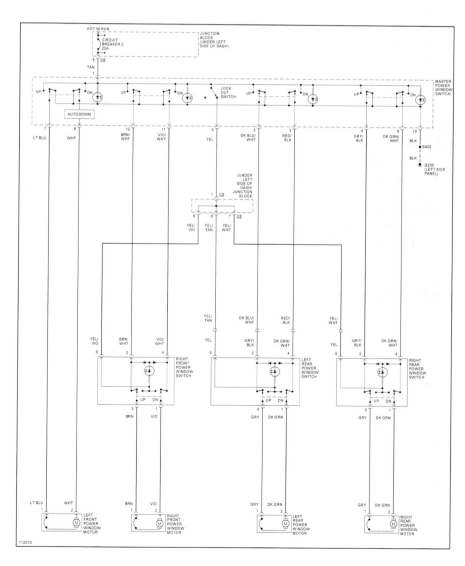

Fig 9-1—Manufacturers' wiring diagrams are one of the best electrical tools for understanding the nature of any electrical problem.

Courtesy Mitchell 1

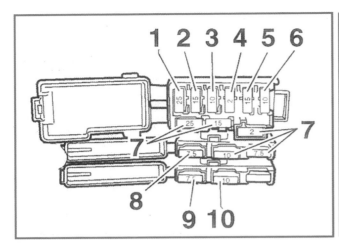

Fuse Number	What's It For
1	Radio Fuse
2	Rad Fan Fuse
3	Clock Fuse
4	Heated Seat Fuse
5	Ignition Fuse
6	Turn Signal Fuse
7	ABS Control Unit
8	Tail/Running Lights
9	Hazard Fuse
10	Charging Fuse

Fig 9-2 —Fuse locations are provided in most owner's or service manuals. Even though fuses are labeled as to what they provide power to, additional electrical components may also be powered by the same fuse but not listed. Check a wiring diagram to see exactly what each fuse is protecting.

In addition to using all of your senses (and your wits, if you haven't lost them by now), other clues undoubtedly exist about the nature of a particular problem and should be explored. First, determine the conditions under which the electrical problem occurs. Does heat or cold affect the problem? Is it intermittent or does it only happen under specific operating conditions? Did it occur right after an aftermarket accessory was installed or after someone worked on the motorcycle? Evaluate the problem(s) to see if any other circuits or components are, or might be, affected. Test other related circuits for proper operation, since there may be more than one thing wrong. Use the owner's manual and service manuals as essential reference materials—these can be invaluable for locating fuses and identifying wiring harnesses, connectors, junction blocks, and other electrical components located on the same problem circuit. However, the most valuable information about electrical problems can be found on the vehicle's wiring diagram and owner's manual. These two tools will save you loads of time and provide you with possible test points within the problem circuit.

"THE STARTER THAT DOESN'T": A CASE STUDY

Consider the following hypothetical scenario: Your long-time friend calls to say you his motorcycle won't start. For the past month the starter has cranked slowly, and now it won't turn the engine over at all. Your friend wants to buy a new battery, but you tell him to wait until you can check it out. Now is as good a time as any to put your diagnostic skills to the test, so you ride over to inspect the bike.

The first step to solving this, or any, electrical problem is to verify the complaint. Then determine if anything else might be wrong. In this hypothetical case, when you try to crank the engine, nothing happens. In addition, no instrument lights come on when the ignition key is in the RUN position. In fact, nothing seems to be working. Before any testing is performed, the battery needs to be checked. Your friend says he left the battery on a charger overnight, so it ought to be charged. And he's right. After connecting your DVOM directly to the battery, an open circuit battery voltage is displayed—12.8 volts. This indicates the battery is indeed 100 percent charged—good enough to continue battery testing. Just to be sure, you connect a hand-held battery tester to the battery, and after holding the load switch for 3 seconds, voltage remains above 10 volts, indicating the battery is, in fact, good. So the problem with the bike isn't the battery. Now, it's time to pick up your test light.

Given that the battery is charged and tested, the next step is to see how far the voltage is traveling within the starter circuit. Using a test light is a quick and easy way to

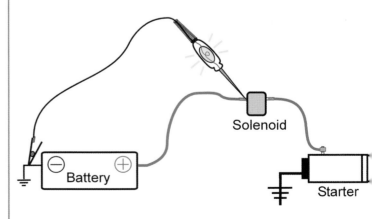

Fig 9-3—When you aren't concerned with how much voltage is present in a circuit, a test light is a quick and easy way to verify that power exists at various points.

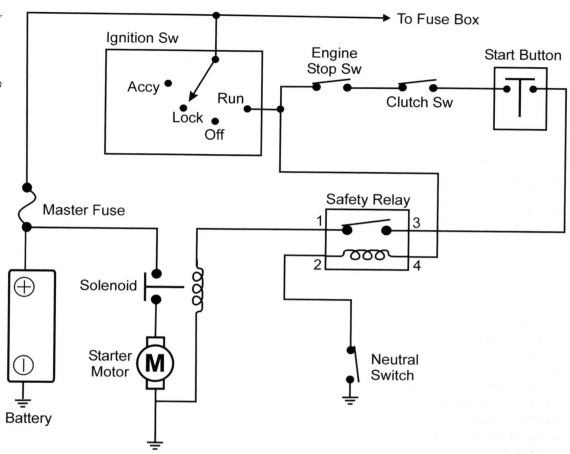

Fig 9-4—This starter circuit uses a safety relay to prevent the engine from starting with the transmission in gear. In addition, the engine stop switch and clutch switch both have to be closed before the start button will crank the starter motor over.

To Fuse Box

Ignition Sw

Accy   Run

Lock   Off

Engine Stop Sw

Clutch Sw

Start Button

Master Fuse

Safety Relay

1   3

2   4

Solenoid

Starter Motor (M)

Neutral Switch

Battery

visually confirm there is voltage at the starter solenoid. Be sure to always check your test light *before* testing to make sure the bulb is lighting. With the test light's alligator clip connected to battery ground, touch the test light probe to the positive battery terminal. The test light should light up. (Don't spend hours testing wires for power, only to find out later the bulb in your test light is burned out.) You connect your test light as shown in Figure 9-3. The test light lights up when touched onto the starter solenoid's battery terminal, confirming there is voltage at the starter solenoid.

The next step is to find out where the voltage is supposed to be and where it's missing—it's time to take a look at a wiring diagram.

Wiring diagrams show all of the components of a circuit and how they are connected within the circuit, thereby providing an overview and allowing identification of the possible areas where problems might exist. The wiring diagram in Figure 9-4 shows 11 potential trouble spots: (1) battery, (2) starter, (3) solenoid, (4) master fuse, (5) ignition switch, (6) safety relay, (7) engine stop switch, (8) clutch switch, (9) start button, (10) neutral switch, and (11) the wires connecting all of the components together.

The wiring diagram in Figure 9-4 shows a master fuse connected directly to the battery's positive terminal. From here, power goes to the ignition switch. A good rule of thumb for electrical testing is to test the most accessible component(s) first. The ignition switch is in a tank panel, and will have to be removed before access to the wires at the switch can be gained. However, the master fuse is located in a fairing panel that's easy to get to—so we'll start testing there. Since you only want to know if voltage is present, continue to use a grounded test light to check for power. Touching the test light probe to the connector on the battery side of the fuse makes it light up. However, when the probe is touched to the other side of the fuse, the light doesn't come on, indicating an open or burned master fuse (see page 132, Figure 9-5). Problem solved? Maybe.

After replacing the master fuse, recheck it using the test light. Uh oh, the new master fuse melted even before the ignition switch was turned to the ON position. Since the ignition switch is off and nothing else on the motorcycle is turned on, the new master fuse must have melted from a direct short-circuit to ground, located somewhere on one of the circuits it protects. The circuit's power wire,

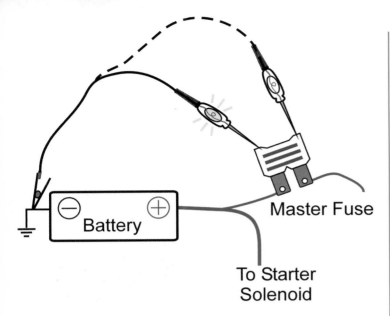

Battery

Master Fuse

To Starter
Solenoid

Above: *Fig 9-5—A grounded test light shows the master fuse is open (burned). Because this fuse powers everything on the motorcycle except the starter motor, it may be the cause of our hypothetical problem.*

Below: *Fig 9-6—A resetting circuit breaker or turn signal flasher unit both make good short finders. The breaker takes the place of the master fuse and will cycle off and on as long as a short to ground exists. As the circuit breaker clicks on and off, a compass can be used to sense the magnetic pulse in the circuit. By moving the compass along the wiring harness, the short can be located.*

protected by the master fuse, may have worn insulation, or have become pinched and its copper strands of wire have come into contact with ground—probably on the frame or engine case. As a result, the next step in the discovery process is to find out exactly where the physical problem with the shorted wire is located.

To find out which wire or circuit in our example has shorted to ground, the open circuit at the melted master fuse needs to be temporarily reconnected. This can be accomplished by using a short finder, as discussed in Chapter 3, Electronic Testing Tools. A simple short finder can be made using a resettable circuit breaker or a turn signal flasher. The short finder takes the place of the master fuse, cycling on and off as it heats and cools. A turn signal flasher is actually easier to use for this purpose, since it makes a loud click as it turns on and off. In order to narrow down the problem, start by unplugging every connector that is part of the circuit powered by the master fuse. If unplugging one circuit stops the short finder from cycling or clicking, that is the section of wire that has shorted to ground. As shown in the wiring diagram in Figure 9-4, the master fuse supplies power to the ignition switch and the fuse box. After disconnecting the wiring harness at the ignition switch and fuse box, the short finder keeps cycling (or clicking) on and off. This means the short still exists. It also means the wires going to the ignition switch or fuse

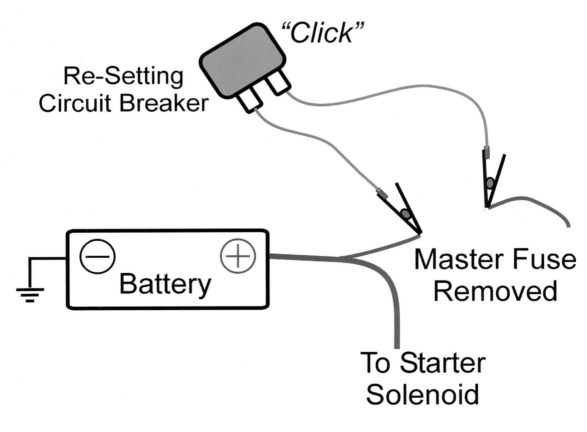

"Click"

Re-Setting
Circuit Breaker

Battery

Master Fuse
Removed

To Starter
Solenoid

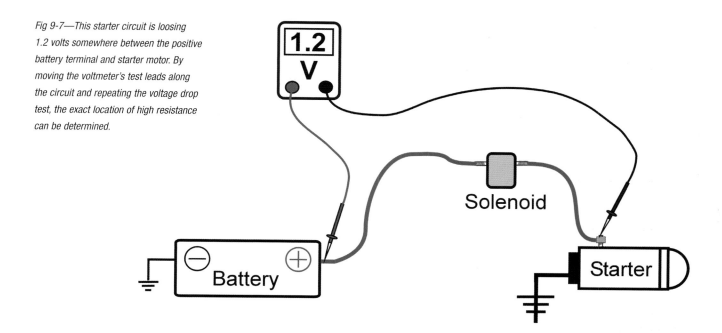

Fig 9-7—This starter circuit is loosing 1.2 volts somewhere between the positive battery terminal and starter motor. By moving the voltmeter's test leads along the circuit and repeating the voltage drop test, the exact location of high resistance can be determined.

box are not causing the short. This only leaves the wires going from the battery's positive terminal (located under the seat) to the master fuse in the fairing as the possible location of the short to ground.

After taking a closer look at the wires near the master fuse, you notice some nonfactory wires disappearing inside

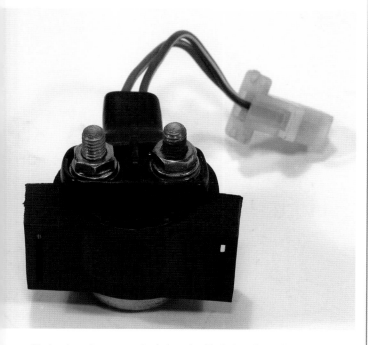

Most motorcycles use remote starter solenoids that can be easily checked for high resistance using a voltage drop test. The contacts inside the solenoid should not exceed a drop of 0.2 volts during starter cranking. Courtesy Twigg Cycles

the fairing. After asking your friend what they are for, he tells you he had a 12-volt ice cream maker installed in his trunk several weeks ago. He said he was tired of programming all the Tasty Freeze locations into his GPS, hence the ice cream maker. Wires that are not original to a vehicle are always suspect as the cause of electrical problems, since you never know how much skill or care was taken during their installation. After pulling the harness partially out of the fairing, a purple (nonfactory) wire is revealed; it has been pinched against the frame and there is a section of bare wire where the insulation has worn off from rubbing against a mounting bolt. After repairing the broken section of wire, and replacing the master fuse again, the instrument lights light up when the ignition switch is turned on and the engine starts and runs. Problem solved? Perhaps—well, almost.

Unfortunately, the engine still cranks very slowly. Slow engine-cranking speed was one of the complaints your friend had, along with the no start condition. There are three common problems that typically cause a slow turning starter: (1) excessive engine friction; (2) a physical or electrical problem with the starter; or (3) high resistance in the starter circuit. The first one, excessive engine friction, can be eliminated in this case because once the engine starts, it actually runs smoothly and does not overheat or have smoke coming out the exhaust.

The second potential source of the problem is a little trickier. In order to eliminate the starter as the problem, you need to know if starter amperage is excessively high or low. If starter amp draw is high, it's most likely caused by a shorted starter field coil or armature; if amperage is low, it's probably caused by unwanted high resistance somewhere in the starter circuit.

You take out your inductive ammeter to measure starter current draw. First, the ignition system fuse will have to be removed so the engine won't start. This allows enough time for the ammeter to read starter amps when the engine is cranked over. After clamping the current probe around the battery cable at the starter solenoid, the ammeter is ready to measure starter amperage. When the starter is cranked, the ammeter reads 82 amps—this seems too low because the five-cylinder engine in a this bike normally would require around 125 amps to start. Furthermore, low amperage in the starter circuit indicates high resistance is present. Now it's time to use a voltage drop test to isolate the unwanted high resistance.

A voltage drop test determines where the high resistance is located within the starter circuit. Start by checking the positive side of the circuit. Connect the red lead of the voltmeter to battery positive, and the black lead to the battery cable located at the starter motor. Once the engine is cranked, the resulting voltage drop is 1.2 volts—too high for this type of circuit. As discussed in Chapter 2, Voltage Drop Testing, the most likely place for high resistance in any circuit is at a switch.

The switch in this starter circuit is the starter solenoid—it acts like an overgrown relay. The ignition switch sends a 12-volt start signal to the solenoid, which in turn connects the positive battery cable directly to the starter. If the contacts inside the solenoid are dirty, they could be the cause of the high resistance, so you need to connect a voltmeter to both sides of the starter solenoid and repeat the test. Sure enough, the voltage drop is 0.8 volt, indicating the high resistance is inside the starter solenoid. After replacing the solenoid, the starter now cranks at normal speed and the engine starts quickly. Finally, all of the electrical problems are solved. Case closed—time for some ice cream.

As can be seen from the foregoing hypothetical case study, a logical approach is diagnosing electrical problems is always more productive than a haphazard method. In the sample "no start" case, it turned out more than one thing was wrong with the motorcycle. But, a step-by-step approach and methodical checks uncovered all the problems.

Be sure to always keep in mind the "Three Things" every circuit needs in order to function—power, load device, and ground return. The previous case study illustrates how to check for open circuits, shorts to ground, and unwanted high resistance. In addition to the three common electrical foul-ups mentioned, there are three other common electrical problems with circuits (of course!): (1) bad grounds, (2) crossover circuits, and (3) parasitic amperage draw.

BAD GROUNDS

Bad ground connections cause a fair amount of electrical problems. Many technicians have trouble checking for bad grounds because, quite frankly, they don't know exactly what they're looking for. Ground wires are not supposed to

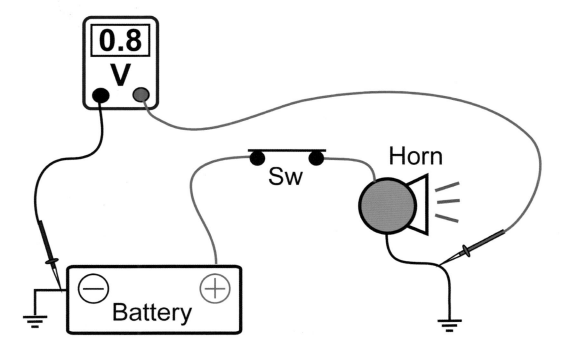

Fig 9-8—A voltmeter reading of 0.8 volts is too high for the ground return on this horn circuit. The bad ground is "stealing" voltage from the horn, causing it to sound weak.

have voltage on them and if they do it's somewhat confusing. By contrast, checking for power is simple and straightforward—either 12 volts (or less) are present or they're not.

There are several ways to check for bad grounds. By far the most accurate method is to use a voltmeter to perform a voltage drop test as outlined in Chapter 2. Figure 9-8 illustrates how a voltmeter is connected to measure the voltage drop on the ground side of a horn circuit. It's important to remember that the horn must be operational for a voltage drop test to work. A good ground return will have almost no voltage present. If the horn (the load device in this circuit) doesn't use up all the available voltage, the ground connection is bad and the bad ground is using voltage intended for the horn. Consequently, the horn sounds weak because it doesn't have enough voltage, or electrical energy, to operate at full potential.

A test light can be used in place of a voltmeter to check for a bad ground, but it has inherent limitations. When touched to the ground side of a circuit, a test light will only lights up if there is enough voltage left to illuminate its bulb. Thus, a bad ground has to be bad enough and have high enough resistance to divide up the voltage between the test light and the component being tested in order for the test light to confirm its presence. If the ground is not quite bad enough, the test light won't light up, and it's impossible to recognize the presence of the bad ground.

Another low-tech method for finding a bad ground is to substitute a ground wire in place of a suspected bad ground. A jumper wire connected between the ground terminal of the load device and a known good ground will help to determine if the original ground has high resistance. If the load device works with the jumper wire in place, the load device's ground wire has high resistance (see figure 9-10).

CROSSOVER CIRCUITS

If a load device is switched on, and another unrelated load device also turns on at the same time, a crossover circuit is present. A crossover circuit is created whenever control wires (power or ground side controls) touch each other. This unwanted contact or connection is usually caused by

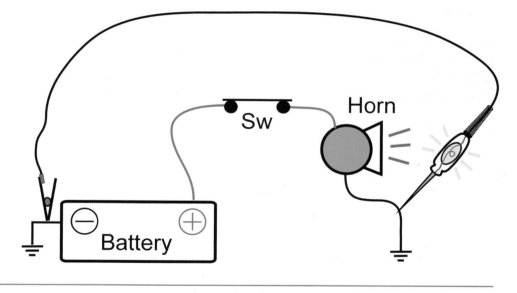

Fig 9-9—A test light can be used to check for a bad ground; however, the ground has to be bad enough in order for the test light to light up. With this limitation in mind, it's obvious a voltmeter is a better way to find a bad ground.

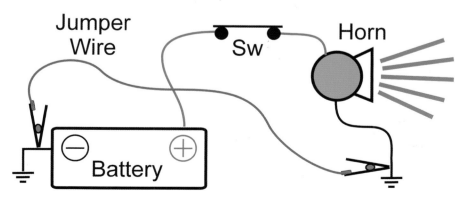

Fig 9-10—A low-tech, but effective, method for discovering a bad ground is to use a jumper wire as a temporary ground wire. When testing with this method, if the load device works as it should, a simple repair of the ground return wire will fix the problem.

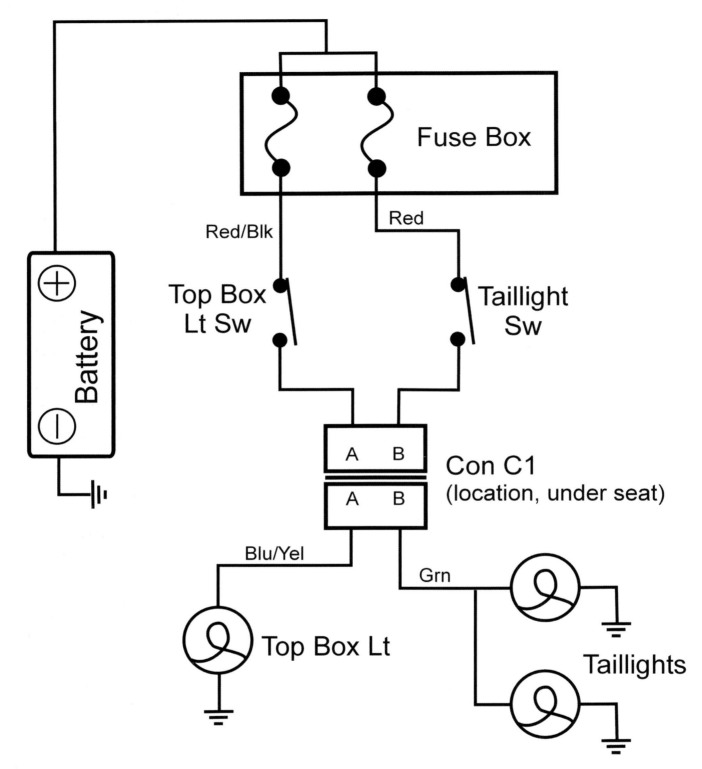

Fig 9-11—A crossover circuit exists between the taillights and top box light. The blue/yellow and green wires are touching—shorted—between the connector and each of the load devices.

wire insulation chafing at a connector or inside a wiring harness (where two wires contact each other). Another common cause for crossover circuits is a defective electrical component. Some circuits are designed so that one component will cause another circuit or component to turn on. Consequently, a defect in the controlling electrical part may cause other circuits to operate unintentionally. A final cause of crossover circuits is the idiot electrical technician—when misconnected connectors have been forced together by an unskilled technician, crossover circuits result. Following is an example of an unwanted crossover circuit.

This motorcycle has a crossover circuit (see Figure 9-11). Every time the top box is opened and the top box light comes on, the taillights come on as well. The circuit controlling the top box light is also unintentionally controlling the taillights. The wiring diagram in Figure 9-11 shows both the top box light and taillight circuits. As can be seen, they share a common connector labeled C1. By unplugging connector C1 and connecting a continuity tester (a common function on digital multimeters) to Terminals A and B on the power side (the half that goes to the fuse box) of the connector, it can be determined if the crossover exists on that side of the connector. If the meter indicates continuity between the terminals, the crossover is on that side of the connector. *Before* connecting the meter, pull the fuses to shut off power to the other side of the connector—you don't want to damage the ohmmeter by putting 12 volts through it.

However, if there is no continuity (no beep from the meter) between the two terminals in the connector, then that side of the connector is not the problem. The meter test leads need to be moved to the other half of the connector. The meter should now beep, confirming the green and blue/yellow wires are touching somewhere between the connector and the top box and taillights. By wiggling the wiring harness while listening to the meter, you should be able to find out exactly where the wires are touching each other and causing the crossover. The meter will beep intermittently when the wires are wiggled, locating the bad section of wiring harness. By simply unraveling the wiring harness, you can repair the broken wire insulation and fix the related electrical problem.

PARASITIC AMP DRAW
Parasitic amp draws occur often enough that knowing how to diagnose this condition is a good idea. For example, if a motorcycle hasn't been driven for a few days and doesn't start up because of a dead battery, there may be some electrical circuit that is on when it should be off, drawing power from the battery. This condition is known as parasitic

amperage draw. This problem is commonly caused by lights that are not visible on the outside of a bike—top box or saddlebag lights. These lights are supposed to switch off when these compartments are closed.

Parasitic amp draw also occurs when a relay gets stuck on. Relays are often used to control power to lighting and EFI computers. A relay that is stuck on while the ignition is in the OFF position will also drain the battery. Unfortunately, these conditions usually aren't noticed until it's too late, and the battery has completely discharged.

Similarly, on-board fuel injection computers, digital radio memory, or other computer-related memory components all use power from the battery to keep their electronic memories alive. However, by contrast, these are normal conditions and should not affect a battery's ability to start an engine, even after several months. Normal amperage draw for these solid state components should not exceed 50 milliamps (0.050 amps) and is usually less than 40 milliamps. Amperage loads exceeding 50 milliamps will draw current from the battery, leaving it dead after a few weeks, or even days.

To find a parasitic amp draw, a series ammeter, test light, and jumper wire are needed. Many digital multimeters can read series amperage up to 10 amps. These meters are usually, but not always, protected by an internal fuse so that once connected to a circuit with more than 10 amps, the fuse melts instead of the meter.

HOW MUCH AMPERAGE?
Before finding the cause of an unwanted amp draw, you must determine approximately how much amperage is being sucked out of the battery. Knowing the amount of amperage draw will help narrow down what type of electrical component is likely causing the draw, and also helps prevent against blowing a fuse in a series ammeter.

First, disconnect either the negative or positive battery cable. Connect one end of a test light to the battery terminal and the other end to the battery cable. If the amperage draw is high enough (above 4 amps), the test light will light up. On some vehicles, a computer-controlled relay may turn on, causing the test light to light up. To eliminate this occurrence as a potential cause of amperage draw, temporarily connect a jumper wire between the battery terminal and battery cable while leaving the test light in place (see Figure 9-12 on page 138). After removing the jumper wire, the test light may go out—but if the light stays on, the amperage draw is above 4 amps. However, be warned! Since you don't know how much more than 4 amps are being used in the circuit, don't connect a series ammeter to the circuit, as it might cause the internal meter fuse to blow!

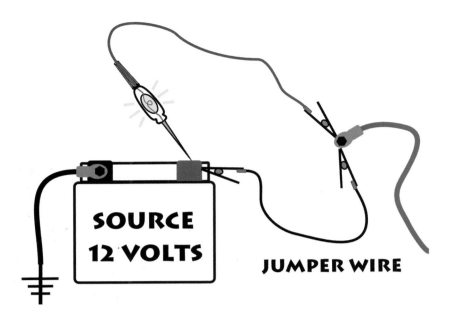

Fig 9-12—In some motorcycles, a computer-controlled relay may be left on, causing the test light to light up. Using a jumper to temporarily reconnect the battery terminal to the positive battery cable in the manner shown will cause the relay to turn off. Parasitic amp draw testing can be continued once the relay is off.

If the test light is out, the amp draw is less than 4 amps; unfortunately, it may still be high enough to cause a dead battery. To find the parasitic draw, connect the leads of a series ammeter to the battery terminal and battery. If the ammeter reads between 0.8 and 1.0 amp, a light of some type is probably on and causing the draw. If amperage is closer to 4 amps, suspect a bad alternator or rectifier diode as the cause of the draw on the battery (see figure 9-13).

LOCATING THE PARASITIC DRAW

With either a test light connected in series with the battery terminal and cable (where the draw is above 4 amps), or a series ammeter connected in the same manner (amp draw is less than 4 amps), you can start locating the source of the parasitic draw. While watching the test light/ammeter, disconnect the wires going to the alternator or rectifier. If the light goes out, or the meter reading changes, a leaky diode is causing the amperage draw. If disconnecting the alternator/rectifier doesn't change the test light or ammeter, start removing fuses from the fuse box. If the test light or meter changes when a specific fuse is removed, the circuit causing the problem has been isolated. Use a wiring diagram to determine what electrical components are powered by the fuse and start unplugging them one at a time; any change in the state of the test light or ammeter when one of the circuits has been disconnected means the parasitic amperage draw has been identified and the problem can be repaired.

Fig 9-13—A series ammeter can be connected between either positive or negative battery cables and the battery to measure parasitic amp draw. Make sure the amperage draw is not higher than the meter's capacity to read series amperage, or it could be damaged!

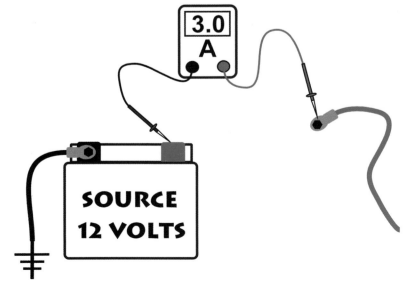

CHAPTER 10
ELECTRICAL ACCESSORIES

Adding electrical accessories to your bike is a great way to make motorcycling more practical and fun. Extending your riding season can be easily accomplished by using heated clothing, including vests, pants, jackets, gloves, and even electric shocks. Knowing how lost you really are is even more fun with a GPS guidance system, and listening to "tunes" on long stretches of interstate can be relaxing. If you're not careful, too many accesories can also unknowingly drain the battery as you ride, only to find out that your motorcycle won't start the next time you take a break. Calculating electrical loads for the accessories you want to use and determining if your motorcycle's charging system can handle the extra power output requirements is something you should do before purchasing and installing. Information regarding calculating excess electrical capacity comes from Powerlet Products. More information on Powerlet and other companies featured in this chapter can be found in the Sources section at the back of this book.

HOW MUCH IS TOO MUCH?

So exactly how many electronic gadgets can your motorcycle's charging system power? That depends on the year, make, and model of bike, and ultimately how much electrical energy in watts the charging system can produce. A motorcycle's excess electrical capacity is the charging system's output minus the normal operating loads. Excess capacity is what you have to work with when adding electrical accessories.

As discussed in Chapter 1, a watt is a measurement for electrical power. To figure out how many watts your charging system can produce, you need to know charging system voltage and amperage. Watts = amps x volts. For example, if you have a charging system that puts out 35 amps, you would multiply 35 amps times 14.5 volts (charging system voltage) for a total of 507.5 watts (35 x 14.5 = 507.5). Fortunately, you shouldn't have to do any math, as charging system output specifications in a service manual are in watts and most electrical accessories are listed in watts as well.

Make	Model	Year	Fuel Delivery	Peak Charging Output
Buell	Blast	2001	Carbureted	297 watts
BMW	R1150RT	2003	Fuel injected	700 watts
BMW	K1200LT	2003	Fuel injected	840 watts
Ducati	996	2000	Fuel injected	520 watts
Ducati	ST2/ST4	2002	Fuel injected	520 watts
Harley	Heritage	1998	Carbureted	360 watts
Harley	Electra Glide	2002	Fuel injected	585 watts
Honda	Shadow 1100	2002	Carbureted	329 watts
Honda	ST1300	2003	Fuel Injected	740 watts
Honda	Valkyrie	2000	Carbureted	546 watts
Honda	GL1800	2003	Fuel Injected	1100 watts
Kawasaki	Vulcan 1500	2000	Carbureted	377 watts
Kawasaki	Vulcan 1500	2001	Fuel Injected	588 watts
Kawasaki	ZX6R	2001	Carbureted	305 watts
Suzuki	Bandit 1200	1999	Carbureted	405 watts
Suzuki	V-Strom	2002	Fuel Injection	360 watts
Yamaha	FJR1300	2003	Fuel Injected	490 watts

Fig 10-1—This table will give you a ballpark number for charging system output in watts for a variety of motorcycles. For better accuracy, use the service manual for your bike to get an exact figure. Courtesy Powerlet Products

To calculate your bike's excess electrical capacity and to figure out how many electrical extras you can safely operate, follow these three steps:

1. Look up your motorcycle's charging system output in a service manual, or for a generic value use the chart in Figure 10-1 (on page 139). In general, smaller bikes have less charging capacity than larger models, and electronic fuel-injected motorcycles have higher output charging systems than carbureted models. In addition, a motorcycle's charging system will not produce anywhere close to its peak output at idle. For example, a Harley-Davidson Ultra Classic Electra-Glide will produce only 380 watts at idle. At 3,000 rpm (cruising speed), the charging system makes 578 watts, and above that, peak output is 589 watts. Take this into consideration if you plan on using electrical accessories with the engine running at idle speeds.

2. Calculate the normal operating loads for your motorcycle. This is the total of all factory installed electrical devices that will be in operation during normal riding. Don't add any aftermarket electrical accessories at this time, and don't include items such as turn signals or horns, as they are only used intermittently. Generic operating loads for most carbureted bikes are around 195 watts; fuel-injected models run about 285 watts.

To conserve power, many motorcycles automatically turn off the low beam when the high beam is on, however, this isn't always the case and operating both high and low beams at the same time should be taken into account. Many larger bikes have additional lighting and miscellaneous loads, including stereo radios, amplifiers, CD players, and heated grips, seats, and backrests, so make sure all of the items that operate continuously while riding are included in your calculations.

Component	Load
High Beam	65 watts
Low Beam	55 watts
License Plate	5 watts
Brake/Taillights	21 watts
Instruments	2 watts
Computer	25 watts
Fuel Pump	60 watts
Cooling Fan	60 watts
Ignition	50 watts

Fig 10-2—This table provides a generic approach to calculating your motorcycle's normal operating electrical loads. Most service manuals (and some owner's manuals) will give you more specific wattage numbers for your bike. Courtesy Powerlet Products

3. Subtract the operating load from the peak charging output; this calculation will predict the approximate excess capacity for your motorcycle. Exceeding the peak charging output for short periods of time is not a problem—the battery will make up the difference between what the charging system can produce and what the electrical accessories require. However, if extra power is needed from the battery for long periods of time, the battery will eventually go dead while you ride. Another factor to consider is how robust your motorcycle's charging system is or isn't. Factories design excess charging capacity into the system for a

Example	Peak	Operating	Excess Capacity
Buell Blast	297 watts	195 watts	102 watts
Kawasaki ZX6R	305 watts	200 watts	105 watts
Ducati ST2/ST4	520 watts	285 watts	245 watts
Suzuki V-Strom	360 watts	285 watts	75 watts
Honda Valkyrie	546 watts	250 watts	296 watts
Vulcan 1500 FI	588 watts	340 watts	248 watts

Fig 10-3—Here are some examples of excess charging system capacity. As you can see, the number of watts available to run electrical accessories varies widely between motorcycles. In general, the larger the bike, the more charging capacity it will have. Courtesy Powerlet Products

Accessory	Watts
Heated Vest	70w
Heated Jacket	100w
Heated Gloves	30w
Heated Socks	25w
Aux Lighting	35-100w (each)
Laptop	40-60w
Cell Phone	1-3w
Radar Detector	1-3w
GPS	2-6w
Portable Music	1-3w

Fig 10-4—This table shows how much power many common accessories require. By far, heated clothing and auxiliary lighting are the big power users. Small items, including cell phones and portable music, are inconsequential. Courtesy Powerlet Products

No more guessing if the charging system is doing what it's supposed to. The chargeGuard monitors not only voltage but charging amperage as well. In addition, ambient temperature is also displayed at the touch of the mode button. Courtesy Kisan Technologies

reason. In part so you can add nonfactory electrical accessories, but also to prevent the charging system from being overworked. If you plug in enough electrical stuff to keep the poor charging system right at its peak output, the generator/stator/regulator/rectifier could all quit working. Alternators, stators, rectifiers, and diodes get hot when they work, and they can only take so much heat before meltdown occurs.

Heated clothing adds up when you consider both rider and passenger. Add two electric vests or jackets and two pairs of heated gloves, and more than 250 watts can be reached easily. If you want to light up a dark road like it's daytime, driving lights can add significant electrical loads to your motorcycle's charging system. Honda Gold Wings with excessive Christmas lights in addition to all the normal Wing accessories need a high dose of electrical energy to power them. Fortunately, late-model GL 1800 Wings have a 1,300-watt charging system—enough to power a small town.

ELECTRICAL ACCESSORIES/PROJECTS

In recent years, editors of several motorcycle magazines have asked me to write reviews on electrical accessories. I have installed and used most of the gadgets in this chapter—some on more than one motorcycle. Thank you to the editors of

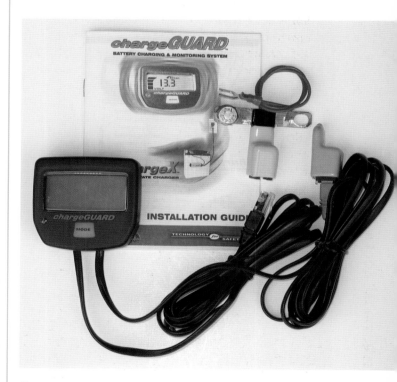

Pictured are all the parts in the chargeGuard kit. The charge monitor plugs into an RJ-11 (phone jack) on the negative battery shunt that allows the unit to measure and display amperage. The sensor at right is an outside temperature sensor. Courtesy Kisan Technologies

Motorcycle Consumer News, RoadBike, and *Friction Zone* magazines for giving me the opportunity to first write the reviews, and now to include this useful information in this book.

KISAN CHARGEGUARD

It's a fact. Many motorcycles don't have an alternator light included with the other idiot lights. Typically, the only indication that a charging system has just quit working is when the engine dies, or at night when the headlight dims to a level suitable for a romantic dining experience—just before you have to pull off to the side of the road. It would be really nice if motorcycle manufacturers gave us a little more warning, but with limited real estate on the dashboard, a charge indicator light takes up too much space—I guess! Fortunately, Kisan Technologies has come up with a solution that does more than just monitor your motorcycle's charging system activity, or lack thereof.

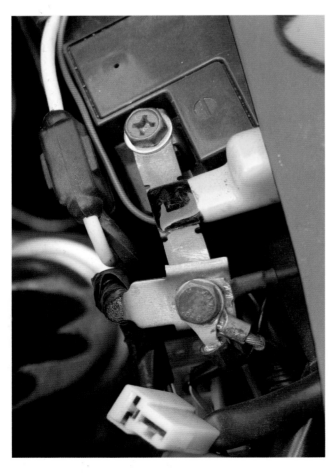

The chargeGuard's shunt is mounted between the negative battery terminal and the battery cable. This allows the chargeGuard to monitor charging amperage. The yellow cover is the phone jack that's plugged into the charge monitor. Courtesy Kisan Technologies

The chargeGuard monitors two electrical functions: battery voltage and alternator output amperage. Both functions are displayed graphically and digitally. The characters are large enough (3/8 inch) to read from a normal riding position. A segmented bar graph adds or takes away bars as voltage or amperage fluctuates. Voltage numbers are displayed in tenths of a volt and amps are rounded off to whole numbers. The numeric display range for battery voltage is 0 to 19.9 volts, while the bar graph indicates 10 to 14 volts. Charging system amperage reads from -99 to +99 amps, and the graphic bars display 3 to 15 amps. In addition to volts and amps, ambient temperature can be displayed in both Centigrade and Fahrenheit. As temperatures approach 32 degrees Fahrenheit (0 degrees C), the display's background color changes to red and flashes "ICE" for 10 seconds. The warning stops if the temperature continues to fall below freezing point. A single Mode button is pressed to cycle the display through all the functions.

The display is somewhat large (2 5/16 x 2 1/8 inch) for a sport bike, but touring motorcycles should have no problem finding a place to mount it. The unit comes with a handlebar mounting kit that uses zip ties to attach the bracket to the bars. If handlebar space is limited, the chargeGuard can be mounted on any flat surface using weather resistant, two-sided tape. Two telephone-type cables exit the bottom of the display—one for the temperature sensor and the other for voltage/amperage. The temperature sensor should be mounted away from engine or radiator heat. I taped it just under the fairing and above the front fender on my FJR 1300. The cable for volts/amps from the display ends in a standard RJ-11 phone jack and plugs into the current sensor or shunt. Amperage is measured via a shunt, which is a copper strip about 3/8 inch wide with a hole at each end and a female RJ-11 jack in the middle. One end of the shunt is connected to the negative battery terminal and the other connects the ground cable(s) while a small red wire from the shunt is connected to the positive battery post. The shunt can be bent in two places to accommodate tight battery compartment dimensions.

In use, the chargeGuard works as advertised. The mode button is easy to operate while wearing heavy riding gloves. The backlit display is visible even in bright sunlight and dims automatically at night. Monitoring system voltage when using heated clothing provides a unique and interesting perspective on a motorcycle's charging system performance.

As my vest and gloves were turned on, the voltage started dropping—not a problem with only one rider, but riding two up with everyone plugged in to keep warm taxes the FJR 1300's less-than-adequate alternator output, and voltage displayed was less than 13 volts indicating the battery was becoming discharged. When checked with a high-end digital voltmeter, the chargeGuard's reading is typically within a tenth of a volt. Monitoring amperage gives the same result, and when the amp number goes negative, it's time to turn off the driving lights or unplug your electric vest. With the engine off and no electrical activity, the chargeGuard automatically turns off the display after two minutes. Pressing the mode button reactivates the display, and amperage draw can be displayed to alert you to any electrical drain on the system. You can also monitor charging amperage or voltage from a battery charger.

POWER FOR TANK BAGS

Most people agree that the factory hard bags included with the purchase of a 2005 Yamaha FJR provide enough room to carry just about anything needed on a ride. The problem is that the bags detach easily and the bike looks great without them. With the luggage gone, you can pretend that you're on a sport bike when riding through the local mountains on a Saturday afternoon. Unfortunately, without the bags it was back to stuffing jacket and pants pockets with a cell phone, Autocom, MP3 player, wallet, glasses, ear plug case, maps, and a candy bar or two. No room for a water bottle or clear face shield for rides that last into the evening hours—must get tank bag. . . .

With all the electronic junk most riders carry when riding, having a 12-volt outlet inside the tank bag seems like a great idea. Powerlet Products makes this easy with their

PowerMate Tank Bag Power System that uses a molded, flange mount SAE plug and anodized backing plate with four screws to attach to the side of any tank bag. The external SAE connector plugs into a Powerlet plug, which are the same types used on BMW, Triumph, and Ducati. I installed a panel connector on my FJR and the bag plugs into it while riding. Inside the bag is an SAE/cigarette Y connector that connects to the adapter, making it easy to power a cell phone, Autocom unit, bike-to-bike radio, or MP3 player while riding. No more dead batteries. Powerlet has numerous types and styles of connectors to power just about anything you could want on a motorcycle. Here's how the PowerMate adapter was installed on my tank bag.

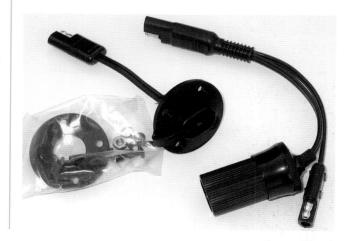

Upper right: Here is the PowerMate tank bag kit and interior Y connector. Black oxide, stainless steel screws with stainless Ny-lock nuts are used to attach the inner backing plate to the tank bag. This will provide a water resistant connection from the motorcycle's 12-volt electrical system to the interior of the bag. Courtesy Powerlet Products

Right: This RoadGear Sport Tank Bag looks sharp on my FJR. It's easy to take on and off and gives me a convenient place to store riding essentials. Now all it needs is power.

1. The first step is to mark the bag using the backing plate as a template. Choose an area of the bag that will be facing a power source on your bike. Courtesy Powerlet Products

2. A hot carpet knife will make a clean cut through the bag's Cordura material. Heat from the blade will seal the edge of the material and keep it from fraying. Courtesy Powerlet Products

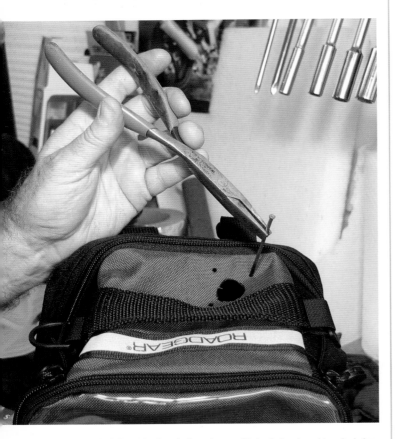

3. After the hole is cut for the adapter, a large nail is heated and used to poke holes in the bag for the PowerMate's mounting screws. Courtesy Powerlet Products

4. After installing the backing plate and PowerMate adapter, the Ny-lock mounting screws need to be tightened—you're almost ready for a 12-volt party inside your tank bag. The PowerMate adapter comes with an SAE connector as shown. Courtesy Powerlet Products

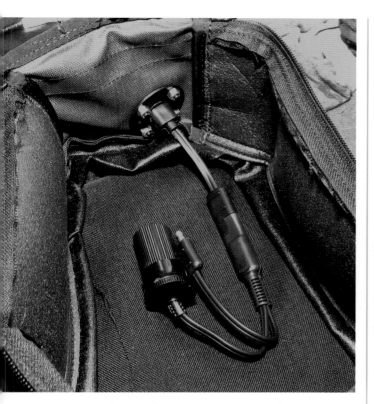

5. Two sources of power are available with the SAE/Cigarette Y connector plugged into the PowerMate adapter. Powerlet has numerous adapters to power just about anything that you use when you ride. Courtesy Powerlet Products

6. My FJR already had a Powerlet panel socket installed. Connecting the tank bag is simply a matter of plugging them together. As an alternative, you can permanently install an SAE connector to your motorcycle's electrical system and plug the SAE plug directly into the PowerMate adapter on the tank bag. Courtesy Powerlet Products

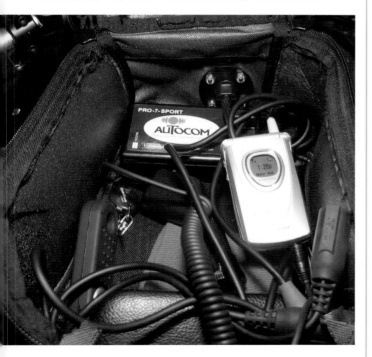

7. Now I can use my Autocom and charge my cell phone during a ride. With other adapters, a CD or MP3 player can be connected. No more running out of battery power. Courtesy Powerlet Products

8. Pictured is a dual outlet Powerlet kit for a Yamaha FJR 1300 and several adapters. All model-specific Powerlet plugs are compatible with stock BMW, Triumph, and Ducati outlets and accessories. Most kits do not require the modification of any stock components; most include waterproof automotive ATO fuse holder and feature high-quality connectors. The aluminum mounting bracket is anodized in black, gold, or silver. Courtesy Powerlet Products

The tailBlazer is available in single (1034) or dual contact (1157) bulb styles (brake light only or combination tail and brake light) that will fit most motorcycles. The bulbs come in pairs or as a single bulb. Courtesy Kisan Technologies

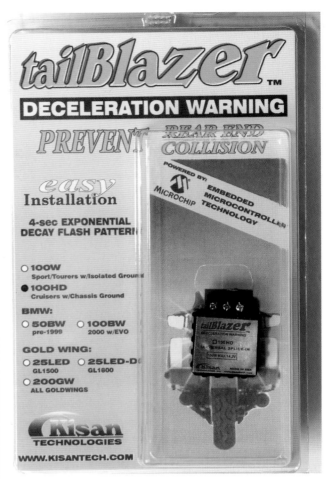

Some motorcycles that have ABS brakes or bulb-checking diagnostic circuits will not trigger the tailBlazer bulbs. The 100 HD tailBlazer will work on these or any other bike. It simply is spliced in between the brake light(s) power wire and the lights. Courtesy Kisan Technologies

KISAN TAILBLAZER FLASHING BRAKE LIGHT

Typically, a 10-mile-per-hour rear-end accident in a car is no big deal, but the same collision when riding a motorcycle could prove disastrous. Even if you don't get hurt, your bike could suffer major damage to bodywork, paint, mirrors, and controls. Every time you make a stop at a busy intersection the potential for getting hit from the rear increases. Do approaching cars and SUVs really know that you're there? As motorcyclists we face this potentially dangerous scenario whenever we go for a ride.

Motorcycle Foundation Safety instructors recommend to their students to pump the brakes several times while stopped. This practice of manually flashing brake lights works only if you consistently remember to do it every time you stop. Instead of having to remember this trick, a more effective solution would be to have the brake light automatically flash when the brakes are applied. Kisan Technologies has made this practice easy with modern electronics.

The tailBlazer brake light modulator is available in two forms: a halogen bulb that replaces a standard brake light bulb and an electronic module that flashes the brake light circuit. In the halogen bulb variety, the electronics causing the light to flash are hidden within the base of the bulb. When the brake switch sends power to the tailBlazer, the microelectronics initiate an exponentially decaying flash pattern. In other words, when your brake light comes on, the light starts flashing at a rapid rate and then slows down over a five-second time period until it eventually remains on. Installation is simply a matter of replacing your stock brake light bulb with the tailBlazer. The tailBlazer is available in single (1034) or dual contact (1157) bulb styles (brake light only or combination tail and brake light) that will fit most motorcycles. The tailBlazer uses a standard,

Left: *With a clear plastic cover to insulate power terminals and a 30-amp rating for individual circuits, this Blue Seas 6-circuit fuse block is an ideal way to cleanly add electrical accessories, and all the wires that go along with them, to your motorcycle. You can find this fuse block and other cool electrical stuff at www.bluesea.com. Courtesy James Haig, FJR 1300 owner*

Below: *Fig. 10-5—Here is the wiring diagram for the fuse box and switched power relay. When the ignition is ON, power from the taillight triggers the relay. Power is switched on at the fuse box to power all the accessories. Individual fuses within the fuse box protect the various electrical components and circuits that are connected to it. The ground panel is a convenient place to attach ground wires from electrical accessories. The relay uses a Bosch numbering system that is found on most automotive aftermarket relays.*

Fuse Box

Switched Power Relay

30   87

86   85

15 → Autocom
10 → Powerlet Plug
15 → CD Player
25 → Ice Cream Maker
5 → Garmin GPS
10 → CB Radio

BATTERY

From Taillight (on with ignition)

Grounds for Accessories

Ground Panel

automotive type, 10-watt, G-4 halogen bulb and though the life expectancy of these bulbs is more than 2,000 hours, a spare bulb is included.

The tailBlazer 100 HD module is designed for motorcycles that can't use the bulbs, such as bikes that are often equipped with ABS brakes or an automatic bulb diagnostic circuit that prevents the tailBlazer bulbs from triggering the flash pattern. The 100 HD module will work on any bike and is simply installed between the brake lights(s) and the brake light power wire.

ADDING A SWITCHED FUSE BLOCK

If you ride a sport touring or touring motorcycle, the number of electrical accessories you can add to the bike are amazing. But with all those accessories comes lots of wire. Rather than have power and ground wires running all over the engine, inside the fairing, and under the seat, adding a powered fuse and ground junction block makes for cleaner installation. Parts such as fuse blocks, relays, and their wiring harness are available at places like Radio Shack and local auto parts stores.

The wiring diagram in Figure 10-5 is but one example of how to wire everything. James Haig and Jeff Paries, members of FJR 1300 Owner's Association at FJR Forum (www.fjrforum.com) and FJR Owner's Association (www.yamaha-fjr1300.com) were kind enough to lend photos of their installations.

ELECTRICAL ACCESSORIES

Above: *Here are the parts required to make a switched power fuse panel. The fuse panel and the relay wiring harness are from The Electrical Connection, www.electricalconnection.com. Radio Shack can supply connectors, fuses, and other components.* Courtesy Jeff Paries

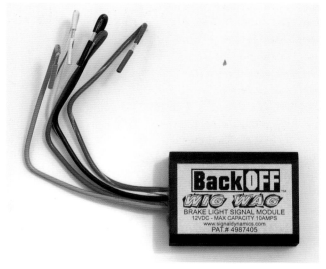

Right: *The BackOff-Wig Wag module is simple to connect to your brake light circuit. The black wire is ground; white/red and red/white wires go to the individual brake lights; and the red and orange wires determine which operational mode the module will use—red for mode one, and orange for mode two.* Courtesy Signal Dynamics

Here is the fuse panel installed under the seat of an FJR 1300. The big red wire comes directly from the battery. The big round thing (lower left) is a servo for an aftermarket cruise control. Courtesy Jeff Paries

Signal Dynamics manufactures single, dual, and quad LED license plate frames. Finishes are available in both chrome and black powder coat. The frames are simple to wire to your existing brake/running light circuit. Sizes fit the standard, 49-state mounting bolt pattern and plate size, and they even have a frame just for the state of Maryland with its odd-ball-sized motorcycle license plate. Custom designs are available as well. Courtesy Signal Dynamics

SIGNAL DYNAMICS BACKOFF-WIG WAG AND LED LICENSE PLATE FRAME

Motorcycles equipped with twin brake lights and pose a unique challenge for riders wanting to be noticed when applying the brakes. Signal Dynamics manufactures an electronic module that alternately flashes the two brake lights. The BackOFF-Wig Wag brake light signal module is designed for use with motorcycles equipped with dual side-by-side brake lights. This compact, solid state electronic module converts your ordinary brake lights into your choice of two attention-getting visual alerting signals: (1) mode one emits five quick alternating flashes of the left and right brake lights, followed by three short flashes and four short flashes of both brakes lights. The four short flashes automatically repeat as long as the brakes are held. (2) mode two emits a visual signal of five alternating quick flashes of the left and right brake lights, followed by three short flashes of both brake lights and then the brake light remains steady until the brake is released. Either operational mode is selected when the unit is installed. The Wig Wag module is designed for 12-volt systems and it can handle up to 10 amps. Its compact size—2-1/4x1-5/8x5/8 inches—makes finding a place for it under a seat or tail section of a bike easy.

For even greater visibility and safety, consider combining the installation of the BackOFF-Wig Wag module with an LED license plate frame, also from Signal Dynamics. Many motorcycles have only one brake/running light bulb that is not as visible to other drivers as many motocyclists would like. This LED license plate frame can be used as a back-up brake light, and because the LEDs are wired for both high and low intensity, they can serve as additional running lights as well. Signal Dynamic's LED frames are quality crafted and come in mirror finish chrome or black powder coat, with respective chrome and black mounting hardware. Figure 10-6 shows the wiring diagram for both the Wig Wag modulator and an LED license plate frame. I included my already installed Kisan tailBlazer unit to make the license plate LED flash.

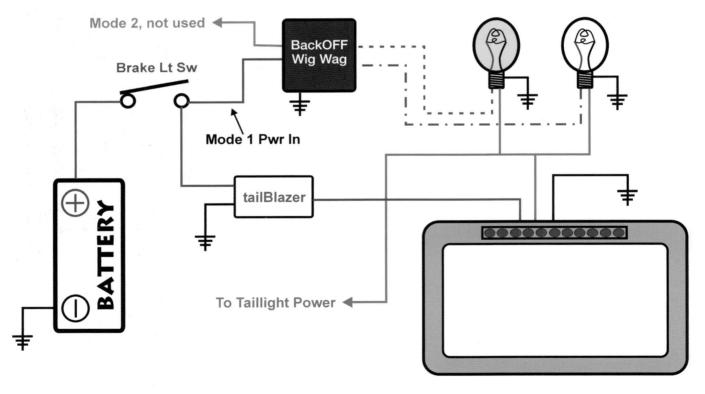

Above: *Fig 10-6—The BackOFF-Wig Wag has two power input wires. The red wire is for mode one and the orange is for mode two that is unused for this installation. The license plate LED serves as a brake light that flashes through the Kisan tailBlazer and a third taillight.*

Opposite, top: *Here is the installation in progress. The most difficult part was getting the bodywork off my FJR to gain access to the wiring harness. Wiring the BackOFF-Wig Wag module, Signal Dynamics license plate frame, and tailBlazer unit was straightforward.* Courtesy Signal Dynamics

ELECTRICAL ACCESSORIES

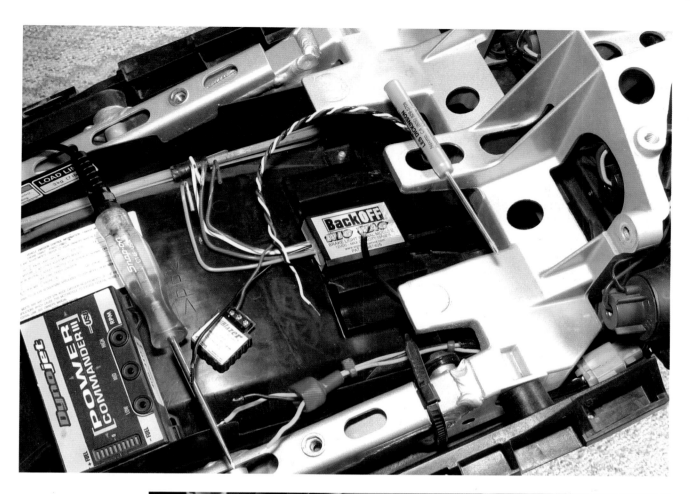

Right: *Here is the finished result. Now when I hit the brakes, the right and left brake lights alternate back and forth rapidly, followed by three short flashes, then four short flashes. The lights flash together for as long as the brake switch completes the circuit. The LEDs on the license plate flash as well— a virtual light show every time I brake. In addition to being more visible, this photo is the tail "end" of this book as well.* Courtesy Signal Dynamics

SOURCES

I would like to thank the following motorcycle dealerships and companies for help with the images and information contained in this book. Their kind assistance made this a better book from technical as well as artistic perspectives. All of these dealers and manufacturers offer great products and services for professional and do-it-yourself technicians alike. Contact information is listed for each company—check out their websites.

bobsbmw.com

Bob's BMW

Bob's BMW is one of the most respected BMW motorcycle dealerships in North America, and the winner of several awards for overall excellence, customer satisfaction, and community service. From its convenient location near Columbia, Maryland, Bob's serves riders throughout the Washington, D.C.; Baltimore; and northern Virginia region.

Beyond the local level, Bob's is a destination of choice for BMW enthusiasts from far and wide, thanks largely to the thriving mail-order parts business which, since 1981, has become nationally renowned as the BMW rider's prime source for parts, accessories, and apparel—and not only to owners of new models, but also collectors of classic and vintage BMWs too. There is even an on-site vintage museum at Bob's, featuring rare bikes and artifacts that illustrate the complete history of BMW motorcycling.

Bob's BMW is more than just a full-service dealership in the conventional sense. There's a feeling about the place: where the special camaraderie shared among the many BMW riders who make Bob's their meeting place creates what we call the "BMW environment." And it's what sets Bob's apart from all other BMW motorcycle dealerships.

Bob's BMW Motorcycles
10720 Guilford Road
Columbia/Jessup, Maryland 20794-9385
301-497-8949
Website: www.bobsbmw.com

Twigg Cycles

Twigg Cycles celebrates its 75th anniversary in 2006. H. William Twigg sold his first bicycle in 1932 and established Twigg Cycles as an Indian motorcycle franchise in 1936. The family owned and operated dealership has carried 42 brands since that time, including Matchless, ATS, CS, Jawa, Triumph, BSA, Airel, Zundapp, Ducati, Benneli, American Eagle, Wizzar, and BMW. Today they sell Yamaha, Suzuki, Kawasaki, and Honda. In addition to motorcycles, they carry watercraft, including Polaris and Sea-Doo.

Twigg Cycles has satisfied thousands of customers in the Maryland, Pennsylvania, and West Virginia area. Twigg Cycles provides every customer with guaranteed satisfaction above and beyond their expectations and creates an environment of friendliness and superior quality for maximum enjoyment of the unique motor sports lifestyle offered by its people, products, and services.

Twigg Cycles, Inc.
200 S. Edgewood Drive
Hagerstown, Maryland 21740
301-739-2773
Website: www.twiggcycles.com
Email: sales@twiggcycles.com

Harley-Davidson of Frederick

Harley-Davidson of Frederick is a full-service Harley-Davidson and Buell dealership. Their Harley-Davidson certified service department has services that include quick bay services while you wait, Maryland state inspections on all brands, dyno test station for all brands, and the area's most highly trained and certified technicians. In addition, they house a full-service, high-performance and customer fabrication machine shop featuring state-of-the-art equipment and a talented crew of dedicated professionals.

Now with their newly expanded showroom, H-D of Frederick can show and sell more new and used motorcycles than ever before. There is a huge selection of MotorClothes and collectibles as well as parts and accessories to personalize your ride. Harley-Davidson of Frederick has recently started converting two-wheeled motorcycles to trikes, and services them as well.

No matter what your motorcycling needs, chances are they can help. The Harley-Davidson of Frederick team is dedicated not only to exceeding the highest standards of professionalism and technical achievement, but to unparalleled customer service as well.

Harley-Davidson of Frederick
5722 Urbana Pike
Frederick, Maryland 21704
301-694-8177
Website: www.hdoffrederick.com
Email: info@hdoffrederick.com

Yuasa Battery Inc.

Yuasa Battery Inc. has been manufacturing motorcycle batteries in the United States to uncompromisingly high standards since 2000. They are the largest American manufacturer and the largest distributor of batteries for motorcycles, snowmobiles, scooters, all-terrain vehicles, and personal watercraft. In addition to their vast replacement business, Yuasa is the preferred original equipment supplier to many of these same markets. By producing batteries that generate more power, last longer, and require minimum maintenance, Yuasa Battery Inc. has achieved a leadership position in small engine starting batteries. Continuous research and development, along with unvarying standards of manufacturing quality, help maintain Yuasa's position as market leader around the world.

Website: www.yuasabatteries.com

Motorcycle Consumer News

Motorcycle Consumer News is the monthly consumer resource for unbiased reviews of motorcycles and related aftermarket products and services. Combined with in-depth technical features and top-notch investigative reporting, it is considered "the Bible" for serious motorcycle enthusiasts. Unlike other power sports publications, *MCN* has no advertising and relies only on reader subscriptions as its source of income. This allows them unprecedented editorial freedom to write the truth regarding how well a product or service really works—or doesn't. If you want to know what brands of jacket, gloves, riding pants, bike cleaning products, electronics, tires, helmets, and a whole host of other motorcycle-related products are best, and how they compare to the competition, this is the magazine that is unafraid to tell it like it is.

In-depth reviews of new motorcycles let readers know before they buy what they're getting for their money. Columns on "Mental Motorcycling" and motorcycle design trends make for interesting and informative reading. A quarterly "Used Bike Value Guide" can make purchasing a second-hand motorcycle a more enjoyable experience. The monthly column "Proficient Motorcycling" provides readers with valuable riding skill tips and techniques. Bulletins regarding factory recalls and letters from manufacturers and readers all add value for motorcyclists.

Editorial information:
Motorcycle Consumer News
P.O. Box 6050
Mission Viejo, CA 92690-6050
949-855-8822
Subscription information:
Motorcycle Consumer News
P.O. Box 37191
Boone, IA 50037-0191
888-333-0354
Website: www.mcnews.com
Email: MCNcuserv@cdsfulfillment.com
Email: editor@mcnews.com

Signal Dynamics Corporation

Signal Dynamics Corporation

Signal Dynamics Corporation's primary business is the manufacturing of electronic products for the power sport industry. SDC has been in business for nearly two decades, manufacturing a large variety of products from LED lighting to complete electrical power distribution systems. Two of their best-known products are BackOff and LINX. The BackOFF line includes Brake Light Signal Modules that help make motorcyclists more visible to following drivers, and the LINX line is the most advanced wiring system available to custom bike builders.

LINX is essentially a network bus system that simplifies the wiring installation for a motorcycle and provides many advanced features that are not normally available on custom-built motorcycles. Signal Dynamics also does contract engineering and manufacturing of electronic parts for many different industries. Over the past two decades, Signal Dynamics has introduced and manufactured many new products that have now become industry standards.

Signal Dynamics Corporation
6500 NW 21 Avenue, Suite 1
Ft. Lauderdale, FL 33309
800-785-1814
Website: www.SignalDynamics.com

Kisan Technologies, Inc.

Kisan Technologies Inc. designs, develops, and manufactures motorcycle safety accessories. The Kisan engineering team specializes in microelectronics, which allows the products to be small enough to fit the tight space requirements of motorcycles. Embedded microprocessors provide the flexibility of upgrading to a new version of software to keep up with the newer models of motorcycles. Kisan products are designed to be "plug-n-play" and engineered for durability. Kisan products meet or exceed DOT standards, UL specifications, and CE requirements. Check their website for a list of all the great products they offer.

Kisan Technologies Inc.
1219 Lake Plaza Drive
Colorado Springs, CO 80906
Website: www.kisantech.com

Powerlet

Powerlet offers a line of high-quality products tailored to the power sports industry. With more than 220 wiring products to choose from, Powerlet power adapters can adapt to any battery-powered vehicle. Products range from prepackaged socket kits that mount easily into a panel or frame boss to adaptive and power cables ready to power any type of appliance. Based on the accepted industry standard, Powerlet is your source for powering appliances.

Powerlet products permit riders to power everything from GPS and radar detectors to heated gear, all from the comfort of their motorcycle or power sports vehicle, further enriching the riding experience. Their lines of Luggage Electrix products enable riders to power stock luggage, bags, or tail trunks. Once their bulkhead is adapted to the piece of luggage, riders can store, charge, and power appliances with ease and be permitted the simplicity of one simple point to disconnect.

Being Powerlet equipped means enriching the ride experience with peace of mind products. Kits start at $29.95 and go up to $124.95, with cables starting at $7.95 and Luggage Electrix products starting at $24.95. Increase your riding comfort and get both you and your vehicle Powerlet equipped today.

Powerlet products can be purchased at many fine resellers of motorcycle accessories or purchased direct on line.

Powerlet
5520 Chicago Road
Warren, MI 48092
877-752-7835
Website: www.powerlet.net
Email: marketing@powerlet.net

TecMate North America

TecMate has been developing and manufacturing unique electronic products for the power sports and niche vehicle sectors for more than a decade. They do nothing else; they are therefore uniquely specialized in this field. In addition to engine diagnostic tools, the development and manufacturing of automatic, smart battery conditioners and chargers with diagnostic capabilities is TecMate's particular specialty.

TecMate's products are in service in more than 45 countries worldwide, and there are active distributors in more than 30 of these. They manufacture private label or custom products for a number of outstanding companies. Their products have been ordered by and/or are being recommended or directly distributed by the global power sports OEM networks in more countries than any of TecMate's competitors.

Their philosophy places strong emphasis on service, whether in response to technical enquiries or in providing after sales backup. Equally important is maintaining a continuously high level of product quality. These principles underscore the close relationships TecMate has been able to develop with a number of motorcycle manufacturers.

TecMate North America
1100 Invicta Drive #22
Oakville, ON L6H 2K9
Canada
905-337-2095
Website: www.tecmate.com
Email: sales@tecmate.com

Rick's Motorsport Electrics Inc.

Rick's Motorsport Electrics Inc. has been an industry innovator for more than 25 years. Their goal is to provide their customers with quick, friendly, dependable service. Rick's build and test their products, and they understand the concerns and needs of the technician when replacing a starter motor or diagnosing a charging system problem. Rick's believe that their products are a high-quality, cost-effective alternative to the OE manufacture.

Rick's Motorsport Electrics Inc.
30 Owens Court, Unit #2
Hampstead, NH 03841
800-521-0277
Website: www.ricksmotorsportelectrics.com

Cycle Electric Inc.

Cycle Electric Inc. manufactures electrical charging systems for Harley-Davidson motorcycles. Their products can also be used on any motorcycle using a similar motor, such as S&S, TP Engineering, Delcron, or Merch Performance, to mention a few.

All Cycle Electric Inc. products are built to last. They start with a rugged design and use only top-quality materials. Cycle Electric craftsmen take the extra time throughout the manufacturing process to make sure everything is just right. All parts are tested individually and then again as an assembly. All this adds up to one thing: products that work and keep on working.

Cycle Electric Inc.
8734 Dayton Greenville Pk.
Brookville, OH 45309
937-884-7300
Website: www.cycleelectricinc.com

MC Advantages

MC Advantages is a premier distributor of high-performance aftermarket V-Twin parts. They carry the full line of Spyke Acculight Ignition Systems, which is the only ignition on the market to boast three sparks per compression stroke. Spyke AIS Ignition Systems are optically triggered, so they produce much more accurate, stable, and consistent sparks. This allows them to be easier to install and time, while producing more horsepower and lowered emissions.

The Spyke AIS Ignition is available in the convenient preprogrammed single- and dual-fire configurations, as well as an infinitely programmable ignition known as the AIS FP. This FP ignition is perfect for racers and OEM builders looking to maximize the horsepower potential of their bikes. It works great with nitrous and auto-shifting setups.

MC Advantages also offers the complete line of Spyke electrics to help build or repair almost any V-Twin electrical system. This lineup includes the powerful SuperStart Battery line, SuperFlex Battery Cables, Spyke Charging Systems, Spyke 80,000-Volt Coils, Spyke Quick-Install Distributors, Firstryke Bolt-On Compression Releases, as well as Spyke Stealth and SuperTorque Starters. All of these parts are designed to work extremely well with each other and integrate seamlessly with thousands of OEM configurations.

MC Advantages
10440 NW 54th Avenue
Grimes, IA 50111
800-726-9620
Website: www.mcadvantages.com

Fluke Corporation

Fluke Corporation is the world leader in the manufacture, distribution, and service of electronic test tools and software.

Since its founding in 1948, Fluke has helped define and grow a unique technology market, providing testing and troubleshooting capabilities that have grown to mission critical status in manufacturing and service industries. Every new manufacturing plant, office, hospital, or facility built today represents another potential customer for Fluke products.

From industrial electronic installation, maintenance, and service, to precision measurement and quality control, Fluke tools help keep business and industry around the globe up and running. Typical customers and users include automotive technicians, engineers, and computer network professionals—people who stake their reputations on their tools, and use tools to help extend their personal power and abilities. The Fluke brand has a reputation for portability, ruggedness, safety, ease of use, and rigid standards of quality.

Fluke Corporation
P.O. Box 9090
6920 Seaway Blvd.
Everett, WA 98206-9090
(800) 44 Fluke
Website: www.fluke.com

SPX/OTC

SPX/OTC is a major manufacturer and supplier of vehicle electronic diagnostic instruments, automotive fuel system maintenance equipment, special service tools, general purpose tools, pullers, heavy-duty tools, shop equipment, and hydraulic components. For more than 75 years, automotive service professionals have depended on the quality and durability of OTC's heavy-duty tools and shop equipment. OTC's full range of tools and equipment has been designed for the professional service technician, representing the highest standard in quality and reliability. Engineered in the United States and backed by a lifetime marathon warranty, OTC-branded tools and equipment set the standard by which all other tools and equipment are measured.

OTC/SPX Corporation
655 Eisenhower Drive
Owatonna, MN 55060
800-533-6127
Website: www.otctools.com

Weller, A Division of Cooper Hand Tools
The Weller Advantage

Weller has come a long way from its humble beginnings back in 1945, when Carl Weller, a home radio repairman, wasn't satisfied with the bulky, slow-heating soldering irons that were the tools of his trade. The technology he pioneered, combined with his own design ingenuity, created the first soldering gun, an invention that revolutionized the electronics manufacturing and repair industries. Today, the Weller brand is still synonymous with electronics design innovation, but in a very different way. Weller is now the most respected name in specialized soldering and de-soldering products for production, rework, and repair of through-hole and SMT boards; products for contact removal of ICs and QFPs; noncontact hot air products; and much more. Weller's latest line of products again breaks new ground—this time in the fast-growing arena of lead-free soldering technology. Weller Silver Series stations have the power to handle the extra demands of lead-free soldering and the versatility to tackle a wide array of applications. As always, the famous Weller blue signifies products that help maximize productivity with a combination of innovation and value. See for yourself; the time has never been better to get the Weller advantage.

Weller
3535 Glenwood Avenue
Raleigh, NC 27612
(919) 781-7200
Website: www.cooperhandtools.com

INDEX

Absorbent glass mat (AGM) batteries, 53
AC circuit, 15
AC pickup coil, 91, 92
Accessory circuits, 26
Alternators
Flywheel, 68
One-piece, 64, 65
Three-piece, 65–68
Amp hours (AH), 45, 54
Amperage, 13
Measuring, 34
BARO sensors, 102, 111–113
Batteries,
Absorbent Glass Mat (AGM), 53
Chargers, 55, 56
Charging, 51, 52
Chemical reactions, 46–48
Conventional, 52
Discharging, 48–50
Gel, 53
Primary jobs, 44, 45
Ratings, 54, 55
Types of, 52–54
Battery
Activation, 56, 57
Condition of, 70
Tester, hand-held, 58, 59
Testers, 40
Testing, 57
Bob's BMW, company information, 152
Carburetors, basics, 99, 100
Charge indicators, 69
Charging, 51
Charging systems
Primary purposes, 60, 61
Testing, 70, 71
Charging circuits, 25
Chemical reactions, 46
Circuits,

Accessory, 26
Charging, 25
Computer, 26
DC versus AC, 15
Starter, 25
Testing, 27
Closed loop operation, 104
Coil tester, 37–39
Cold cranking amps (CCA), 45, 54
Computer circuits, 26
Continuity, 21
Conventional batteries, 52, 53
Crankshaft position sensor, 102
Crossover circuits, troubleshooting, 135–137
Cycle Electric Inc., company information, 155
DC circuit, 12-volt, basic concepts, 11–15
Amperage, 13
Necessary physical components of, 9–11
Resistance, 13, 14
Resistance-amps relationship, 14, 15
Voltage, 12, 13
DC generators, 61, 62
Testing, 75
Detonation, 104
Digital voltmeter (DVOM), 31–34
Auto-ranging feature of, 31, 32
Common buttons, 33
Measuring amperage, 34
Rotary switch positions of, 32, 33
Diodes, checking for bad, 74
Discharging
Dynamic battery load testing, 58
Dynamic testing of circuits, 23
Electric ignition, 90, 91
Electrical accessories, charging system output, 139–141
Electrical capacity, calculating, 140, 141
Electrolyte solution, 50
Electronic fuel injection, 100–107
Basics, 100, 101
Starting, 101–103
Temperature, 103–107
Test drive, 101
Fluke Corporation, company information, 156
Fuel injectors, 115, 116
Gel batteries, 53, 54
Generator polarizing, 75
Ground return, 10
Grounds
Bad, 134
Troubleshooting, 134, 135
Hall-effect switch, 92, 93
Harley-Davidson of Frederick, company information, 153
High energy ignition (HEI), 39
Idle air control, 115
Ignition circuit, secondary, 96–98
Ignition coils, 83–86
Testing, 86
Ignition dwell, 89
Ignition modules, 94
Testing, 94, 95
Ignition spark tester, 39
Ignition system
Computer controls, 90, 91
Contact points and condenser, 88–90
Electronic, 90
Disabling, 78, 79
Primary jobs, 82, 83
Triggers, 91–94
Ignition timing light, 39
Jump starting, 51
Jumper wires, 36, 37
Kisan Technologies Inc., company information, 154
ChargeGuard, installing, 142, 143

TailBlazer, installing, 146, 147
Knock sensor, 104, 114, 115
Lab scopes, 40–43
Load device, 10
Logic probe, 34, 35
Magnetic induction, 61
MAP sensors, 111–113
Mass airflow (MAF) sensors, 113
Mathematical formulas for circuits, 15, 16
MC Advantages, company information, 156
Mechanical voltage regulators, 63
Motorcycle Consumer News, company information, 153
Multimeters, 30, 31
Noid lights, 35
Ohm, Georg Simon, 14
Ohmmeter, problems when voltage drop testing, 21, 22
Open circuit voltage test, 57, 58
Optical sensors, 93, 94
Oxygen sensors, 110, 111
Parallel circuits, 17–19
Parasitic amp draw, 137, 138
Points and condenser, 88, 89
Port fuel injection, 101
Power source, 9
Powerlet, company information, 154
Rectification, 64
Rectifier testing, 73
Relays, 116, 117
Resistance, 13, 14
  Relationship with amps, 14
Rick's Motorsport Electrics Inc., company information, 155
Series circuits, 16, 17, 19
Short finder, 35, 36
Signal Dynamics Corporation, company information, 154
BackOFF-Wig Wag, adding, 150,

151
Soldering tools, 43
Spark production and distribution, 82
Specific gravity, 50
SPX/OTC, company information, 157
Starter
Amperage issues, 79–81
Circuit, 25
Motors, 75, 76
Solenoids, 77
Troubleshooting, 130–134
Stator testing, 73
Switched fuse block, adding, 147–149
Tank bags, installing 12-volt outlet, 143–145
TecMate North America, company information, 155
Temperature sensors, 108–110
Terminal jacks, 33
Test lights, 29, 30
Testing
Charging system components, 70–73
Circuits, dynamically, 23
Coils, 86–88
DC generator and regulator, 75
Diodes, 74, 75
Ignition modules, 94–96
Starter, 78
Stator and rectifier, 73, 74
Three things, 9
Throttle position sensors (TPS), 108
Transistorized electronic voltage regulators, 63, 64
Twigg Cycles, company information, 152
Vehicle speed sensors (VSS), 115
Voltage, 12
Voltage drop, 24–26

Testing, locating bad switch, 26, 27
Testing, purpose of, 20, 21
Voltmeter, measuring voltage, 22
Weller, company information, 157
Windings, primary and secondary, 83
Wiring diagrams, 118–128
Practice, 122–128
Reading, general, 118, 119
Samples, 119–122
Yuasa Battery Inc., company information, 153

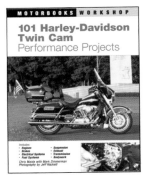
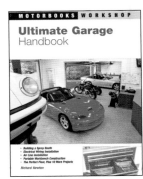

MOTORBOOKS
WE'D LIKE YOUR INPUT!

Name of Book Title: _____

How would you rate it? ___ Excellent ___ Good ___ Fair ___ Poor

Was this a gift or personal purchase? _____

Can you suggest a way to improve this book? _____

_____

Can you suggest other titles we should publish? _____

_____

Your name: _____

Your e-mail address: _____

Any other comments: _____

_____

Thank you for your comments,
Your friends at Motorbooks
For more information, go to www.mbipublishing.com or call 1-800-826-6600
Online form available at http://www.mbipublishing.com/feedback.html

$ 26.95 US
£ 16.99 UK
$ 33.95 CAN

Motorcycle Electrical Systems
Troubleshooting and Repair

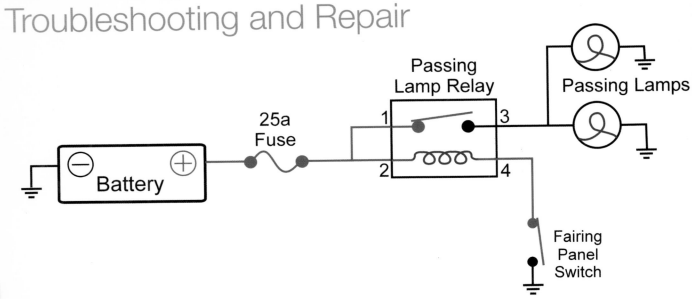

Motorcycle electrical systems can be a mystery to the weekend mechanic and even to the experienced professional. No longer shall you fear the mass of wires under your fuel tank or seat, or behind your headlight. *Motorcycle Electrical Systems: Troubleshooting and Repair* explains the principles behind motorcycle electrical systems, describes how they work, and reveals proper testing tools and techniques to find out where the problem's source is.

From Ohm's Law to reading wiring diagrams to specific electrical scenarios, ASE-certified master technician, author, and motorjournalist Tracy Martin takes you on a guided tour of your motorcycle's electrical system. Martin details the various tools, such as multimeters and test lights, that can be used to evaluate and troubleshoot any bike's electrical system, dishing out handy tips to help you banish your electrical gremlins.

Don't get lost in the dark again. The information in *Motorcycle Electrical Systems: Troubleshooting and Repair* is your best tool for understanding your electrical system and diagnosing problems with your motorcycle.

Side tabs:
OHM'S LAW
VOLTAGE AMP TESTING
ELECTRONIC TESTING TOOLS
STORAGE BATTERIES
CHARGING AND STARTING SYSTEMS
IGNITION SYSTEMS
FUEL INJECTION SYSTEMS
WIRING DIAGRAMS
TROUBLESHOOTING ELECTRICAL SYSTEMS
ELECTRICAL ACCESSORIES

MOTORBOOKS

Visit **motorbooks.com**
or call **1.800.826.6600**

Printed in China   MW241

ISBN-13: 978-0-7603-2716-6
ISBN-10: 0-7603-2716-5

MBI Item # 144121